T0265477

'A wise elder once told Annie Worsley that in order
to learn anything about land you need to have an open
mind and your feet on the earth. "Watch, wait and listen.
The land speaks to you but you must be patient and careful."
In *Windswept*, Worsley has followed that advice to create
a book of great insight and beauty, charged with gorgeous
colours and sound'
CASPAR HENDERSON

'*Windswept* is an elemental lesson in how to belong;
how to watch, listen and wait, and not miss a thing.
Annie Worsley paints this extraordinary Highland
coastal crofting landscape, its winds, tides, mountains,
wild inhabitants and sea, with dynamic, fully immersive
sweeps and fine sensory detail. Reading it is to feel like
being out in the wildest, most exhilarating storm, before
being warmed by myrtle-scented sunshine. Breathtaking'
NICOLA CHESTER

WINDSWEPT

WINDSWEPT

Life, Nature and Deep Time
in the Scottish Highlands

Annie Worsley

**WILLIAM
COLLINS**

William Collins
An imprint of HarperCollins*Publishers*
1 London Bridge Street
London SE1 9GF

WilliamCollinsBooks.com

HarperCollins*Publishers*
Macken House
39/40 Mayor Street Upper
Dublin 1
D01 C9W8, Ireland

First published in Great Britain in 2023 by William Collins

2

ISBN 978-0-00-827837-3

Typeset in Dante MT Std by
Palimpsest Book Production Ltd, Falkirk, Stirlingshire

Printed and Bound in the UK using 100% Renewable Electricity
at CPI Group (UK) Ltd

For my husband, for our children and grandchildren.
Listen up, stories incoming.

Who has seen the wind?
CHRISTINA ROSSETTI

Happiness comes the way the wind blows.
MIKHAIL LERMONTOV

The wind is us – it gathers and remembers all our voices,
then sends them talking and telling through the leaves
and the fields.
TRUMAN CAPOTE

CONTENTS

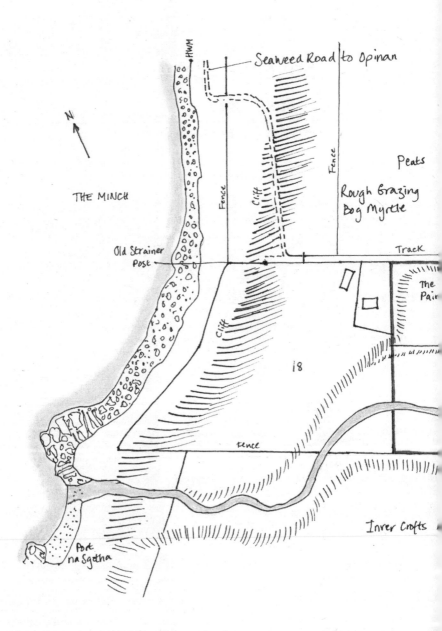

N

THE MINCH

HWM

Seaweed Road to Opinan

Fence

Cliff

Fence

Peats

Rough Grazing
Bog Myrtle

Old Strainer
Post

Track

The
Pair

Cliff

18

Fence

Inver Crofts

Port
na Sgatha

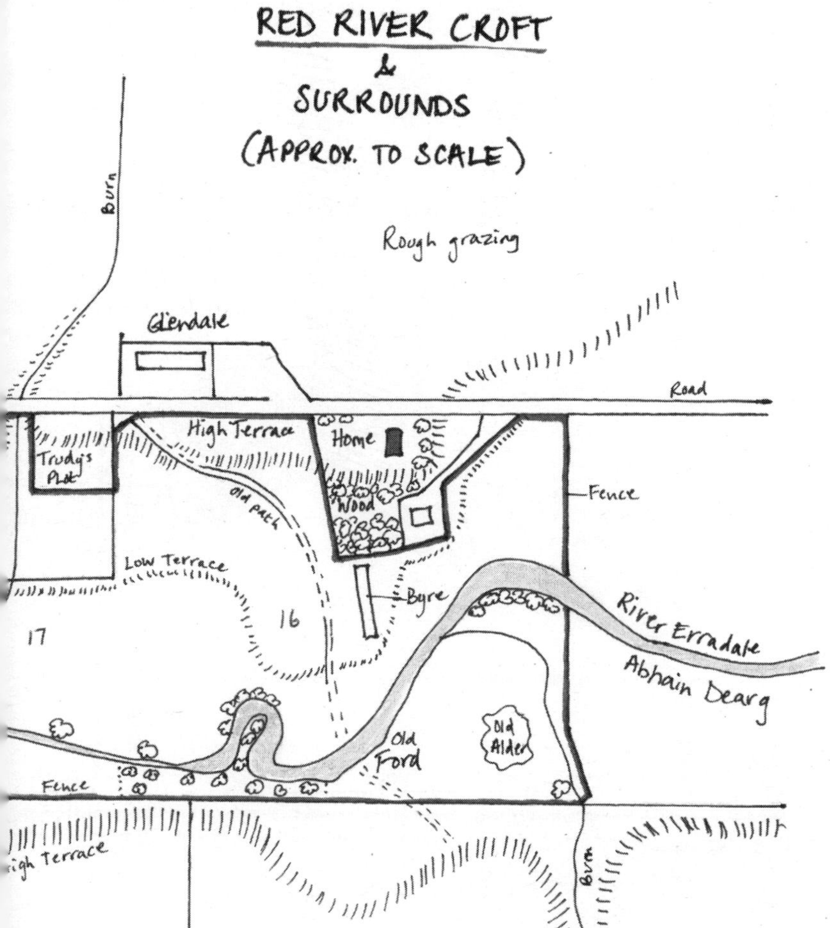

RED RIVER CROFT
&
SURROUNDS
(APPROX. TO SCALE)

Rough grazing

Burn

Glendale

High Terrace

Home

Road

Trudy's Plot

Old Path

Wood

Fence

Low Terrace

Byre

River Erradale

Abhain Dearg

17

16

Old Alder

Old Ford

Fence

High Terrace

Burn

3
"America"

N

PEATS

TO OPINAN

SEAWEED ROAD

WATERFALLS

PORT NA SGOTHA

FORD

PEATS

P... BRI...

TO RED POINT

SOUTH ERRADALE
TOWNSHIP AND RED RIVER CROFT

APPROXIMATELY TO SCALE

RUTTING GROUNDS

TO OPINAN

CNOC AN FHUARAIN

TO BADACHRO

RIVER
ERRADALE

MAOL RUADH

AW.

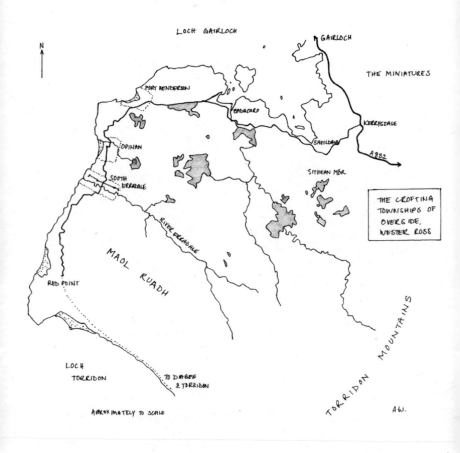

N

LOCH GAIRLOCH

GAIRLOCH

THE MINIATURES

PORT HENDERSON

BADACHRO

KERRYSDALE

OPINAN

SHEILDAIG

A 832

SOUTH
ERRADALE

SITHEAN MOR

RIVER ERRADALE

THE CROFTING
TOWNSHIPS OF
OVERSIDE,
WESTER ROSS

MAOL RUADH

RED POINT

TORRIDON MOUNTAINS

LOCH
TORRIDON

TO DIABEG
& TORRIDON

APPROXIMATELY TO SCALE

A.W.

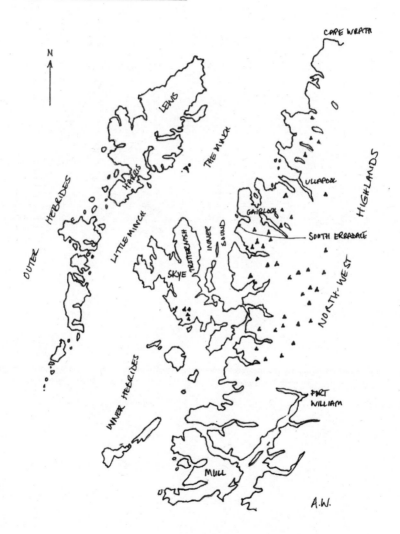

SOUTH ERRADALE AND
THE HIGHLANDS & ISLANDS

N

CAPE WRATH

LEWIS

THE MINCH

HARRIS

OUTER HEBRIDES

HIGHLANDS

ULLAPOOL

GAIRLOCH

SOUTH ERRADALE

LITTLE MINCH

TROTTERNISH

INNER SOUND

SKYE

NORTH-WEST

INNER HEBRIDES

FORT WILLIAM

MULL

A.W.

FROM A WINDSWEPT PLACE

A faint smear of rosy brightness hangs out in the west – a September haar, sea mist reflecting the sunrise. A gentle wind runs up from the shore to ruffle the remaining tufts of summer greenery. The biting insects have retreated. I taste salt and clarity, things midges detest. Change is coming. The grasses will not be green for long.

Across the sea the teardrop shapes of islands begin to pop up along the horizon. From my cliff-top vantage point it is impossible to pin down when or how the dawn pastels become a palette of bright acrylic paints. This is how the seasons change here too. There is no slow bleeding from one state to another but a sudden rupture of light and colour.

Gusts begin to sculpt waves. They carry sea-bird cries and a whiff of iodine. The sun appears. I take a couple of photographs – glisks of light on the water and swift-moving clouds. Yesterday I took dozens. Yesterday was so volatile no single image could have captured its essence. Sea colours, cloud types, shadows and shapes, weaving complex tales in organic combinations of the oceanic, terrestrial and atmospheric.

Clouds thicken and darken; sea birds tumble in the strengthening wind. This is how to read the incoming weather, by watching large-scale atmospheric phenomena and the minutiae of animal behaviour. I love wind because it trades so much light, sound, colour and scent, and because it is powerful.

Winds can sculpt stone, move great quantities of sand, disrupt the flow and fall of water and mould thought. They bring air masses filled with stories of the high Arctic or deep Atlantic or tropical south. Here the seasons are multiplied by weather systems tumbling in from every compass direction. At this north-western edge of mainland Britain they are visible long before they arrive. A single day may catch snippets of summer and spring, or morsels of autumn and winter. Weather rewrites the terminology of landscape and the natural world, creating new seasons, new sensations, new memories.

Together air and sea have communal voices and vibrant natures. In Wester Ross they interact with the powerful presence of ancient rocks and landforms and complex configurations of coast and high mountain ranges to create a special magic and generate a visceral sense of being inside story-telling and history-making. They alter the dimensions of life, warping space and time, extending and compressing distant horizons and immediate surroundings; they can bewilder and disorientate, yet create such a strong sense of belonging that one feels part of the living and intricate narrative of earth, sea and sky.

This is a windswept, elemental place, filled with colour and energy created by the interplay of air and water with ancient geology and living organisms. Once, at day's end, after a mustard-yellow and soot-black storm, I watched the last cloud, domed like a cauliflower, its tops glowing red, sail past me from north to south. For a few moments it stuttered and emptied a purple shower into the sea. On one side was a rainbow, on the other a flash of lightning.

*

The wind begins to whip my face and I notice a long band of indigo thickening out to the west. Only moments ago, the horizon was a thin pencil line, topped by the faint shapes of distant islands, but now it writhes as it swells. Strong winds are at work out there, over the Hebrides, and soon they will arrive here on the mainland. There are changing colours in every direction. This is what happens as competing energies run towards us. Their purposes are revealed in hue and chroma, light and sound. Almost as if some giant invisible hand is pouring paint, the Minch turns green, then yellow, then grey. In a heart-beat it is blue, the sapphire of a summer sea. Then there is a sudden burst of sunshine and heat on my back, summer still prodding my body into action. I turn for home and the whole valley shimmers in the sunlight.

Back indoors I scribble a few notes – reminders of the sea colours and birds spotted down on the shore. My diaries report, decode and deconstruct the seasons here, breaking them down into smaller pieces and wrapping them back into distinctive parcels. Inside are bite-sized mini-seasons, each distinctive in their own way, with characteristics based on the vagaries of the weather and natural phenomena seen on croft, hill and shore.

I rummage through a pile of old calendars. I create one every year for the children and grandchildren so they have small slices of this place in their own homes. Each year contains a mixture of sunsets and sunrises, pictures of the croft, meadows, peat bogs, mountains and coast, and photo-graphs of approaching storms, plants in bloom, the river in flood, birds on the shore, insects feeding on wildflowers, and lambs, ponies and cattle grazing. They are my versions of calendars based on the natural world, each with pictures of phenomena unique to both month and place. Short phrases pop into my head, prompted by the images in front of me – hints of possibility, ways of describing, of articulating how our year changes.

*

We are all linked across time and space – from the understanding of long-term solar and lunar changes to my photographs of sunsets and sunrises. Ancient communities would measure and predict seasonal change by looking to the heavens; they transposed and interlinked the astronomical with the earthly, partnering the movement and phases of the moon and stars, the procession of equinoxes and positions of solstices with the practical needs of their communities – when to harvest grain, plant seeds and pick fruit.

At a site known as Warren Field in Aberdeenshire, archaeologists found stones that record phases of the moon across a year, but when matched up to features in the landscape, create a calendar that can stretch out across hundreds and hundreds of years. The 'Warren Field Calendar' is thought to be ten thousand years old. Scientists say it would have enabled the builders to track much larger and longer periods of time, millennia before the 'civilisations' of Babylon, Greece or China created their own complex calendrical systems. There may be one like it here somewhere, buried in deep peat; there is enough about to conceal all kinds of mysteries.

In ancient Egypt, calendars were based on the Nile's flood history as well as the stars, a beautiful marriage between geomorphology and astronomy. One Babylonian calendar used agricultural events as well as lunar cycles. It referred to a multiplicity of specific seasons, ones much smaller than ours, with delightful titles such 'barley is at the quayside' and 'first fruit offerings'. In the Far East, the earliest Chinese calendars incorporated the lunisolar year with ecological descriptions, environmental phenomena and key dates. They evolved into a specialised system based on the sun's position in the zodiac, akin to some Celtic traditions, including Warren Field. The year was subdivided not into four seasons or twelve months but twenty-four solar and twelve lunar periods of variable length principally used to guide farming activities. Eventually they came to influence broader aspects of society.

The Chinese calendar is still in use. Each subdivision of the year is tied closely to events happening in the natural world, to types of weather or to specific agricultural activities, and it includes beautiful names such as 'locust trees blossom' or 'white dew'. The latter marks the start of autumn, when morning and evening temperatures are cool enough to cause the formation of dew and mist. By the seventh century the Chinese calendar had spread across the Far East and today the Japanese version of seventy-two *sekki* and *ko* is well known. It also uses beautiful descriptions of small changes to environment and weather or to events in the natural world. Although its modern version is more firmly rooted in the Gregorian calendar of the West, the Japanese have retained many of the original Chinese descriptors, enchanting names such as 'first peach blossoms' or 'plums turn yellow'.

I remember reading about a druidic calendar found at Coligny in France, almost two thousand years old and carved into bronze. It was based on both the moon and the sun, similar to the calendars of the Near and Far East, and just as the Warren Field stone calendar in Scotland appears to be. Subdivisions or micro-seasons with names adorn it – 'time of ice', 'shoots show' and 'seed fall' – testament to a deep understanding of astronomy and the natural world. Thus, similar ideas about the measurement of seasons and natural phenomena were present across western Europe too.

*

I am a writer and crofter, a mother and grandmother, and a former geographer, who loves to take photographs and fill my notebooks with descriptions of this scent or that, of colours and sounds and changes observed over the years here in the Northwest Highlands. The books and camera files are filled with the smaller truths of life, and about the natural world; they contain evidence of not four seasons but dozens and dozens and dozens.

Living here means we are coastal *and* montane. Coast and people are conjoined to sea and mountains elementally, historically, physically and emotionally. We occupy a charged space, an edgeland, rich in biodiversity and full of character, one in which the 'elementals' described by Nan Shepherd – light, air, water, earth, sound and scent – are our constant companions. This place churns with energy, we are pulled this way and that by the magnetic lure of some of the most dramatic mountain landscapes in Europe, by the deep, pulsing, charismatic and ever-changing stretch of sea and by the wrinkled horizon of distant islands.

This complex country is dominated by powerful forces – climatic, thalassic and terrestrial – combining to colour all aspects of our lives. Their relative influence changes many times each day so trying to define or describe this place merely by its geology and landform, or by its land-use and human activity, or by weather and wildlife, does not always work. Weather is volatile, landscapes powerful, the sea dynamic. Together they expose the deep and intricate relationships between people, crofts, communities, coast, sea and surrounding hill country. I see these bonds running through the waves, clouds and rippling grasses; they are present in the river and gusting winds and play of light on mountain tops.

I live with my husband Rob in a little house on a croft – an agricultural smallholding of just a few hectares known as Red River Croft. The croft contains a complex collection of different types of habitats – meadows, ditches, paths, scrub and woodland, a sinuous river and small peat bog. We are close enough to the sea to see it from any west-facing window and from anywhere in the fields. Our eastern views are dominated by mountains. The croft sits in South Erradale, a tiny settlement in a small river valley, surrounded on one side by the rugged peaks and sparsely populated country known as 'the Great Wilderness' and on the other by the sea.

We came to live here a decade ago after a lifetime of visits, first as youngsters wanting to explore, then on our honeymoon and later with our extended family on holidays. Eventually, encouraged by family and friends, we gave up our full-time, well-paid jobs to take on a croft within a busy crofting community. Although he loved wild places, Rob had worked for thirty-five years in busy pharmacies in Liverpool and Lancashire. Over the same period, I obtained my doctorate on environmental change in New Guinea, left work to raise our four children, and then returned to full-time academia.

Rob was ready for change. I was ready to leave an increasingly difficult working environment. We both wanted to do more of the things we love. The children had gone successfully through university, each had good secure employment and moved away. At first we were anxious about making ends meet, and then Rob began part-time work as community pharmacist in Gairloch. In the last decade all four children married and became parents themselves. Now there are eight grandchildren, and our home is very busy once again, filled with noise and bustle.

Our aims were straightforward – we wanted to create a new family hub in the Highlands, climb mountains and manage our croft. But after a few years I was reduced to sleepy muddleheadedness and painful hobbling by a strange infection – Lyme disease and a range of autoimmune conditions were discussed. Doctors and testing followed two main lines of inquiry – a flu-like virus of some sort or a long dormant tropical insect-borne infection sparked into life perhaps by a tick bite. Whatever its origins, the infection that had begun so suddenly resulted in repeated vicious and nasty bouts of acute illness followed by chronic deterioration and debilitating pain. Almost immediately all the higher wilder places were out of reach. My health waxed and waned. On good days I could manage a slow walk around the croft or a short walk to the coast. On bad days Rob would drive to our neighbour's gate and help me negotiate the last short stretch to the cliff-top. There I could lean against an old fence post, wriggle my body into the tiny bit of shelter it granted, breathe deeply and let the wind course through me.

Over the next few years I would watch storms run in from the Atlantic, thundersnow over the mountains, sunsets as they passed back and forth through the seasons, full moons cresting Baosbheinn and dipping into the Outer Isles, the Aurora Borealis lighting up both the heavens and the sea, and all manner of astronomical phenomena in between, including Jupiter rising, Venus setting, the Milky Way running overhead. I wrote about what I had witnessed or felt or sensed, drew sketches of changing landscapes and natural phenomena and, every day, took photographs.

In this little space by an old and unassuming fence post at an unimposing cliff edge, where my feet became rooted, complete lunisolar years unfolded in front of me. What emerged from the photographs and notes were stories of life here, of the natural world and changing time and space. The years were embedded with a mixture of the solar and earthbound in narratives akin to the old Celtic calendars whose subdivisions do not quite align with twenty-first-century months and dates but run across them with names belonging to trees and phases of the moon as well as the sun.

The tiny vantage point, embraced by winds from every compass direction, surrounded only by the whispers of grasses on the croft and waves on the shore, by birdsong and otter whistles, yet unnoticed by the wider world, became for me the centre of a celestial and terrestrial calendar, one created by spectacular arrangements of ancient geology and sea, by high mountain peaks, distant islands, and the valley in which I live. The wooden post made a convenient marker and axis from which to measure changes in the natural world. The croft, river and coast became the beating heart of all the calendars and a pivotal force in my recovery. Here I felt connected to the earth like never before, more than in all my previous lives, from undergraduate to professor, daughter to grandmother.

Just as the Chinese, Babylonian and Celtic calendars accounted for myriad seasonal changes with simple words and phrases, similar cycles of change and repeating patterns have emerged here. Together, they tell the story of this place, and, in a small way, they are my story too.

This book ties nature, place and memory to the solar year. It is a calendar of place with markers crafted from deep time in a unique partnership of landscape, sunrises and sunsets. Its myriad seasons are characterised by natural weather phenomena – storms, snow, floods – by the arrival of nature's own markers – orchids in bloom, cuckoos arriving – and by activities on the

croft – haymaking and tree planting. Created by the configurations of mountains, islands, sea and croft, no other calendar is
as singular, not even the great stone calendar of Warren Field.
There are other threads too – my family and friends, illness and
recovery, loss and great joy – but through it all flows the wind,
my companion and healer.

★

I pause and tidy the piles of books and papers. Through the
window the fields now look like they have been spread with
butter. Everything has a yellowy tinge. I open the window wide
and take a photograph with my phone. Somehow the camera
has made the landscape appear even more diffuse and golden.
The air is thick with light. I might include this image in next
year's production, as one of September's very special days. It
could be named 'golden dew glistens', or 'honey-coloured haze'.

Part One

Autumn Equinox to Winter Solstice

1. Sunrise northeast of Creag an Fhithich on Baosbheinn, sunset beyond Ben Volovaig on north Trotternish, Isle of Skye, Celtic month of Ivy (September to October), Harvest Moon

(i) Greens fade to gold, purples to grey

For more than forty years we came to Wester Ross in the Northwest Highlands to climb the ramparts and crenelations of mountains such as Liathach, Beinn Eighe and An Teallach and walk the lesser-known trails from Knoydart to Sutherland, holidaying with family and friends or working. Eventually we decided to stay, arriving in South Erradale during a golden and turquoise September under the gaze of hills so clear it was possible to see the crags and gullies and detailed forms from our new home without the aid of binoculars. For almost two weeks, even as autumn approached, the days were cloudless and almost defiantly azure. Not all Septembers are so blessed but in most years since then the Erradale valley has been brightly gilded with gold and polished copper, the surrounding moorland deeply bruised with purple and green.

The shifting moods of early autumn are revealed again and

again by rapidly changing colours. Soon after the equinox the once purpled hills turn the colours of burnt toast and the fierce orange of cinder toffee. Meadows turn from golden-blonde to silver-grey, lanced here and there by tall shards of bronze and copper. Eventually, despite even their implied metalled strength, the last of the tall wildflowers and grasses simply topple over. Only rushes remain rigidly, defiantly upright.

Sea breezes carry the intermingling melodies of breaking waves and birdsong through the croft and sweep up the river valley towards the distant hills. Often the air remains rich with the lingering perfumes of heather, for it continues to flower at the coast long after it fades on the hills. But as October draws closer fine mists are slowly replaced by salt spray rising up from the sea. On such days I can taste it on my tongue; it is both sweet and savoury.

*

Wester Ross has a population of only six thousand, with a little over six hundred living in and around the parish of Gairloch. Red River Croft sits some kilometres south of Gairloch village in the tiny hamlet of South Erradale, one of several settlements known as 'crofting townships'. These coastal edgelands are part farmland, part open country, and merely a fragment of the expansive grandeur known as 'the Scottish Highlands'. To some they may only be a tiny faded watermark in the intricate map of more familiar Scottish history, but croft-lands, along the western margins of the Scottish mainland and on the Outer Isles, are the important, integral, living heart of a fierce and intoxicating country recognised the world over for its isolated and rugged spaces and for its unique and wonderful variety of wildlife. These crofted lands characterise rural life in the west both here and on the islands, and have done so for almost two hundred years. Yet the crofting way of life contains echoes of long vanished farming practices that once filled the glens inland.

Red River Croft itself is a busy, life-filled space. The landscape around our home is wide open and views can stretch for more than fifty kilometres. The natural energies of this place appear to hinge on the river valley and flow out from the great mountain wall, always running down to the sea, but in reality the pulse of life moves from mountain to valley to sea, from sea to atmosphere, from sea to islands and back again, just as it has done for millennia.

A croft is a field used for agricultural purposes. In this part of Wester Ross, most crofts are roughly two hectares in size, fenced with post and wire and tending to be square rather than long and narrow. Red River Croft is a combination of two, about four hectares in total. In general, many crofts have a house and outbuildings, though not all have homes built on them. Where they do, a portion of ground would have been 'de-crofted' and no longer legally used for crofting purposes but given over to a house and garden.

The pattern of croft boundaries is relatively modern and in this area dates from 1845 when the townships were laid out by the Gairloch Estate under the supervision of its factor, Dr John Mackenzie, brother of the absent laird Francis. Originally families would have grown cereals, vegetables and hay in order to feed themselves and their animals, but eventually that practice of subsistence production gave way in the second half of the twentieth century to large numbers of sheep, with incomes derived from government and European grant schemes and family members needing to seek alternative means of work. But the effect of this way of life over the last hundred and seventy years, largely free of artificial products in spite of the changes to the practice and nature of crofting, has culminated in a patch-work of micro-habitats that today support a great variety of birds, insects and other wildlife.

Our small house and garden are enclosed by a high green hedge adjoining a small woodland of pine, oak, alder, willow, birch and hazel. Although some houses and gardens have protective screens of larch or spruce, our abundant hedging is unusual but provides much-needed, vital protection from the strong and scouring salty winds of winter. Woodland, garden and house are themselves enclosed by the large meadows making up the croft. Many of our neighbours' fields comprise grass pasture but Red River Croft is bisected by the River Erradale, resulting in a remarkable and complex variety of habitats including peat bog, flood meadows, dry grassland, wet flushes, riverbanks, burns and ditches, scrub and trees.

Adjacent to our house and garden is an old stone byre. One end is home to bats and, in the middle, nests line up along the main roof-supporting rafter. Previous owners added ropes and pieces of wood for extra purchase so that from end to end there are more than a dozen cupped and precisely made swallows' nests.

*

During our first autumn we investigated the nooks and crannies of our fields and buildings, noting the tree and shrub species and watching the way water moved after heavy rains. Rob checked the old fences and field drains, and chopped wood, while I did my level best to identify bugs, birds and dying meadow plants. One morning I wandered along the riverbank, watching the water reflect a bright blue sky. The river crinkled like cellophane where it ran over bright rust-red pebbles and around great black and grey boulders. Bubbles occasionally broke the surface and at its margins horsetail and sedges trembled in the gentle breeze. Even this late in the month insects dashed back and forth in the warmth. There were dragonflies, damselflies and clouds of small dancing, non-biting midges. A long branch of an old alder swayed back and forth and its outermost twigs trailed like fingers through the water.

I was suddenly aware of another voice above the birdsong and looked up to see a woman clambering over the fence, calling out and waving to me. She was small, slender and lithe and climbed the high barbed wire easily.

'Hello,' she said, 'I'm Cathma, from the house just up the bank there. "Cathma" is short for "Catherine" but there are so many of us here that some call me "wee-Cate". Well, that was at school and the name stuck. My grandchildren call me "Katack".' I could not compete with her list of names and laughed. 'I thought I'd come down to say hello and ask you and your husband to come for tea and maybe a scone or whatever it is I've been baking.' Her voice sang lightly, in tune with the river. 'I'm Ann,' I replied. 'But all my friends call me "Annie". I always hankered after a longer name or at the very least an extra "e" on the end of it.' We shook hands. 'Yes, a cuppa would be lovely, thank you.' 'Welcome to South Erradale, to the Highlands,' she said. 'I hope you will cope with the weather, and with us.' Her Highland face was open, honest and full of mischief; her eyes twinkled with the colour of skies on an autumn morning, blue-grey with flecks of russet; her hair was straight and almost white. 'Cuppa? What is that?' I laughed again. 'A brew. As folk say in Lancashire. A cup of tea.' 'Aye, yes, well there's always lots to learn, even at my age.' We carried on along the riverbank towards her croft, exchanging pleasantries about the weather. Then Cathma took her leave and with long strides quickly crossed the tussocky ground and jumped the fence again.

Cathma Thomson is a Mackenzie. Her family have lived here and worked the land for generations, probably since long before the township and crofts were designated. She is of this place; her bones and muscles are made of rock and peat, her blood flows as rustily red as the river that passes through our croft and hers. She loves the land, the sea and the air; she loves her animals and the flowers in her garden. For some years she taught business at the secondary school in Gairloch. How a woman so obviously wrought from the magic and life of this place, who has surely descended from the fae, could have been interested in what to me are the insipid mechanics of a business curriculum still puzzles me and has provided ample opportunities for teasing and laughter. But her crofting wisdom and knowledge have been invaluable. Cathma quickly became our link to crofting practices and the wider community of crofters, but she also provided powerful connections to the past and the old ways of living in this place.

For crofting communities to have survived and flourished for so long required deep mutualistic ways of working. Cathma herself recalls how crofters in South Erradale who owned horses and implements not only ploughed their own patches but also did the work for others. Most families owned a cow but they would be communally herded onto the surrounding hills after milking on summer days, returning 'to the call' in the evenings. When the cows began to 'go dry' in the autumn, people shared what milk remained, the deliveries made by the children. At shearing and dipping time all the able-bodied crofters from South Erradale and the nearby crofting townships of Port Henderson and Opinan worked together to round up the sheep. Once the ewes and lambs were gathered into an enclosure known as a 'fank', the men sheared, the women and children gathered up the wool. All foods for animals and people had to be home-produced and the growing of crops such as potatoes, turnips and carrots was communal. The cutting and lifting of peats to provide heat and energy for cooking, the cultivation of land, animal husbandry, the management of food supplies and exchange of goods created a necessary reciprocity, a system developed out of a long-shared history predating the establishment of crofting by thousands of years, a symbiotic relationship between people and place borne out of need. Today, although the traditions of crofting have changed, that same sense of interchangeability and shared responsibility continues, rooted in people and in place. It was into this unique landscape and community we hoped to settle.

*

The great complexity of life and landform on the croft and surrounding coastal and mountain landscapes creates an ever-changing panoply of colour, texture, light and shade. No two days are the same. Flux and motion are constant companions. As autumn progresses, these complexities intensify; they become louder and bolder, overwriting the golden calm usually associated with September until the days themselves lose their gentle gold and silver fragility.

A week or two after the equinox, autumn spreads down from the hills and in from the sea. Large swathes of hill country, once so richly purple, darken. There are shadows on the hills like spilled tea. In the summer-green flashes where bog-cottons and moor grasses dance, there is a dry crispness, as if everything was made from tattered strips of parcel paper. But even these colours fade – rust to grey, cocoa to flax. More of the detailed shapes and forms of the fields and riverbanks become visible. Lumps and bumps appear everywhere; ditches and steps are revealed; the remains of houses, old fence lines, boulders and tree stumps emerge. In those early days, what Cathma had disclosed through our growing friendship began to emerge in the physical characteristics of the valley as vegetation decayed. In the low golden light of our very first autumn, the land slowly began to disclose its secrets. In subsequent years, secrets turned into stories.

(ii) Meadows die back

The landscape around the crofting township and beyond to the hill country is wide open, and by gaining just a little height the views can expand and stretch for tens of kilometres. Many parts of this country are so devoid of trees its secret forms are revealed by the autumnal dying-back of ground cover, its essential structure now visible like bones and blood vessels seen under the translucent skin of an old hand.

Across South Erradale there are patches of scrub here and there, dense clusters of gorse growing in odd corners. And sitting atop old walls or alongside unkempt ditches the brambles provide pounds of fruit in late September. One day I wandered about intent on blackberrying but also curious about the few remaining walls, old tracks, old fences and strange, scattered heaps of stones and ruins. Many of these features were illuminated by the late afternoon sun and almost all were accompanied by bramble growth or rushes to a greater or lesser degree.

I had asked Cathma about them and she showed me some of her maps of South Erradale and the old crofts and recommended a series of booklets published by the Gairloch Museum. She herself had contributed memories of life here, including stories about who lived where, what was grown in which fields and where the peats were cut. Historical gossip. The museum booklets led on to a raft of maps and Ordnance Survey archives revealing the history of our croft, the valley and wider Northwest Highlands. Stories of landscape and environmental change in time and space.

Underneath the spiky tangles and below the modern crofting landscape is a history reaching back to the last vestiges of retreating ice. The whole place is a palimpsest. Stacked upon the natural and geological are layers and layers of settlement structures and the remains of agricultural activity, now crowned with thorns and rich purple-black fruit.

One of the most interesting maps was the very first – South Erradale, drawn in 1845 by the Gairloch Estate when the township and crofts were originally laid out. Crofts were allotted to individuals and families who had been removed from other settlements inland or relocated in the reorganisation of coastal communities when estate land was restructured and repurposed for sheep and deer. The allocation of crofts continued the long tradition of controlling land and people in order to secure the viability of the estate's financial outputs in the form of cattle, sheep and other produce, but it was also one more step along the road of deliberate depopulation as landlords strove to follow the latest fashions and means of making money. This final clearance, however, created the South Erradale we know today.

The estate map showed Erradale's crofts laid out in grid-square fashion. Although it did not detail croft-house sites, it marked a huddle of pre-1845 buildings whose remains can still be found today straddling the northern edge of the township, and several clusters of other features that may once have been huts or dwellings. How long ago they had been built or how many years they had been inhabited is lost to time and turf but it was interesting to note the larger houses sat above the contour line delineating the shape and extent of an ancient estuary.

The story of each individual field is one of shared family ownership, of co-ownership and inheritance. Each croft had an identifying number, from 1 to 28, and today they are all still known as Croft/*Lota* 1 or Croft/*Lota* 22 and so on. We own numbers 16 and 17. But each number on the map had a family name, listed as original tenant on the estate records. Croft 16 is recorded as *Lota Dhomh'ill Eachainn*, or 'Donald, Son of Hector's Croft'; Croft 17 as *Lota Banntrach Eachain*, or 'Hector's Widow's Croft'. Hector was presumably a Mackenzie because his surname was not included, whereas others from different clans, such as Macgregors, were. Some assignments had names referring to their position or their environment – for example, Number 10 was *A'Lub Dhubh*, or 'the Black Corner'; Number 20 *A'Faithir Ur* or 'Croft by the Beach'. There were crofts assigned to 'Fair John', 'Grey John', 'John, son of Roderick', and others to the women of Erradale: *Lota Banntrach Ali* ('Alick's Widow's Croft') and *Lota Curstaidh Ruaridh* ('Kirsty, Daughter of Roderick's Croft').

The 1845 land boundaries in South Erradale have persisted into the twenty-first century and continue to represent a reworking of community structure, land-use and landownership with both a dark past and great symbolism. Crofting represents an overwriting of much older environmental conditions, settlements and ways of life. Building materials have been reworked and repurposed – walls and houses, in many instances, built from even older remains. Whatever was available in the landscape was put to good use so that the remoter origins of settled life in Erradale lie under the modern fences and beneath layers of turf.

★

On either side of the township the valley sides slope gently upwards, covered in thick heather and tussock grasses growing on peat. While the fields of the valley floor grow pale and thin, the heathers grow darker and sedges flush to bronze. The long curling leaves of purple moor grass are clustered into tough tufts and glow with threads of palest beaten gold. Clumps of deer grass fall open to reveal richly textured and earthy browns, the colours of a red deer's hair

One afternoon, spurred on by another long discussion with Cathma, I decided to have a wander upriver and uphill. Here and there on the low hills the long linear forms known as 'lazy beds' – part of the old 'runrig system' of agriculture, constructed for growing crops – were picked out by shadows created by the late afternoon sun playing over the shallow differences in ground surface height and also by variations in plant species growing in the alternating wet and dry rows. The labours of the past, hidden by the living blanket of life, are occasionally revealed by the passage of the seasons or play of light. Here, on the slopes, bog-cottons, plum-red mosses and the dark-brown dead leaves of flag iris sat in damper hollows, while heathers and scattered crimson autumnal leaves of tormentil marked the drier raised ridges. In a few places old buried walls or houses were revealed only by dried and withered remains of wood sage and stonecrop. As with so many British landscapes, it was apparent the long and complex stories of people living here were not simply explained in any linear history but in the braidings and weavings of reuse, in the reworking and repurposing of land and materials as families adapted to social and environmental changes.

I was armed with a photograph kindly given by another neighbour and, leaving the old path, I turned uphill to see South Erradale from a higher vantage point. Our croft and house are overlooked by a small hill – Cnoc an Fhuarain ('hill/knoll of the springs') – one of a small chain of hills forming the north side of the Erradale valley. The photograph had been taken in the 1960s from an elevated position somewhere on the Cnoc. I wandered about for a while trying to find where the photographer had captured the view. The changes over sixty years were marked. In the picture the absence of trees and hedges was striking, more so than the absence of modern houses, including our own. Most of the view was given over to grassland; there was little in the way of heather, gorse or bog myrtle then. Both in the photograph and the view before me the layout of croft boundaries was unchanged. Just as in 1845 there was a checkerboard of large square fields with two 'roads' crossing each other in the centre of the township. But since the photograph was taken clusters of small trees had grown around many of the houses along with straggles of hedges. From the vantage point it was also clear the once grassy hillsides had almost all been consumed by heather moor, testament to the falling number of sheep and cattle in the intervening years. The valley, it seemed, had been slowly rewilding.

Together the 1845 township map, various modern Ordnance Survey sheets and the museum booklets provide clues to the changing story of the valley. The entire township of South Erradale was once enclosed in a great dyke, known as a 'head dyke', a wall of stone perhaps topped by a hedge or wooden fence in the remote past. However, it eventually succumbed to time and gravity, subsumed under heather and grass. From the Cnoc I could pick it out on the north side of the valley where, for a short distance, it ran parallel to an ancient route, once the main 'road' out of South Erradale. Also marked on the map and described in the booklets to the southeast is the *Garradh laruinn*, the 'iron dyke', so named because it contains large pieces of bog-iron found around the Erradale valley. It may well have been part of the main head dyke. The museum booklets suggested some early ironworking took place here, although there is little physical support for this view apart from remnants of bog-iron held within the dyke. And from my vantage point I could see no evidence of anything other than agricultural activity.

Cathma has no recollection of anyone knowing what these dykes looked like in all their glory, and since they are not marked on any later maps they presumably predate the crofting system of fields and meadows, but she does remember a post and wire fence surrounded the township in its entirety, and gates permitting entry in and out from the road to Gairloch. Seventy years ago she and other local children would get excited when visitors came, hoping to receive a penny or two for their services opening and closing the gates. Where the ancient rock and turf dyke might once have protected homes from wild boar or wolves centuries earlier the twentieth-century fences prevented cattle and sheep from raiding the food and fodder crops grown on the crofts during the summer months. In those days few fields inside the township were sectioned off by wood, wire or hedge; however, today each individual croft is fully fenced and the outer gates to the township are long gone.

From the small bare hilltop of Cnoc an Fhuarain it was possible to visualise both the Erradale of Cathma's childhood and the ancient settlement outlined by the crumbling sections of the old dyke. I sat contemplating older geographies and older maps. History and geography swell and subside in the curving and straight lines drawn on paper and I hoped more would be explained in the features slowly revealing themselves as the vegetation died back even further.

The modern grid of fence wires glinted in the sun. The river crimped and twined through the fields as it has done for centuries. Apart from the thick green hedge of our croft-house, there were only a few sparse hedges, little more than thin bedraggled stripes, better than nothing and more than could be seen in the photograph. And around almost every house, trees of all kinds.

The day was getting colder. Hooded crows quarrelled through the air. Upstream beyond the last croft, the river was a coiling band of silver reflecting the pale smooth quilt of cloud scurrying in from the west. The sun flared between clouds and for a few moments the multi-coloured patchwork of crofts and riverside meadows appeared to be hatched by other thin lines – trails made by animals and people as well as by the strews of fencing. Together they created threads, landscape bindings, fastening all the components together. The contrast to the rolling, hedged countryside of some parts of rural England could not have been greater.

I set off downhill, traversing the slope and heading for the road. Once down on the valley floor I passed an old remnant hedge and counted the hazel, willow, alder, dog-rose, honeysuckle and bramble that have survived the scavenging of deer and sheep. It is said the number of woody species counted in a one-hundred-foot length of hedge multiplied by one hundred can tell you its approximate age in years. These thin and spindled accidental non-hedges were neither long nor dense but I counted the species anyway, an old habit. Could it really be almost sixty years old, I wondered. The hedge was filled with great quantities of blackberries and rose hips and among their dense thorns and curling barbs came susurrations of insects and chattering of birds, and the secretive rustle that might have been field-mice or voles.

By the time I reached home the sun was dipping down to the west. Beams of strong amber light poured out from under the cloud-quilt. What had been drained of colour now flared with it. The fields were gilded with gold and rose, trees and hedges rusted to iron. Straggles of bramble, briar and thorn and bolsters of furze still hummed with insects and bustled with birds. Then, as swift and disquieting as gun shots, two grey raptors swooped low to my left, one skimming over the hedge. Small birds startled out from the shrubbery in raucous disarray. The second hunter pounced in a grey-brown jumble and then luminous grey wings pulsed with coral as they dipped away towards the sun. I stooped down and picked up a small, pale, dun feather. A sudden cool gust of wind whipped and plucked the tiny thing from my fingers and carried it away over the fields.

(iii) Birch leaves turn yellow

In a Highland autumn by the sea, the last trickles of golden stickiness are quickly shredded and the few remaining leaves on the old thin hedges stripped by sharpening breezes. Pale-gold autumnal days are spliced by fickle and feisty bouts of turbulent weather. All the seasons, in every possible combination, may be experienced fleetingly during a single day.

A sensation of shifting and progression grows. Encroaching darkness takes unmistakable and expanding bite-sized chunks out of each day. There are spells when the world is grey, dull and sunless, and rain-showers are dragged slowly from sea onto land. Such dreich days seep and slither into darkness. Thick bands of cloud press shadows down onto the fields like squid discharging ink, others are rimmed with white-hot light. And there are days when striae of clouds trundle in from the sea and tangle in gridlock on reaching the mountains. The ferocity of change is exhilarating. Life pulses in tune with the volatile light. The hills, valley and coast bristle and brindle with colour. The extreme beauty of all the decay and dying spreading around us is akin to gilding on a medieval triptych.

Vegetation and wildlife form a significant part of the character of the Highlands, alongside the dramatic physical features created by geology and landforms. Plants create a thick living blanket respiring, growing and dying and being reabsorbed again and again. It is colourful, scented, light-reflecting, light-absorbing, and has the ability to alter and cover up the past. Writers and artists often portray Highland landscapes as treeless heather-clad mountains but the reality is many different vegetation communities live cheek-by-jowl. Small yet complex varieties of habitat occupy what at first sight might seem to be a relatively species-poor countryside. Different types of grassland and wild-flower meadow sit next to wetlands, raised mires and blanket bogs next to sand dunes. Moorlands of heathers and tufted grasses cloak the hills next to ancient woodlands of oak, hazel and Scots pine. From high mountain tops tundra-like dwarf shrubs overlook deep gorges and glens of birch and alder, reed-fringed lochs and meadows tended by crofters with ditches full of marsh marigolds and meadowsweet, and, fringing our coasts, the dune grasslands and machair.

South Erradale and the other crofting townships are situated on a peninsula known as 'Overside'. Loch Torridon and Applecross lie to the south, the Gair Loch and Gairloch village to the north. Woodland is relatively scarce but there are sessile oak woodlands along Overside's northeastern coast. This mature oak forest has been protected from deer for many years. Old trees at Kerrysdale, Shieldaig and Badachro are the remnants of ancient mixed decid-uous woodland, the rich temperate rainforests of the eastern Atlantic fringes which escaped earlier widespread forest clearance and were perhaps preserved because they were once actively managed for charcoal production. As autumn deepens, these great deciduous trees lose their leaves and reveal underskirts of luminous grey and delicate frills of olive green. Even their smallest branches are covered with thick colonies of lichen. In the more sheltered parts, away from the sea, long trailing beards of pale-grey *Usnea* add to the sense of time passing much more slowly than our senses can discern. In the constricting daylight of dawn and dusk, woodlands glow richly, their lichen coats afire. And in the middle of the dullest, wettest days, when thick shawls of cloud are pulled across the forests, strange ethereal light emanates from the branches of oak trees. The effervescent alien lichen-glow is beautiful and otherworldly, flourishing in the pure clean air and hinting at forests long vanished.

*

In Erradale trees are scarce although most houses have rowans planted nearby. Many ruins still have a rowan tree (*Sorbus aucuparia*, or mountain ash) growing beside them. This beautiful tree has long been associated with motherhood and birth as well as protection from evil, and while some legends speak of men originating from the mighty ash (*Fraxinus excelsior*), they also say women came from the rowan tree. The red berries have a calyx shaped like a five-pointed star, an ancient symbol of protection – an explanation for being planted close to the door of a house. Although the berries were once widely used, some of the folklore surrounding this species remains, and their association with witches, menstrual blood and the moon are widely remembered. Women and blood-red rowan berries create powerful magic. To fell a rowan tree would bring years of bad luck, so they are never cut down on purpose, even today.

In moorland peats it is possible to find tree stumps, remnants of forests long gone. Cleared by people over millennia, the remains of pine, oak and birch, gnarled and blackened by time, their rings, knots and bark beautifully preserved, are evidence of a land once rich in woodland. Just as a book is ordered in numbered pages, the concentric rings of a tree stump are layered. Seasonal variations are expressed in thicker or thinner rings – a spring and summer that are warm and benign produce a thick ring, while in a cooler year only a thin ring develops. The resulting tell-tale patterns can be translated into the tree's own particular story and a history of changing climate.

While clearing an area of dense bramble on the croft so we could repair an old fence, Rob found a large oak stump. Almost three hundred discernible annual growth rings on its finely ridged cut surface meant it had lived through at least as many years. If this tree was felled when Erradale's crofts were laid out in the mid-nineteenth century, it would have waved its sapling leaves at the sun during the late 1500s, perhaps as Mary Queen of Scots was beheaded. When the last wolf was supposedly killed in Killicrankie at the end of the seventeenth century, this oak could have been almost a hundred years old. By the time General Roy completed his 'Military Survey' in 1755, the Jacobite Rebellions had been quashed and major land-use changes had begun. Woodlands not managed for timber, charcoal and tanning bark were clear-felled to make way for sheep, just as inland settlements were cleared of people. Yet this tree survived.

We debated whether a cluster of very thin rings represented the first half of the nineteenth century when weather conditions worsened at the peak of the Little Ice Age. Global climate was affected and summer temperatures across the northern hemisphere were suppressed by ash from the Tambora volcanic eruption in 1815. During the following year, the 'Year Without a Summer', such was the impact of the disruption from intense rainfall and cold it led to the telling of fireside stories and ultimately the publication of Mary Shelley's great gothic novel *Frankenstein*. In the Highlands the effects of extremely poor weather over subsequent years enhanced the already desperate plight of communities during the 'Clearances'. Our tree survived but, in all likelihood, by the time the Scottish Industrial Revolution reached its glorious peak with the building of the Forth Railway Bridge, and as the Erradale townships and crofts were fully established, the oak was finally cut down. The stump remained in place, a library-book record of the croft and testament to the many seasons experienced, enjoyed and endured here.

Whether or not you live among trees or close to woodland, it is difficult to imagine an extensively wooded Highland Scotland, especially in the face of a modern landscape whose many hills and glens have been treeless for so long that most of us are not aware of their wooded ancestral past. But across Wester Ross names appear on Ordnance Survey maps attesting to the former presence of trees and more extensive forests. Such is the importance of trees to Gaelic that letters of the alphabet used to be symbolised by species: 'a' is *ailm*, elm (*Ulmus*); 'b' is *beithe*, birch (*Betula*); 'c' is *calltainn*, hazel (*Corylus*). Around South Erradale several places have names associated with trees, though the trees themselves are long gone: *Druim na fearna*, 'ridge of the alders'; *Doireachan nan ubhal*, 'grove of the apples'. The word *beithe* or *bheithe* appears frequently, probably because the birch tree is a fast-growing invasive species which happily regenerates where other trees have been cleared or where grazing intensity has fallen. Today, however, there are no groves of apples, and where tree names appear on modern maps there are often no woodlands of any kind. Yet the names remain as echoes of the former mixed and complex mosaics of woodland, shrub and open ground widespread throughout the Highlands thousands of years ago.

Modern maps of the area also include species associated with the more open moorland landscapes of today: heather (*fraoch*), reed (*cuilcean*) and cotton grass (*canaich*). Since all three species are found around us now, such place names probably date from a post-forested world, when woodland had already been cleared to make way for sheep.

In the same way that maps contain Gaelic names for lost woodlands and associated species, they also refer to the fauna. In the hill country around South Erradale there is *Creagan Fhithich*, 'hill of the ravens', *Creagan na Feannaig*, 'hill of the crows', *Lochan nam Breac Odhar*, 'little loch of the grey trout', and various names for landscape features that intriguingly refer to the long-vanished wolf and hare (*madaidhean, maigheachan*).

*

The story of Wester Ross's forests made the few trees on our croft seem even more precious. We discussed the idea of our fields becoming native woodland and I mapped out where trees could be planted – a cluster here, a broad band there – wild cherry, willow, hazel, oak and aspen. I rang a crofting consultancy and a forestry expert and organised site visits.

The outcome was disappointing. Transformation to a 'woodland' croft would be impossible without the agreement of our sheep-rearing community and local 'Grazings Committee'. In addition, the entire croft would need to be refenced with good, strong 'deer fencing', at least two metres high, with two new river gates as well as all the necessary field gates. Consultancy, financial wrangling and form filling confirmed the potential costs would outweigh any financial support. One by one, difficulties were placed in front of us like fences. 'This is good pasture and always has been,' I was told by one crofter. 'Why would you plant trees?' asked another. 'We've never had them here.'

My enthusiasm plummeted. I gave up the idea of creating a new woodland croft and agreed to have the ground grazed intermittently by our neighbours' sheep and cattle. We drew up plans to create hedges and small groups of trees, thinking they would ultimately enhance biodiversity and supply additional mulch and organic matter to depleted soils. Our tiny saplings would be planted with protection we made ourselves, cobbled together from old fencing materials. Any return to woodland must wait.

And yet a small woodland sits next to our home, planted more than forty years ago with oak, ash, rowan, pine, hazel and willow. There is a crab apple tree and a delicate aspen growing from the ruins of a building that may once have been a house, and lots of birch saplings. The trees produce many seedlings. They are so prolific the garden is rapidly turning into forest, a rewilding of sorts, forest regeneration in action. Tree babies sprout everywhere, every year, and show how quickly forest regeneration could begin if it was allowed to do so.

Often new plantations are on poorly developed soils or in areas absent of any active tree growth for long periods of time, or they are in places so heavily grazed that all the tree seedlings are eaten before they have a chance to develop. The net cumulative effect is that soils become depleted of the seeds, fungi and soil organisms vital to forest health. But on the croft the life support systems for forest regrowth appear to be healthy and active. In the past few years I have gathered as many seedlings and small saplings as possible, potted them on and planted them out along the field margins. There are new splashes of proto-hedge and one area over the river is already promising a woodland for the future. At this time of year, as the garden and meadows swell with the fruiting bodies of fungi of all shapes, sizes and colours, I imagine forests everywhere.

All across the croft, as grasses pale and shrivel, the turf sprouts with bright iridescent colours of all kinds, daubs of unmixed acrylic paints on a fading watercolour. Purple, red, yellow, white and all shades of brown, beige and cream, small forests of fungi, radiant fly agaric, chanterelles and many more. They are symbolic of a rich underground network of mycelia transmitting food and information along a quasi-neural network. Threads are woven between fungi, tree roots and other plants, between insects and soil fauna, symbiotic, mutualistic and vital chemical exchanges. Above ground the air is filled with spores, moving about invisibly on currents of air.

The torrent of leaves grows apace. Strangely, our birches are the first trees to lose their vibrant summer greens, perhaps prompted by cold, salt breezes from the sea. As winds strengthen, their yellow leaves flutter like butterflies and their bark begins to darken from rusty brown to dark purple. Yet they are resilient and often the last to shed their leaves, and when they do, there is a cascade of bright yellow pennies. The ground is covered with a beautiful lemon carpet, woven with the very last whisper of summer. Leaves even gather in the river, caught by boulders, stones and gravels. For a short time the river turns from red to a pale butter-yellow. Soon the winds scoop up the leaves and carry them away and those trapped by the river darken until they sink into the riverbed or are carried off down to the sea.

2. Sunrise over Beinn Alligin, sunset between Ben Edra and the Bealach Uige, Trotternish, Isle of Skye, Celtic month of Reed (October to November), Hunter's Moon

(i) Water flows more strongly

Modern Ordnance Survey maps label the river running down the valley through the township as the 'Erradale', but on those from the early twentieth century and in John H. Dixon's 1886 book *Gairloch and Guide to Loch Maree* it is named *Abhain Dearg*, the 'Red River'. In other documents the river appears as *Abhain Ruadh*, also red, but subtly different. *Dearg* hinting of a colour more reddy brown, and *ruadh* the colour of red hair or bracken – both meanings can be found in the waters here. Although historical numbers allocated to each croft must remain the same, it seemed fitting to assign a name to our new home – Red River Croft.

Geology and topography have controlled the movement of water and thus how water has shaped the character of the valley. On a battered old Ordnance Survey map I had marked the watershed in pencil. The lines outlined a river catchment shaped like a human lung. The wet springs and sumps were alveoli, trickling streamlets the bronchioles, and larger burns the bronchi. Where the mature river ran through and bisected the township, it looked strong and thick like a trachea. There are repeating patterns in any fluvial landscape – fractals and bifurcations – and if you look hard, they pop up everywhere on maps and throughout the natural world. They can be seen in the branches of stunted alders on our croft, in *Cladonia* lichen clinging to clumps of heather and in deer antlers found discarded on the hill. When I stood on the small hill above our valley, the patterns made by streamlets, burns and river matched the blood vessels in my hand and dendrites in my brain. Water-glisks from streamlets were riverine thoughts, glints from wet rocks flashing synapses. Erradale is filled with the motion of water. Everywhere.

Highland Scotland is blessed with rain. As a result, the whole landscape acts as a sponge, soaking up water and releasing it quickly. After a storm dozens of burns and streams materialise. Autumnally brown hillsides are speared by dozens of white, fast-moving threads and ribbons. They are responsible for carving up these hills and slopes, though for much of the time they are invisible, hidden under overhangs of heather, peat and stone. But when they do appear, their power and determination are tangible. Then, just as quickly, they vanish, their ephemeral forms absorbed into the slopes once again.

In periods of prolonged downpours, or after sudden, heavy rain, the lower Erradale valley becomes animated with the movement of water. Water effervesces from the earth and here, too, streams emerge where none had been seen before. Abhain Dearg appears to possess its own special nature and character. The river swells soundlessly at first, then forges forward in great bursts of noise. By watching how quickly river levels could rise and fall we began to understand a little more about the enigmatic role of water in this place.

One morning I decided to go in search of the river's source in a space on the Ordnance Survey map pockmarked by small pools. The day was overcast but still bright. A keen wind blew off the sea. From the crossroads in South Erradale a track runs east in a straight line between two ancient collapsed walls. On my right the river waters sang lustily, the music full of light and shade, tone and depth. From a five-bar gate straddling a quag-mire, a tortuous, narrow and very rough path headed upriver. It wandered between remnants of old walls and heaps of lichen-embroidered stones and eventually came to an oval field, an unusual and stark contrast to the squared-off crofts downriver. One of several lobed fields drawn on the older maps of South Erradale and labelled 'sheep folds', it may therefore predate the nineteenth-century crofting layout. These curving stone walls must have once completely enclosed the fields but are now mostly hidden by grass and heather, having collapsed years ago. Only a few upright remnants were still visible. Several tall fence posts supported dangling wires which perhaps once hoped to restrain deer. Cathma described how one crofter had ploughed the field and planted potatoes, but the whole crop was plundered, wires snapped by hunger, driven by need. Since then, the culti-vated ground has surrendered once more to a dense cover of tussock grasses.

Beyond the old fields any semblance of a track thinned to a trickle matching the convolutions of the river. Water drummed over rock steps as the valley rose gently eastwards. There were heathered and moss-covered lumps everywhere, made mostly of large rocks and occasional tree stumps, which made the walking difficult. The river behaved more naturally here, free of the restraints and fortified embankments common on the crofts. It swung in grand, sinuous calligraphy, back and forth between the rounded valley sides. Clusters of boulders increased in size, room for booted feet shrank. Some rocks were as big as byre doors, others larger still. Small grey-brown birds hopped about on them, their colours dulled by a growing blanket of grey clouds, making them impossible to identify.

Even though the trail was contorted, it gradually gained height. Behind me Erradale's houses looked small, the square fields neat and compact, the river meanders map-drawn tidy. I could hear other watery sounds and clambered up onto a large boulder to look about. It was a landscape of peat and black bog pools flanked by crisp tufts of heather, rusty-brown deer grass, golden tussock grasses, grey-haired dwarf willow and sweet-scented bog myrtle. Dozens of small burns and smaller rivulets, each with their own individual song, coalesced and together created the impression of a choir backed by the tinkling of hundreds of tiny bells. The sounds were unlike anything I had heard before. The air soughed in accompaniment; the same noise that waves make as they run onto a beach. Township noises, from cars, tractors, sheep, cows, people, and especially the sparrow rabbles around the houses, had dwindled to nothing. Haunting voices emanated from the moorland. I could identify the river's voice, the sounds of smaller cascades and then the trilling of curlews. A stranger ululation, snipe perhaps, came from a smear of green, a wet patch of grassland. To the west the neat fields and houses looked strangely remote, as if they belonged elsewhere. Up here, the valley was bound tightly by invisible threads of passing time and semi-wildness, tangled in unseen music and rooted by the braiding river.

The afternoon was passing quickly. It began to feel that locating a single source was an almost impossible task. Any one of a dozen springs or sumps or wet peat hollows could claim that title. The upper catchment, an enormous area of gently sloping land continuously feeding water into the river system from waterlogged ground and almost immeasurably deep peat, brimmed with water. Like a giant sponge, the land seemed to hold wetness in the peat beds and pools and in its very bedrock.

I had been walking for a long time and realised the head-waters were still a considerable way off through even more tough, energy-sapping country. I gave up my search. Instead, I sat down and then lay back in a dense bed of heather, feeling bone weary. Overhead, what had earlier been a formless shield of grey cloud began to tear into strips like paper. After a few minutes of watching the sky and breathing in the clean, precise notes of bird calls and water music I stood up and turned for home. Before me, countless small pools of water were now visible, some black, others grey, some pale blue, each one smaller than a kitchen sink. The hillside was covered with splashes of water like tears. Millions of them.

I began to pick my way downslope, accompanied at first by a single filament of silken water made from merging tear-pools. Another strand appeared, then another, and another. Twisting and spinning, they thickened and brightened and melded together, slowly at first until they became a silver bracelet. The waters, yet to find their red blush, skipped on faster and faster, leaving me far behind.

★

My childhood was spent on the banks of the River Mersey, whose currents, in the days before environmental regulation, ran choc-olate brown, occasionally luminescent green, and often carried orange, floating scum and other nameless rankness past my home and out to the sea beyond Liverpool. Swimming was forbidden. Small streams and ditches leaked foul-smelling sludge into the margins of the great river and occasionally foamed with bright-coloured bubbles. The sucking muds exposed at low tide stank and plants were grey and wraith-like. Riverbank chimneys poured with bitter-tasting sulphurous-yellow smokes which crept unwelcomed into lungs and blood. Each day, my mother would wipe black grit from the window sills. And, as a child, I had dark thoughts about those nameless vapour-creepers, while adults around me had darker words about dying too soon.

Such foul air chased us out of town every year. We headed for the open countryside of mid-Wales and the sands of Borth in Cardigan Bay, to clean salt-air, grassy cliff-tops, purple-blue mountains and ancient oak woodlands. To a child of a northern chemical town in England this holiday-country was a sunny and expansive place, with big seas and bigger skies, and light-strewn hills. It was the land of Welsh legend, of Taliesin and Merlin, the Mabinogion and the drowned forests and fields of Cantref Gwaelod. I clutched my tattered books of birds, flowers and insects and vigorously coughed up industrial grime inhaled over the previous year. There was a river here too, the clean, sparkling Leri, so different to the Mersey. A narrow path followed its course for many kilometres, a secluded trail for the most part hidden by tall reeds and rushes until it passed by the edges of the great, vast bogland of Cors Fochno. There my mother showed me dragonflies and strange, striped spiders sitting on rafts, bright-belled heathers and shy bog rosemary, grasses with inner tubes like straws and brazenly orange sundews that trapped flies. The walk was a mother-led wandering where we collected wild-flowers and tried to identify birds and bugs, and it set me on a long path, into the world of geoscience and natural history.

The Erradale is a much smaller watercourse than the Leri, yet it has the same strong bond with mountain, moorland and peat bog. Thronging in the tiny pools and damp hollows of the river's upper reaches were the same plants I had seen as a girl, the same species that blessed the great bog of Welsh legends and lost worlds. I wondered if these deep, wet mires and bog-covered hills might hide similar secrets, the stories of remote, long-vanished peoples, perhaps.

I began to think I had the measure of water in the Erradale valley. Its springs and sumps, bog pools and wet flushes, stream-lets and burns were all part of an interconnected whole along with the peat-covered moorland and carefully tended crofts. Water, it seems, rises and falls through them all in unison, in the same way a living organism breathes, in a lung-shaped catchment with alveoli, bronchi and trachea active at the landscape scale. The Red River controls the pace and nature of water movement from hill to sea, from head to heart to lungs and back again.

At this time of year moisture-laden air pours in from the sea and sweeps up-valley, upriver, up-mountain. It is a period of atmospheric flux. Flash-mob showers can be so swift and sharp they create rainbows again and again, moving together as swiftly as cars racing. Tall narrow arcs, great broad bands, triple rain-bows, rainbows that can outpace a galloping horse, low bows that appear to descend into the earth, rainbows whose reflections in lochs form complete circles, all shapes and sizes and dizzying levels of vibrancy and animacy. They run upslope or downriver, from sea to hill or hill to sea, and generate a sense of connection between the tiny bog pools, streamlets and burns and cloud-filled skies. A day of rainbows almost becomes a narrative, as if the elemental was in deep conversation with the geological. The dizzying displays of light and colour and motion of air and vapours are the visible, tangible expressions of an exchange of energy between atmosphere, water and earth, and the ever-present connections between peat, rock and running water. Together they are evidence of both the continual movement of water in this landscape and its power.

(ii) Rivers flood occasionally

Autumn deepens. The spread of colour becomes a deluge. Greens shrivel, overwhelmed by bursts then torrents of rich, deep browns and oranges. Even the lichen on rocks and boulders flare with seasonal colours. All across the croft and up on the valley slopes, the tones and shades of autumn gel and thicken. Tussocks of deer grass deepen to rust, leaves of tormentil turn crimson, mosses prickle with red, orange and yellow and the tips of tall grasses turn from purple and green to butterscotch and cream. The riverbank myrtle, willows and alder variegate to yellow, vermillion and then brown. Only the gorse bushes remain defiantly green.

For most of autumn the River Erradale trundles slowly through the lower meadows. Abhain Dearg is aptly named. River bedload, derived from rusty-red sandstones, gives the water its hints of henna and titian. Water held within peat or travelling slowly through it takes on the dark brownness of coffee, while bog-iron adds its rusting effects to the overall ruddiness. But this appearance of relative slow-moving steady calm is very quickly overturned. An overnight deluge may cause water to bubble up from just about anywhere and ooze out of the peat. It can create new burns that run down the hillsides and merge together in white frothing cascades. As a result, the river churns with foam under the arches of the nearby road bridge. What appears as a thinly branched watercourse on a map is overwritten by multiple white threads sewn across the slopes, stitching skies to valley. The flux and flush of water are swift; the river is red no longer. And with it comes considerable power. In full spate the Erradale, usually a channel some three metres wide, can swiftly become a flood zone of thirty. The old crofting map shows the course of Abhain Dearg in 1845, while modern aerial photographs, taken for government surveys of crofts over the last twenty years, show contemporary positions of the river channels. By comparing them we see evidence of a very dynamic and change-able river, its meanders roaming liberally and quite naturally from one side of the floodplain to the other.

Channel changes, floods and resulting damage to riverside crofts and the road from one coastal township to another clearly caused problems for the people of Overside in the past. In the 1873 logbook for the school at Opinan the entry for October the twenty-fourth reports the Erradale river flooded so severely that none of the children from Red Point or those living on the south side of the river could get to school. One child almost died as he was swept away while trying to cross. Such events eventually led to the building of a bridge. The bridge is impres-sive, with buttresses, and fourteen arches through which the river cascades; but despite its solid construction, floodwater was still able to cause trouble. In 1877 the Erradale changed its course so dramatically the entire bridge was left 'high and dry', while water ran freely around and past it to the north in a great wide curve.

Today the arches span a broad area of meanders and continue to help control the direction of flow while carrying the modern single-track road running north to Gairloch and south to Red Point. But it is likely that one of the original crossings was here on Red River Croft, at a spot marked 'ford' on old maps. The ford's position, on a large sweeping meander, makes perfect sense, for it is downriver from the widest section of braiding but upstream from the narrowing that precedes the waterfalls dropping down to the sea. This ancient crossing place is still used by people, cattle and wildlife, and from time to time the footprints of deer, otters and birds are visible. Often, at dawn and dusk, a small group of deer will be seen crossing the river here en route to the shore.

Where the river threads through our croft, there is evidence of river management and decades of effort. Ropes, metalwork, fishing nets, wood, stonework and fencing were placed to protect riverbanks and pasture from erosion and collapse during flooding. On Red River Croft the meandering river enters a section of the valley shaped like an elongated bowl. At the boundary between Croft 17 and 18 the bowl narrows, and the river makes its final steep, sinuous cut down through solid rock to form a series of short, stepped waterfalls to the sea. In heavy storm rains, the channelled narrowing restricts river-flow so water backs up, filling the basin. In this way the river can rise by as much as three metres, spilling out across our meadows in great, fast gushes. Under such conditions it is easy to see why crofters had to work hard to protect the riverbanks. But the whole system quickly readjusts, the flooded bowl empties, leaving behind fresh sediments and assorted debris all across the valley floor. At this time of year the lower meadows remain soggy even when flood-waters recede, but the sedimentary debris, red sands and gravels, and other detritus, leaves and clumps of soil, eventually bring life too, by forming the nutrient base for plant growth in the years to come.

The intermittent flooding and sporadic wet patches attract many migrants. Geese, in transit on their long journeys south, pause here to splash and rest. For a short time the crofts are filled with the honking and hissing gossip of long-distance trav-ellers determined to feed. Once the waters have receded others come to pick at the spoils – herons, sea birds, pine martens, raptors, as well as hundreds of small birds.

The river rises and falls. With every reduction in water level the shoals and braids of bright-hued gravels and sands change colour. Adjustments in the speed and pace of river-flow cause the sediments to shift. The river's voice, the sounds of water passing over new gravel banks or dropping over boulders, changes too. New music shimmies across the fields. Fresh cuts are made in the unprotected soft banks, small pools are gouged then buried. The scour and scuffling of Abhain Dearg's deposits redraw the features and character of Red River Croft as if the whole river is reorganising and tidying itself in readiness for the big storms of winter.

Away from the floodiness of the valley's lower reaches, the moorland and mountains swiftly become a patchwork of metallic brown, crimson and gold leaf. Autumn rains enhance the shimmer and sheen. Our proximity to the sea augments the light. There can be more vibrancy now than in the height of summer.

This is a good time to walk in the hills. The biting insects have vanished. Gusting winds swirl about the mountains and glens, carrying leaf fragments of every conceivable colour. The heathery slopes turn orange, mosses, lichens and fungi glow on tree stumps and boulders and the peaks crackle with light as clouds hurry by. Intense rain-showers, singular and often thundery, fill the burns and rivers; waterfalls surge. Paths lead up into mist then lift you above it. Colours deepen, then fade. Brightness reigns, then light falls away and everything vanishes under a thick darkness. The first swirls of snow may appear on the highest tops, while in the woodlands and sheltered places multitudes of fungi of every conceivable shape, size and colour sit quietly in remnant golden light.

For a while there is only a winter tickle, a dust-like scatter of white that merely hints at what is to come. It is intermittent and untrustworthy; it comes and goes. This is the time of colour – deep, rich, flamboyant colour. Colour fills up every space, every gap. Orange marmalade mountains at sunset darken into rampant Prussian blue. Cinnabar mountains in a swift dawn cool to jasper under morning showers. And then, as the days shorten, the colours of heat and blood are absorbed back into the earth.

(iii) Salmon return to the rivers

Each autumn, we wait for Peter Cunningham to arrive. He works for the Wester Ross Fisheries Trust, whose aim is to improve the management of wild fisheries and track the populations of oceanic and riverine species. He has been coming for a few years to survey the Red River and check the health of brown and sea trout, ever hopeful of finding salmon.

Crofting communities were once permitted to maintain traditions of sustainable sea fishing and that legacy can still be found today in abandoned fishing stations, net poles, winching gear and long-buried nets. Although no crofters were permitted to take salmon from the rivers, they found other ways of bringing fish home. The men of the township would string nets across the mouth of the Erradale river (Port na Sgotha) when seasonal migration brought fish in from the ocean, a method that is probably older than any of the communities here and one still practised today by the indigenous peoples of the Pacific Northwest coast.

Rivers are also part of the clearance history of this land. Their juxtaposition in the sporting narratives of the great Scottish estates was one of people often denied access to salmon and trout, of overfishing, poaching and control. By the time we moved to South Erradale there had been no salmon in Abhain Dearg for years, at least since Cathma's childhood, although she said there were plenty of small trout and eels, themselves making incredible journeys to find 'home'.

I read in Robert Macfarlane's book *Landmarks* the word *èit*, a term from the Isle of Lewis in the Outer Hebrides. It refers to the placing of quartz stones in streams in the hope they will sparkle in moonlight and hopefully attract salmon to return 'home' to the rivers there. When I asked Cathma about *èit* she was puzzled, but said it was worth a try. We agreed that since magical properties are often accorded both to quartz and the moon it may all be true. With *èit* in mind I began to gather quartz from the local beaches. There was plenty of Cambrian quartzite but suitable pebbles of pure-white quartz were rare so it took several weeks to find just a small handful. On a day preceding a full-mooned night I walked upstream from the mouth of Abhain Dearg and threw a single bright white stone onto every gravel bed I could get to. And then forgot all about the stones, moon and salmon.

*

In 2017 Peter rang as usual, 'If it's okay with you, Annie, I'd like to get into the river today. We've got the same gear as last year and it will be interesting to see what we catch.' 'Of course, yes,' I said, shamefully remembering my initial disinterest about Peter's first visit. I had known little about fish or 'fishing rights' and vaguely recalled something about landownership, the laird and trout. As owners of riverbank crofts, we can fish for trout legally, though only the laird can take salmon since he owns the river. Regardless of any feudal rights, I had assumed a relatively short watercourse like the Erradale would not support a population of breeding salmon and therefore did not think such rules applied to us.

There was a knock at the door. Peter and his colleague Colin Simpson had arrived. 'Thank you for allowing us to come and play again, Annie,' he said. We headed out to the fields. The wind was cold and I explained about the horses who had come to stay for a while. 'They are friendly and won't bother us,' I said. But as we dropped down the embankment the horses came thundering up, wanting to play and seeking treats.

I felt a bit foolish but the two tall calm men did not seem to mind. They were focused on carrying their equipment and deciding where to begin the survey, talking as they walked. We made a merry troupe, the tall men, me, dog and four ponies. Peter settled on a spot where it is relatively easy to scramble down the steep, deep riverbank. He strapped on an array of instruments and picked up a long pole with a coil of thick wire at one end and a tail of thin wire at the other which he plugged into the gear on his back. He clambered down the bank and entered the water up to his thighs. Colin followed behind, carrying a large net and a bucket half filled with river water. A low hum came from the gear as Peter flicked switches on and off. Then they began to walk slowly forward and upstream, Peter sweeping the pole back and forth in front of him with the same smooth motion a metal detectorist uses. When I watched them work in the river for the first time, I had been puzzled by all the gadgets. Peter explained the pole and wires create a small electrical charge in the water to stun the fish without harming them. This made it easy for Colin to scoop them up with his net and drop them into his bucket.

'Colin will catch them before they float away,' he had said. 'Or before I fall over,' replied Colin. Though both men occasionally did slip they were swift and skilful and soon filled the bucket with fish. Peter and Colin clambered out and transferred fish from bucket to bucket. As quickly as possible Peter weighed, measured and photographed each one, calling out data and comments for Colin to record. A few scales were scraped off for laboratory analyses and each fish examined for sea lice or lice damage. 'Lice will latch on and sometimes eat away at the fins. Look, here, Annie, here is a wee bit of tearing where lice were once attached to the fin,' he explained.

We were all so caught up with looking at the beautiful creature we had not noticed the horses gathered around us. Their earlier skittishness and excitement had gone, replaced by calm curiosity, and they slowly sniffed and gently prodded the bags, boxes and buckets. Peter always talks while he completes the necessary data gathering, quietly unleashing a torrent of knowledge about fish, rivers, the sea and other creatures. I expressed concern the horses might damage the equipment, but Colin assured me that Peter's 'incessant blether' would calm them. Both men have the sing-song lullaby-lilt of Highlanders so I laughed, wondering if he might be right.

The survey continued upriver. There were brown and sea trout, and eels. I marvelled as Peter described the life cycles of these incredible animals, and looked at the river in a new light, with wonder and with respect. The pony interlopers followed on. Overhead, clouds scudded by, disinterested. The river sang lustily and a chilly wind had begun to scamper in from the sea when Peter jumped up with a great shout, lighting up the day with his excitement.

'Salmon! We have salmon!' The sudden shout and change of tone caused Colin, following behind, to slip and fall into the water. 'Catch it! Catch it, Colin!' yelled Peter. Colin swung the net, then smiled.

The men scrambled back out of the water. Among the trout and eels was a salmon. I could tell by Peter's raised voice that it was unexpected, though much hoped for. The men tried not to hurry through the procedure of transferring the precious fish into the largest bucket with a drop of anaesthetic, desperate not to cause the animal any undue stress.

'It's a female. She has come home to spawn.' Peter laid her gently down on his measuring mat and called out numbers to Colin. The salmon was singularly enchanting and beautiful; her body was speckled like the river itself on a summer's evening, all wraith-grey, platinum and mother-of-pearl. Her eyes were as deep-dark as the ocean in winter, her fins as clear as summer waves about to break on the shore. I could find no suitable words. This creature had ridden the tides and currents of the Atlantic to come here, to this place, to us, to our small river, to Abhain Dearg.

'Well now, Annie, this is a find. We must keep it quiet for now or all the fishermen of the west will be tramping across your fields disturbing your bees and flowers and teasing the ponies.' I flushed with pride. 'Do you think it was my *èits*?' I asked. Peter looked puzzled. I explained about the Hebridean method of luring salmon into and up the moorland streams by setting quartz stones on the riverbeds where they might catch the moonlight, and thereby attract the salmon. I told him how I had gathered quartz pebbles from the shore, distributed them along the river on suitable shoals and that one of the old crofters had laughed at me, but he said Wester Ross folk might have done the same thing long ago, although he knew of no one using the practice today.

'The river's bedload already contains stones of quartz and quartzite but each one I picked up was coated in algae, so I got a handful from the beach and gave them a polish. I reckon they have done the trick!' As he gently returned the salmon to the river, he laughed. 'It could be so, Annie, but it is more likely to be luck.' No, I thought, it was my *èit*-enchantment, pebbles of shining white quartz set out at a full moon. I had wished the salmon back.

★

Later that day I walked downriver, happy knowing the waters of Abhain Dearg were providing for the young silvery salmon. Where the waterfalls meet the sea is a shingle beach whose large rounded stones and boulders get piled high into giant steps by powerful winter storm waves. It was busy with oystercatchers and ringed plovers. The salmon must have negotiated the stepped sandstone, the tumbling waters and pebbles churning in the breaking waves. Often at sunset, as water pours down from the croft, it takes on the colour of old blood and the waterfall's rock steps deepen to rust and bronze. Here and there small patches of rosy sand caught the late afternoon light. Larger boulders shimmered like armour dropped by warriors in ages past. The shiftings of smaller pebbles and stones vibrated and slurped westwards. It is a secluded and contemplative place, set apart from the business and activity of people. Rewilded remnants of past lives are scattered about, old tyres with myrtle or willow growing in their centres, logs covered by moss and winches studded with rust and barnacles, old stone walls coated with pink thrift and furred with grey lichen. Nearby I spotted a rock slab with rippled surfaces created by the action of small waves passing over sand grains billions of years ago and then frozen in time. I sat down on one of the waterfall's steps and through the clear red-tinted river water could see the same kinds of ripples in the bottom sediments, with similar dimensions, amplitude and length as those of the Precambrian. Both sets of ripples were at once endless and timeless, twins created by the continuous movement of water across sands. The Red River seemed to arc into the Archaean and pull lost landscapes out like teeth.

I thought again about the salmon, of how she had to cope with the raging torrents of a river in full spate or how, after a prolonged period of low rainfall, shallow trickles of river become molten metal slick, when gabbles of water bubble and shimmer across gravel banks and pierce the gaps between boulders, and when precious gems appear to be resting on the riverbed, highly polished and ready for sale – garnet, jade, malachite, amber, jet, sapphire, topaz and diamond. I wondered how any fish could survive such a low water level but remembered that Peter had reassured me. 'They will always find a pool somewhere, underneath overhanging vegetation or beside a boulder, which is why rewilding your riverbanks is so important,' he had said.

But on that evening, as the Red River cascaded down the waterfalls, it trilled in harmony with a sea chorus of brine-slosh over beach cobbles. It seemed that one was calling out to the other, and as the music played and waters sparkled, their laughter bubbled with earthly magic of the purest kind. I knew it then to be a salmon river, with wriggling eels from the Sargasso Sea and colour-changing trout. I realised too that Abhain Dearg is also a light-catcher and sound-bringer, carrying ideas and stories out to the west along with its sediments. The sea must be plankton-full of them.

3. Sunrise over Tom na Gruagaich, sunset across the Old Man of Storr, Isle of Skye, Celtic month of Elder (November to December), Mourning Moon

(i) Winds from the sea blow harder

Red River Croft lies close enough to the sea for its influence and energy to be felt every day. This is a coast of many colours; mixed habitats are plentiful, the grazing varied. Landform and land-use maps of Wester Ross show an indented coastline of cliffs, caves and stacks, geos, sandy bays, estuaries, long sea lochs, islets and skerries, and edgelands of great variety, complexity and richness, fractal piled upon fractal. Coastal geology here is mostly sandstone, with outcrops of gneiss, overlain by an array of deposits left by melting ice more than ten thousand years ago. This distinctive mixture of varied substrates, coupled with the transformative effects of millennial-scale landform processes and sea-level changes, ultimately led to present-day landscapes in which myriad habitats are seasonally abundant in animal and plant life.

Although we are sheltered to some degree by the Inner and

Outer Hebrides, the dramatic physical geography adds extra energy to the capriciousness of weather. Mountain ranges interrupt the passage of Atlantic low pressure systems, focusing winds and enhancing rainfall while the sea intensifies temperature and relative humidity. The relationship between islands, sea, mainland and atmosphere are as intricate and enigmatic as their land-surface and underwater topographies. The waters of the Minch are in a permanent and long conversation with the rivers, valleys and mountains of Wester Ross. Together they exchange radiance and lustre, and supply nutrients and vitality to the sea, making it one of the most enigmatic, dynamic and beautiful stretches of coast in Scotland. Light, colour and sound are interchangeable.

*

All along the west coast, seaweeds were traditionally used to enhance soil fertility. But during the seventeenth and eighteenth centuries kelp was used to produce soda ash for making glass and soap. In Wester Ross it was cut by hand and dried out in the open on 'drying walls' but by the early nineteenth century, when taxes on imported soda ash were removed, the west coast kelp industry died out. For almost two hundred years harvesting seaweeds for cash had meant less was available for use as fertiliser on land and that in turn enhanced the already declining soil fertility of 'lazy beds' and other crop-growing grounds of the local communities. At the start of the nineteenth century the failure of the kelp industry almost certainly added yet another level of stress to the severe social and environmental conditions that culminated in the final phase of clearances. Today kelp forests can be seen up and down the coast from cliff-tops north and south of Erradale, especially at low tide, for they have recovered from intense harvesting and bloom with life.

Each walk from our house along the Seaweed Road to the sandy shore at Opinan is another delve into the past. This short route crosses otter trails marked by spraint mounds, ditches that fill with yellow flag iris in summer, mysterious tumbles of rounded stones, and old fences in various states of disarray. It is a walk accompanied year-round by rock pipits, wrens, oyster-catchers, gulls, terns and curlews, rowdies of hooded crows, ravens and birds of prey, and in spring and summer by wheatears, stonechats, bonxies and skylarks. Much of what was a well-constructed 'road' has been broken up over the years by storms and by burns cascading across it after heavy rains. But it is still possible to see sections of the retaining kerbs and drainage channels here and there.

Although the days of kelp-cutting and seaweed-gathering are long gone, the bond between crofts and coast remains strong. There are other remnants of remoter times: a rusted winch which used to haul fishing skiffs from the shore, old fence posts pitted with lichen and studded with moss, curled and rusting wires and other, stranger crusty pieces of metalwork whose purposes are long forgotten, and fragments of walls once used to dry kelp. Intrigued and encouraged by the old practice of using seaweed to enhance plant growth, Rob and I spent some time gathering seaweed in bags to spread on our raised vegetable beds. Without the right skills, or a pony and trap, the work was hard. We marvelled at the time, strength, endurance and energy needed by the kelp-cutters to earn a living and by crofters deter-mined to keep soils well manured and productive. Our first crops of potatoes, beans, kale and broccoli in those early years were good. I was fit and well then, and we were both determined to grow as much produce as possible.

★

The autumn days shorten swiftly and weather patterns change. Gone are the gentle rains and rainbows. Turbulent moisture-laden Atlantic squalls bring short, sharp showers and thunder. While the Red River pulses, rising and falling in sync with the cloud-bursts, on the croft any remaining upright grasses or flowers are broken or flattened. Winds accompanying the showers whip up crests on the river and, down along the shore, churn breaking waves into a frenzy. Under high, rising cumulonimbus clouds and low light, the sea takes on the mirror sheen of chrome while the river is hand-beaten pewter. The entire coast ripples with motion.

Now the value of healthy kelp beds in dampening down the excess energy is clearly visible. Seaweeds are nature's form of coastal engineering; they protect the beaches, rocky shores, and cliffs from the biting effects of energetic storm waves. Some kelp is uprooted despite its specialist 'holdfasts' and, along with other seaweeds, is brought ashore by the more volatile weather. Great mounds of copper and rusty red, black, olive green and coffee-bean brown appear, only to be sorted and washed away again. As the piles of seaweed are delivered, re-sorted, buried by sands, and then excavated once more by the waves, they attract birds who come to feed on the dead and dying fragments of life from the sea. The scent of salt and iodine and decaying kelp and bladderwrack attract sheep who come to nibble at the sea harvest and lick the mounds for salts and minerals. And, at dawn or dusk, deer emerge from the shadows, having come down from the hills to take their fill.

The sea froths and foams more vigorously. With every strong Atlantic low-pressure system, energy is transferred from atmosphere to sea and from sea to coast, from coast to our croft. Waves are taller, darker and deeper in colour. The noise made as they churn the sands and gravels or boom into geos and rock crevices grows. Sea birds dip low over the waves, light catches the spray and the music of the breaking waves creeps further and further inland. There are many days when we are greeted by their roaring and keening as we open the door. The sands of Opinan may be a kilometre away as the oystercatcher flies but we can hear the slushing backwash of big waves on the beach. On a windy day the sea's spray can be seen as a thick translucent veil drawn across the beach at Opinan and the small cliffs of South Erradale from the hilltop road. And, on the croft, the air begins to coat everything with salt.

*

We knew from the outset we would not manage our croft for rearing sheep or cattle. I had only childhood memories of my grandfather's farm and our former lives were filled with children, academia and pharmacy. We were ill-equipped for a life of animal-rearing. Besides the usual raft of legal documents, it was necessary to inform the Crofting Commission about how we intended to fulfil our statutory obligations as crofters. Our stated aim, one prescribed by the Commission itself – to preserve the croft for future use, conserve and enhance biodiversity and soil quality through habitat management, and manage the land for nature and wildlife – would require a mixed regime of grazing, cutting and periods of fallow in the meadows. Sensitive planting of native trees and shrubs would help protect the riverbanks and water quality in the Red River, and ultimately help fish stocks. We wondered again about creating hedges as shelter belts along one or two of our boundaries. Keen to work in partnership with our neighbours, we asked Cathma if she would be happy to graze her sheep and cattle occasionally. Almost immediately her sheep and cattle came onto the croft to nibble and browse. I watched them move about, noting where they preferred to eat.

The ways animals feed and move across the land have varying effects. Cows grasp plants with their long tongues and then swing their heads to tear the leaves, while sheep use lips and teeth to nip and bite at grasses and herbs close to the soil surface. A range of stock weights influences soil compaction and the extent of bare ground. After a few weeks we agreed to vary the length of time sheep and cattle grazed the croft. There were long periods when the ground was 'rested' or when animals were kept to one part of the croft to 'mob-graze'. Although I tried to monitor the effects of these small changes, at the time I had no idea nature would immediately set to work or that the process of rewilding had slowly begun.

Our plan was to continue with limited mixed grazing by 'borrowing' Cathma's livestock, and to get on with planting trees in more sensitive areas such as the riverbanks, but in the dark autumnal days of 2015 we were asked to help out with an emergency. Danielle is a gritty and warm-hearted Northumbrian who runs a pony-trekking centre. Her business was originally located in Gairloch but for various reasons she needed to move back to her late husband's croft in nearby Red Point. Danielle was desperate to find additional grazing for horses and ponies used to much larger and more sheltered inland paddocks. Many Oversiders offered help. One small troop of ponies came to stay with us temporarily and we put our own slowly developing plans on hold. During their first visit they thundered about the fields, tearing at the turf and eating even the oldest remnant grasses and clumps of rushes. When they finally left to work, we agreed to take on two very old retired Shetland ponies, and Cindy and Toby became permanent residents who were moved from patch to patch as our plans evolved.

Danielle also owns a small group of breeding ewes. They are 'rare breed' sheep known as Zwartbles, large animals with short curly coats of burnt umber. Unlike the ewes of Erradale who are put to the ram for a few weeks, the lambing schedule of these particular pedigrees is organised strictly. In order to synchronise ovulation, hormone-sponges are inserted vaginally and removed two weeks later when a ram, usually a prize-winner himself, is introduced to the herd for a few days. In her first year at Red Point, Danielle asked for assistance with sheep as well as ponies; for some strange reason she thought I could help with inserting the sponges.

'Aha well, you're a mother and grandmother and older and wiser, and you know all that kinda stuff. Sheep canna be that different?' she said. 'The "girls" know me coz I feed 'em, so it'll be better if I hold the head end! I don't reckon they'll kick you, Annie.'

For a time I was gynaecologist to the Zwartbles. With Danielle holding tight, one by one her precious ewes were synchronised. Sheep can be skittish but these tall, broad ladies were calm and patient as we crooned and ordered their lives.

Eventually all the South Erradale ewes are released again to roam in the hills. They wander from hill to hill, from one side of the valley to another. Living between high mountain ranges and the sea means we are subjected to weather extremes, but the wise older ewes lead younger sheep to spaces and places of relative shelter, from one heathery hollow to the next. Occasionally they walk back along the track to Cathma's front gate in the hope of extra feed, glaring at us and the Shetland ponies before they are shooed away again.

*

Our croft fields are exposed and open to winds from the sea and in the trickery of autumn light they appear to churn under gusts fetching in from the Minch. Birdsong, tranquil and leisurely in late summer, becomes fraught and hasty. Migrants continue to straggle by as they head south for winter feeding-grounds. Starlings noisily settle on wires, their spotted shiny feathers blinking as they catch the light, and gossip raucously before setting off again.

And so autumn is a jumbling flow. As kelp tumbles in the breaking waves and sands are dragged back and forth along the beach, both croft and coast are stippled with colour and filleted by sound and light. Yet the oncoming dark is a palpable and growing entity. Sunsets lose their bright iridescence; clouds smear across the sky then crumple into great piles. Birdsong thins, hill colours fade, hedges and woodland edges are lanterned by the last remnant glow of fruit and berry, and nights chill by increment. What begins as a gentle shower of pale copper or silver confetti under birch and alder becomes a frenetic, flamboyant, rustling red cascade in oak woods. Green larch needles quickly flame to orange and carpet footpaths and roadside edges. Soon the wax pennies of deciduous leaves melt into shining coffee-brown sheets and larch needles are stitched into black crusts.

(ii) Stags bellow

As autumn advances, a sensation of shifting and progression grows. Encroaching darkness takes unmistakable and growing bite-sized chunks out of each day and the transition from day to night is swift. Yet there are spells when the world is grey, dull and sunless, when rain-showers are dragged slowly from sea onto land. Such still, dreich days are dusk-less; they leach away light and energy and foment sleep. The crofts look more like an old patchwork quilt, threadbare, worn and colourless. Only the rushes still stand tall, scattered across wetter patches of ground, having resisted the grazers and welcomed the rains. Higher on the peat banks mosses and bog myrtle defy the gales with their lowness and bent backs. On some days thick banks of cloud brush charcoal shadows across the fields; on others, when beams of sunlight are so focused and intense, they act as powerful torches, eye-wateringly, blindingly bright. And there are days when slow-moving ribbons and cushions of cloud roll slowly in from the sea to fumble and swirl and judder into a greyness so deep the mountains vanish.

Yet the ferocity of change is exhilarating. I am turned this way and that, inside out and back to front with the fluxing colours, sounds, scents and light. Wildlife is also on the move underneath changeable autumn skies and the croft becomes a temporary sanctuary, part of a system of natural highways and corridors.

Early one morning I watched a band of deer, young stags, cross the ford and run up through our top field. They passed by in a surge, moving as one, organic and volatile, rippling almost, until they disappeared from view. For most of the year small groups of deer billow and surge around emptier inland hill country. As the weather worsens, they descend to the valleys in search of food. They come onto the croft and rummage among the low and stunted stands of alder and hazel, stripping bark and nibbling any remaining leaves. At dawn they move onto the shore, following the Seaweed Road. Humans and animals twinned by need and instinct.

I tracked their twining trails to the beach at Opinan where the sands were soft and high-banked. Deer footprints were every-where – large splayed, heart-shaped hollows, with smaller dimples from dewclaws. Long spacing suggested they were running as they came onto the beach.

The tide was low. I sat down on a bladderwrack-covered boulder. The wind was made of cold grit; the scorching gusts scoured my cheeks. Salt spray settled on my black coat. The deer were at the far end of the shore. They startled and broke on the sands like a wave and then stopped, looking inland, and I wondered if someone was coming through the dunes. Then they turned abruptly and ran back along the beach towards me. The deer flew past unheeding, perhaps unable to discern human scent underneath salt and sea minerals and seaweed, perhaps called by some far greater need.

*

When sheep are brought onto the crofts to mix with the rams, deer return to the rutting grounds of South Erradale. Each year, the rut plays out on the lower hills adjacent to the river and croft-land. Scents twist through the air in invisible threads, firing neurones in the stags' brains and sending surges of energy through their blood vessels. The stags' response is visceral and profound. It is the start of the rut when they come down from the mountains and up from the shore to fight. All paths lead to our valley.

Sloping down in a large caress from Maol Ruadh to sea cliffs south of the river, the moorland is dark, rusty brown in autumn. The hill forms a barrier to light from the south and here in dark shadows are the rutting grounds. As combat begins, they echo with primal and frenetic roaring. Clusters of hinds break apart and merge as the stags begin to fight, charging back and forth, clashing antlers, breath steaming in great hot spouts. Mist and breath and sweat and steam from their bodies mingle, but as the sun rises voices calm and the herds move higher to feed on the upper slopes, out of the cold and into the light.

There is nothing comparable in this open country to engender such a feeling of the feral than the sound of stags bellowing. One night I woke abruptly, shuddered out of deep sleep by a loud noise. A scent of damp earth seeped in through a sliver of open window. A keen wind was winnowing the night and rattling the roof tiles. I wondered if their clatter had woken me. I got out of bed, pushed the window wide open and looked out at a wolf-pelt grey world. In the moonlight only the dim forms of surrounding hills were visible; their shapes were smeared as if behind frosted glass. The night sky was an inverted silver salver above shadows of charcoal swirling around a pewter lawn.

A gush of sound made me shiver; a roar, guttural and aching with rage. For a moment I did not know who or what had made this noise; this was no badger or fox, and certainly not Cathma's cows. I held tight to the handle and leaned out further. The river's cold shushing slipped over my head and shoulders followed by a hoarse ululation echoing from the crevices and folds of the valley. I knew it then – a stag-bellow, filled with hormonal angst and deep organic need. The night quietened. Then a single, lonely bellow seemed much closer, a trick of the wind perhaps. Across the valley, beams of moonlight brushed across the hill-sides like silver ribbons. I imagined sprites and fairies dancing in the fields, ghosts and spectres on the moors, and Charon the ferryman about to cross our river, its waters no longer red but filled with quicksilver. There seemed to be two groups moving about mid-slope on Maol Ruadh, their antlers pearled, their coats lustrous steel. One stag glowed corpse-white, legend made real. He strode back and forth, cutting through the silver-grey, dragging tatters of mist behind him, fragments of wraiths and trailing livery. A sweet scent accompanied the bellowing, coming from stems and remnant leaves of myrtle crushed by the running deer and from peat torn by thrusting hooves. The stag's roars bounced from rock to rock. Young bucks agitated by perfumes of females, dashed up and down the slope, one moment cresting the hill summit, the next spiralling down, filled once more with bravado. Again and again, the white stag was able to fend them off. My human senses vibrated with the roars and oscillated with an altered, almost alien, sense of space created by the noise and motion. Soon a glimmer of pale lemon-yellow began to crease the hills to my left. White warmed to rust brown. The hinds scattered upwards in a flurry of light-gleam and motion to the moorland tops to my right. Cold and with iced fingers I slipped back into bed, leaving the window wide open.

The rut is nothing short of a fierce battle between dominant rival males who are fighting for control of harems, one large stag for each group of females. Maol Ruadh is perfect for the challenges and displays because it has several flatter areas covered with deep, wet peat. Before fighting commences hopeful stags create scrapes and rub against fence posts or boulders to demarcate their rutting grounds. They wallow in wet hollows, urinate in them and then wallow again, to make themselves more attractive to females. During the rut the largest, strongest and often oldest stag holds court over his 'ladies', most of whom are in oestrus, ready to mate. Individual younger, smaller males range around the harem and try to reach the females. Some may be successful if the dominant stag is either fighting one of his main rivals or too exhausted from battle.

Stags assess each other as they strut and roar. They thrash and paw at the ground; they drag their antlers through the vegetation in order to catch plant debris and make themselves appear larger; they mate as soon as a hind is receptive. For most of the rut they will eat little, only resting during the middle hours of the day. As soon as the morning light whips up across the valley the hinds run and scatter upwards to the crest of the moorland to graze in the warming air. Gradually they all calm as hormones dilute. For just a few short hours when the autumn sun is strongest the stags relax and allow their harems to feed and roam. But as soon as the sun begins to dip towards Skye the rutting ground is cast into shadow once more and the bellowing begins afresh. Thinner and thinner grow the stags, thicker and thicker their throaty roars.

The rut creates sounds of such alien emptiness it is easy to forget the season is earth-coloured and rich. Once it is over, all the deer disperse into their bachelor groups or clusters of females and young and retrace their familiar routes from hill to croft to shore and back again. The utterly exhausted fighters, depleted of calories and nutrients, come down to feed and replenish muscle mass before heading back into the hills again. At this time of year I forgive the deer their raiding parties and thievery. They bring the wild to me, in my head, and in my home. For a brief spell there is no need to follow hill trails or roam by the shore searching for wilderness; it slips in through open doors and windows, in ghostly threads like fingers, and into dreams.

As quickly as rut-hormones seep away in the stags, the last colours bleed from the hills. The transformation of moorland from plum purple to burnt brown toast is complete. Deer herds fragment and disperse, no longer held together by the need to fight and mate, though occasionally lone stags will loiter for a few days to feed and recover before they too vanish. As stars fill the autumn skies the dull inkiness of a cloud-filled dusk is transformed into a thick, blue-black velvet cloak whose dense, soft pile is studded with diamonds. Autumn moonlight, magnetic and wilful, shrouds the valley and surrounding mountains in grey linen; the sea turns to solid alabaster and the Red River to porcelain. On such a night, ghosts and spectres appear to dance across the hills and chase away the roars and bellows of giants. Like *sithean*, fairies enchanted by the moon, this is wild magic.

The rut, played out in the wraith realms of peat bog and moorland, accompanies this marginal time when spirit merges with the living, when the promise of life requires death and decay, when winds turn to the west and north and strengthen and the sea begins to fill with growing waves of aquamarine, gunmetal grey and plum blue. Gusts filled with shards of hail rush up the cliffs and rime the fence posts; they splice and splinter the hormone-filled mists. The scent of ice comes on the wind and the aching roars of stags are replaced by wilder, elemental storm voices weaving through the air.

(iii) Frequent storms may bring snow

Snow may arrive as early as October but more usually in November, appearing on peaks for the first time while crofts and coastal moorlands remain lacquered with autumn. More often than not northwesterly winds blow snow showers swiftly from the Minch past the coastal valleys and sea lochs and onwards into the mountains. We find ourselves clasped inside a picture-postcard scene of serrated mountain tops crisply and surreally Alpine. While all around us the hills are white, we may remain snowless, our valley rippled with terracotta and burnt umber. When it comes, the first tentative kiss of winter is exciting. Landscapes are redefined by snow, resculpted. A skiff of snow in the nooks and crannies, once blurred by summer growth and fine rains, reveals details of the land's shape and form forgotten or mislaid. In the shortening, darkening days of winter's approach the peaks of inland mountain ranges such as the Cairngorms are often permanently white and many small lochs freeze for weeks on end, but in the Northwest Highlands, mountain snow-cover flashes in and out depending on prevailing weather systems – those from the southwest and northwest wash us with warmer Atlantic rains, while the Arctic comes to Wester Ross on northerlies and easterlies.

Snow and ice arrive intermittently and lightly in patches and sprinklings. Only the northern and eastern flanks of the serri-form and notched Torridon mountains might remain snow white and icebound. Their west-facing slopes, open to warmer, wetter air from the Atlantic, will whiten then shadow to indigo and grey as snows come and go. Storms tracking in from the west bring deluges to fill the rivers and burns, and because the air masses are relatively warm, mountain snow melts rapidly, swelling floodwaters and turning rivers and waterfalls into mighty cascades. Again and again the hillsides are festooned with white ribbons. But airstreams coming from the north or east usher in bitter glacial cold, clear days and nights, and deep, hard frost. For much of the time these two types of weather system alternate, and early winter will be an unpredictable confusion of gales and rain or ice-rimmed calm. When the two collide, snow crash-covers the whole landscape and temperatures plummet. The atmosphere over the Northwest Highlands becomes a war zone.

Every aspect of our weather is dominated by wind. After ten years we have become storm veterans, and almost permanently windswept. The violence and speed of change are exhilarating. Weather forecasts cannot keep up. The variety of colours, shapes and sounds of storms is infinite. Greenlanders have dozens of words for snow and ice – *qanik* (Inuit for steadily falling snow), *nunavik* (deep snow you sink into), *puddersne* (Danish for powdery snow) and *snefygning* (blizzard). Gaelic, too, is full of words and phrases concerning the natural world. There are maps filled with names that refer to wildlife, woodlands or features in the landscape. I asked Cathma about speaking weather, about her words for winds and storms. Besides the Scots for cold and snow such as 'glush' or 'gru', Cathma explained how Gaelic combines words to create a specific name for weather conditions – *gaoth feadalaich*, a 'whistling wind' – or richer combinations rather like the first line of a poem. 'As in *Cluinn fuaim na h-ataireachaird*, which translates as "the high surge of the seas",' she said. 'Oh yes,' I replied. 'When a storm comes, it pushes the waves before it.' And I am *leannan gaoith*, 'wind-lover', and therefore, according to Cathma, 'crazy'.

The first potent squalls build out in the Atlantic, ready to sweep past Ireland and into northern Scotland in late autumn. They blow away the last ululations of rutting stags and migrating birds; they send great waves onshore and carry sea birds inland. Extreme low-pressure systems hang on the coat-tails of the jet stream and as the latter undulates through the upper atmosphere, sometimes travelling much further south than usual, it brings winds from every compass point. Small instabilities merge into directed force; the rivers, coastal waters, woodlands and moorland respond with increased internal dynamism of their own.

Winter weather is ruled by the *Cailleach*. Her stories permeate the whole of Celtic mythology. According to legends, she is to be seen riding through storm clouds on the back of a wolf carrying her magical staff. Wolf-pelt grey is the colour of clouds bringing snow and there are many tales of mythical beings striking mountains with their mighty staffs of magic or hammers associated with both storms and rockfalls. In western Scotland she is also known locally as *Beira*, 'Bringer of Winds', 'Bringer of Ice Mountains', 'Storm Wife' and 'Grandmother of the Clans'. Under all her guises this goddess of winter loves the wildest weather and is said to control the land and its climate by raising storms, bringing ice and preventing the return of sunshine and greenery. The battles between Beira and the spirits of spring are supposed to account for periods of good and bad weather and for their famed changeability. Her meanest and most fearsome wind is called the 'sharp-billed wind', or *Gobag*. Used to fend off the spring, it lasts for nine days and is fierce and physically painful for all who live through it. But just as the storms of winter months are peppered with brighter days and melting snows, so too the stories and songs tell of a more benign side to Beira. She is also referred to as 'Gentle Annie' who allows spring to come out from her hiding place somewhere here in the west, a green isle where the sun shines and flowers still bloom. Since the snows mostly blow past us, could Spring hide here, in this small sheltered valley, where a red river sings?

In some Scottish and Irish tales it is said that all winds are associated with colour: black, brown and grey for those blowing in from north to west, green from south to west. A pure west wind is pale dun, an easterly is purple. When gales blow, the sea also fills with colour; it boils with aquamarine and viridian under the westerlies, polished jade and malachite in south-westerlies and with jet and obsidian as northerlies howl. The tempests of these northern latitudes are so filled with colour, our skies tear open with meaning and oceans fragment into shards of light and dark so it becomes impossible to decipher their names or understand where they have come from.

Gales have tangible bodily force of their own. They barge us aside, steal air from our lungs and scrape skin from our faces until our senses becomes blurred and confused. We knew about the winds before coming to live here, had experienced whole holidays of sand-blasting gusts and I once presented wind as one of many mangled explanations to friends for loving this place.

'Winter storms are on our agenda,' I said. 'We are happy to have them as part of our lives.' 'You should have been named "Beira", or "Gentle Annie the storm-lover",' one of my Irish friends said.

*

I love the wind. As wind speeds rise, so do my levels of excitement and contentment. I was born in a winter's blizzard when the chimney of my parent's house was blown down. An unsettled baby, I was put in my pram, tucked in tightly with blankets, pushed outside and left to grizzle and grumble until lulled by the wind. It was the 'done thing' then, though my poor mother must have been desperate to have my pram outside in winter. She always insisted I was 'storm-born'. Whether or not those deep memories of being warm while listening to wind-howls are from babyhood or from other times I cannot say, but the link between windiness and feelings of comfort have stayed with me to this day. There are other deep memories too, of a childhood plagued by coughing and sore throats exacerbated by living in a town whose atmosphere was thickly polluted. In the days before central heating my bedroom window was always wide open to let in the 'fresh' air. Now there is a Pavlovian rush to meet a gale, an embedded reflex, as vital to me as wind is endemic in Wester Ross.

One morning, early in December 2013, our first winter, a fusillade of swelling noise clattered at the door. From the kitchen window I could see banks of cloud rolling in – Davy's grey running with pale bismuth-yellow beams of light. Birdsong was strident and urgent. There was an undertone of deep drumming. Darkness was heading towards South Erradale but it was expected and even anticipated, coming after a chain of damp, leaf-swirling autumn days. Forecasts had warned of a prolonged spell of stormy weather and here it was, a physical, almost animate and growing presence. I was excited at the prospect and wanted to go down to the sea to witness the first stages of this, our first 'big' storm. Rob insisted on coming too, 'You'll find it hard standing up out there,' he said. 'The wind is already very strong.' Blustery, debris-filled air swelled and made my ears pop. Gusts shouted angrily, bumping and jostling. As soon as we left the protective shelter of our garden hedge the full extent of dark and discordant colours displayed by the storm's rapid approach was unmistakable. It had a voice and creaturely energy; its volatility was almost solid.

We reached the gate to the cliff having staggered and stuttered along the track, arm in arm, only eyes and noses exposed to the atmosphere. Beyond the shelter of our neighbour's barn, we were pummelled and jostled and shoved by muscular, grasping arms of air. I clung to fence wire on my left and Rob's arm on my right as we made our way to the cliff edge and the top of the Seaweed Road Clouds spilled cries of intent and yelps of temper over a sea that squirmed and flexed like snakeskin. The surface waters glowed mint green, creased with white streaks where waves were splitting apart but were pinned down by the flattening pressure and speed of the gusts. Every so often a patch burst open, flashing intermittently and brightly, as if the sea had been holding the sun's light for safe-keeping and was trying to break free.

I wanted so badly to watch the waves but was gasping for air despite the protection of a cotton scarf. The livid, shrieking sea then turned mustard yellow, the sky to coal-dust black. I pointed to the west. 'The storm has noticed us.' My outer self was being scraped away, mind and spirit unpicked and released into the turbulence. No one would have known me by my old name. 'I should be Beira.' The gales were aggravating and agitating the sea. Its yellowness vanished as quickly as it had come; the spearmint greens and cobalt blues turned to molten black and boiling sable, then back again. Surface waters smeared the lower atmosphere. Rob nudged me and pointed to home. It was not safe high on the cliff edge in such wildness.

Instead, we drove to Opinan and struggled through the dunes. Huge waves of indigo, chromite and pewter tumbled in white and silver as they broke against the rocks and spread out over the sandy beach in great fans of cream lace. It was impossible to stand, so we lay belly-down in clumps of marram grass to watch. Every so often the waves organised themselves into long, lean ropes, like ships' hawsers; they rolled over and over, finally thumping down as if dropped from a great height only to break apart in a foaming flurry of brilliant white. Froth and water sluiced up the shore slope dragging kelp and stones and rusty-red sands back and forth. The rope-waves tore and collapsed and the sea's edge exploded. Balls of coffee-coloured foam broke away, rolling and skipping inland. With each successive blast of wind, they detonated into hundreds of smaller globules that bounced at high speed towards us and were only halted by waving marram grasses. Here they combined to make castles and minarets that wobbled before bursting open and vanishing over our heads.

The winds boiled with noise; they ransomed thought and squeezed synapses in my brain. Everything disappeared in streaming veils of salt spray and icy grit. I felt irrelevant in the face of such implacability. Time appeared to operate in a different way. Perceptions were altered. Overhead the sky metamorphosed from ink black to glaucous grey and the sea variegated darkly in waves of steel and emerald. Individual clouds began to erupt with light and as they did, coruscating wave crests transmuted again and again into millions of individual rainbows that were eventually hurled ashore along with the foam.

This was the first in a series of prolonged and extreme storms that December. We knew about the potential dangers from intense northwesterlies, but what followed was shocking, even for those who had lived here all their lives. A series of severe weather systems continuously ram-raided the entire month, one after the other. Hurricane-strength winds coupled with thrashing seas and caterwauling rains stripped the land of any last pockets of autumnal colour. According to folk tales, the Gobag storm winds last for nine days and nine nights. But in winter 2013 gusting wind speeds only dropped below eighty kilometres per hour on five days for the entire month. Three Gobagan one after the other. Their relentlessness was almost overwhelming; the atmosphere growled; the sea wailed as if in pain. The volume of sound forced us to talk loudly inside and, when needing to venture outdoors, yell for all our worth. We were rock-concert deaf.

Our fields were compressed flat by the simple raw power of wind and torrential rain. Tiles were ripped from roofs, trees and fences were crumpled and the river threw itself across the lower fields in great booming waves, as if driven demented by the wind. Crofters ushered their cattle into byres, something that rarely happens here. On one of the 'calmer' days we tried to post Christmas cards through the letter boxes of our new neighbours, but they turned to mush in the icy squalls. Power supply came and went, and by the time the merging storms had faded away, everyone, and every living thing around us, was utterly exhausted.

Once, in London's Natural History Museum, I saw pictures of Titan, one of Saturn's moons. Captions explained the rare surface structures, shadowed lakes and dense methane rains. The images were mesmerising and shudderingly stark, like winter storm clouds over the Minch; they made that alien place both terrible and beautiful, yet almost understandable. I tried to imagine what sounds Titan's rains might utter as they fell but could only think of a Gobag storm-yowl.

On December the eighth my little weather station lost part of its protective outer casings and its inner workings were ripped away, never to be seen again. The last wind speed it recorded was one hundred and forty kilometres per hour. That same day the entire roof of Gairloch's Youth Hostel also disappeared over the hills, some of it for good. There was so much damage the local builders were eventually joined by others from much further afield to help restore what had been broken or lost, though for a time we all had to make do as best we could. Repairs took weeks.

Along the shore, much of the coastal path below South Erradale was gone, lost to the sea. Instead, huge boulders and cobbles had been thrown up, partly burying fences and creating new 'walls'. Seaweed and small stones were thrown up onto the cliffs. Opinan's beach was re-engineered – most of the sand was gone and high water was marked by a steep cliff in the sand dunes. Even after the worst weather had abated, showers continued to blow in from the south, dragged back and forth across the Hebrides in long skirts of lavender under high cloud-jackets of ivory and ochre. For a time they alternated with rainbow-edged funnels of diamond hail that swept back down the Minch chased by towers and castles of luminous, thunder-filled white. Daylight was striated by showers. To begin with, the impacts on wildlife were incalculable. On the croft it was impossible to gauge the death toll of small birds, but several months later keen birders and wildlife watchers reported considerable losses in both marine and terrestrial wildlife counts across the Highlands.

This near-continuous bout of stormy December weather was

unusual. It developed from an 'extratropical cyclone' and brought sustained winds, wild seas and hurricane-force winds. Mountain-top gusts were reported in excess of two hundred kilometres an hour. Although the main weather system travelled eastwards to Scandinavia and continental Europe, its long tail carried persistent storm winds that affected the Northwest Highlands until well after Christmas.

Scotland has certainly suffered badly from multiple cyclonic weather systems driven in from the Atlantic. The nineteenth century saw many winters beset by severe storms, with lives lost at sea and even in the relative shelter of sea lochs. Prolonged hurricane-type winter storms were also reported in 1961, 1976, 1989 and 1992, with almost two weeks of severe wind in the 1993 'Braer' Storm. Older residents remembered tales of winters long ago when the Gobag gales blew without ceasing for days on end. But this was the longest spell of damaging winds that anyone could recall and, for the first time in living memory, some described being truly scared.

Everything around us was battered by great columns of soot-black clouds and by mud-grey showers, and deafened by stentorian gusts that whipped and sliced up the air and space around the croft-house and sluiced, keening and wailing, through telegraph wires. Our fields were flooded. The Red River rose and fell in tune with the deluges. After one nasty night of squalls a large sheet of metal appeared in the river, too heavy and cumbersome for us to drag out, and I worried for the sheep and ponies, the deer and otters. By the following morning it had gone. It had been picked up again by the wind and blown completely away. But when the 2013 'season' finally fizzled out, Cathma merely smiled, calmly saying that if we could cope with that, we would cope with anything.

Part Two

Winter Solstice to Spring Equinox

1. Sunrise over Maol Ruadh, sunset beyond Ben Tianavaig on the Isle of Skye and Isles Rona and Raasay, Celtic month of Mistletoe and Birch (December to January), Full Cold or Oak Moon

(i) Darkness deepens

With storms of snow and salt come the darknesses of midwinter. Yet even the shortest days are as varied in hue, tone and chroma as any other time of year. They burst open with sound as well as colours of every shade. At the winter solstice, although the north tilts in extremis away from the sun and we are all slewed, leaning away from a light that remains a cold distant pull on our consciousness, our emotions, senses and awareness are enhanced and they fill with colour. Add the vibrancy of stormy weather and we are swept along by an even deeper dive into wildness.

The unravelling and rebuilding that comes with the arrival of midwinter is wholly governed by streams of volatile weather – calm, storm, freeze, gentle, loud, wild. Reaching the midpoint of winter can be arduous and emotional. Outside, everywhere is stripped of its density, everything is thinned and whittled.

Inside, winter deepens with another peculiar sensation, as if something is running ahead just out of sight or hearing. No matter how hard I try, it cannot be caught.

As light recedes it fundamentally shifts as a concept, and tangles with time. Nights elongate and days contract, but somehow there is more. Strange and different energies prod at the days. December darkness is a tangible wave which grows slowly in a rumbling crescendo to a high peak and eventually overwhelms everything, even our ability to sense the light. It breaks in a torrent of noisy radiance and, in the foaming and tumbling of a winter's day, we hurtle about like pieces of kelp in a storm wave, until once again the darkness begins to build. When we first moved here, I worried about coping with the long nights, fearing submergence by the darkening waves, and drowning. Instead, I cascade and fizzle with the surging and crashing days. The more windswept I am, the better.

On the solstice everything falters for a few short hours. This is the pivot of the year, the pausing, when earth's rotation seems to stop, when mind, spirit and body hesitate, until, from a blaze of darkness, a tangible shift occurs and we all begin to move forward again. Morning light may struggle to reach the croft if the cloud-base is low, but somehow a little brightness will slide indoors. It is a time for bringing in the Yuletide greenery and decorating the house with garlands and candles, and I snip at holly, ivy and pine regardless of the weather. By two o'clock the day begins to fade again. As the sun sets, a short burst of red ice on the mountains or pale-peach rain in the valley holds the promise of life and warmth and renewal. Without fail it is a day for remembering. My mother died in the long night of midwinter; she missed the rebirth of light and hope by just a few hours.

*

In the rabble of 2013's continuous storms we filled the winter solstice with blazes of light and music and all the busyness the advent of Christmas entails. When the children were small, the house was always swamped by the noise and clamour of family life and excitement. When I worked at university, an approaching solstice was invisible amid the tumult of student classes, end-of-term staff meetings and brightly lit university buildings. The dark could not impose itself on me either at home or in my job. But tidily stored in an appropriate mind-drawer was a special folder, never opened or discussed with my family or friends. My mother died at the winter solstice in 1996, three years before I began to work as a full-time academic. My colleagues never knew about her death or its impact, or how it drove me to work harder with each passing year.

As a researcher, I wanted to understand the relationships between air pollution and human health and argued that our environmental histories of pollution could and should be examined alongside records of disease. I was driven by two main factors to work in those urban spaces. First, I was born and raised in some of the most toxic air in Britain, in Widnes, birthplace of the chemical industry. It smelled and often looked vile. Second, my mother's death was appalling. She died of mesothelioma, an incredibly rare form of lung cancer, when she was sixty-six. Some form of toxic pollutant, breathed in over years, killed her.

I developed projects on environmental evidence of air pollution found in the sediments of local Merseyside lakes and ponds and created an archive of changing air quality since the Industrial Revolution. The 'bottom' muds contained 'heavy metals', such as zinc, chromium, mercury and lead, which could only have come from factories and power stations and from traffic. By measuring the amounts of these elements in every half-centimetre of mud, it was possible to 'see' how air pollution had changed over time. Small ponds, once surrounded by fields and farms, only receive pollutants from atmospheric fallout. Gradually, what descends onto the surface water is incorporated into the sediment. The data from multiple sites were therefore records of atmospheric pollution in time and space. It followed that if atmospheric sources delivered toxic particulates to accumulate in the ponds over time, then they could almost certainly also be stored in the human body. Our sedimentary timelines of heavy-metal pollution became a proxy for more general contamination in the wider environment. Worse, they were an indication of what might be found deep within our own bodies. Today it is well known and widely accepted that excess heavy metals in the body can cause a range of serious health conditions and diseases and that various types of air pollution are problematic for our long-term health and well-being.

*

Mesothelioma is a small-cell cancer triggered by long-term exposure to invisible fibrous particles such as asbestos. Mum must have breathed in the stuff at least three decades before her lungs could no longer mask the cell growth. The toxic particles carried deep into her lungs were so small and sharp and fine that they passed through the cell lining of the alveoli and into the pleural cavity where they mostly stayed, hidden and unnoticeable. Some were finer still and moved further into the blood vessels surrounding the pleura and across the outer pleural membranes into the chest cavity. Each tiny individual shard that found its way into the almost infinitesimally small spaces between cells eventually triggered a response in them. The process was terribly slow; there were no clues or symptoms to suggest anything was wrong. Just as a pond in Merseyside absorbed pollutants with no signs at the surface, Mum's body had steadily, slowly and deeply accumulated trouble.

My mother had never come into contact with asbestos. Another micro-material must have been responsible. When she received her diagnosis, it was too late to do much other than alleviate stressful symptoms. As with asbestosis, the outlook was desperately poor, some two to three months at best. Her mesothelioma was uncommonly dispersed, inside both lungs and across both pleural cavities. Multiple metastases, in breasts, armpits and uterus, almost completely overwhelmed her body, but a radical combination of excision followed by a new trial drug therapy was deployed to buy some time. Her post-chemotherapy hair grew back curly, thick and richly chestnut in colour, but the lights in her eyes continued to fade. She endured a spring of chemotherapy and a summer of bright hope, and just as autumn began to sink towards the dark sleep of winter, so did she.

Even as her energy failed, she nourished her family. She watched us with concern and love. She told me to stay strong for my own children and help them deal with her dying. I felt helpless and sorrow-filled, but most of all angry. Mesothelioma had swept through her lungs, enveloping the brachiocephalic vein so it could not drain blood and fluids from her head. She could not see or hear through the swelling. For a short while, radiation shrank the tumour and the terrible swelling reduced enough so she was able to see dimly. In the end her lungs could manage no longer, yet her mind was alert and capable until her last hours. We were encouraged to take her back to hospital so she could have help to breathe without distress, back to the ward where she had endured so much. It felt like a betrayal. Worse, despite assurances, her pain management was chaotic, varied and often cruel: at times she would beg for more. Christmas was rushing ever closer. The wards were busy, Mum was moved into a small room of her own. Periodically she would want to get out of bed and sit up in a chair. As she slept sitting up, I would read to her or snooze, curled up like a foetus on her bed, utterly exhausted, then curse myself for being so weak of mind and feeble of body.

The shortest day was cold and frosty. Mum's skin was hot, the room stuffy. She had not spoken since the early hours, so at teatime my brother took my exhausted father home and I stayed, expecting to stay through the night once again. Her last words were about the solstice, and the power of renewal and rebirth. 'Think of me when the light is strongest on the shortest day,' she whispered. I held her hand and felt her pulse as it flickered and pattered. Somewhere a choir ran through a repertoire of Christmas carols; voices and melodies echoed along the hospital corridor from the main ward to our side room. Occasionally I sang too. As the evening wore on, a dense black fog smothered the view outside the hospital window. I got up and opened it wide to let the cool air seep in. Only years later would I remember that instinctive turn to an old tradition: open a window or door to let out the soul of the departed.

Mist drifted through the slats in the blinds. I turned back to Mum with the overwhelming sensation the room was filled with people; I had to push my way through to get back to her. She left me at ten o'clock. As I spoke out loud, saying goodbye and stroking her head, one of her fingers curled, and I knew she could still hear me.

Her death and funeral were wrapped around the winter solstice. Her house was filled with holly and greenery and lights and parcels and food and the excited laughter of her grand-children, just as it had always been, and exactly as she would have loved.

Midwinter is poignant; I know the winter solstice intimately. I know its shape because in truth it is light-filled. I know its moods, its songs and poems, its words of love and loss. And yet the waves made of darkness and grief no longer engulf me; in this grand, open country the dark is no longer cold and suffocating or formless. Glowing lichen on bare tree branches, the high flow of stars in the Milky Way, the tumbling sheets of neon in the Aurora Borealis, the moon, shooting stars, a lambent sea and the red eyes of animals in the dark bring light and hope. The night air is alive and filled with whispers and snuffling, the pounding feet of red deer, the tickle of cobwebs against cheeks, the Red River's voice, and the distant roar of waves as they break along the shore. In the depths of a dark night I hear trees creak, peat bogs sigh and rock-cliffs groan, feel the comfort and solace given by the mountains and sea and rich, dark sky. On a cloud-free night, prostrate on the ground looking up at the stars, the sensation of earth's rotation seeps into my spine and brain and I register the slow churning of space. Then I am not alone or overwhelmed in the great void but secure and loved as never before, closest to those I have lost. This profound, infinite and wilder dark is my comfort and joy.

*

In 2017 the winter solstice here in Wester Ross was unusually pastel and calm. Down on the beach at Opinan, in the low midday light, shadows stretched fuzzily. My own shadow was long and thin with an unusually swollen head. For one brief, lurching heartbeat, Mum's ghost was wrapped around me in the fierce embrace all mothers give. I turned around; my shadow vanished.

At midwinter the sun's rays are so low-angled the fragile light barely reaches the shore even at noon. Ice magic had delicately picked out the finest tracery of sand grain, kelp-leaf and barnacle. The beach sands were frozen in rose-pink crystals and crunched underfoot. Quartz grains sparkled and glinted and twinkled as merrily as a starry night sky. Ripples of sand had captured iced water in mother-of-pearl bands; shell-studded rocks cast crinkles of indigo shade.

The whole day was muted. There was only a whisper of wind, as gentle as a baby's breath and as cold as the snows on An Teallach. I longed for a fierce clear sunset because I had been hoping to see if a strange cluster of boulders at nearby Red Point was aligned in some way to the setting solstice sun. The great stones sit on top of a hump of rock, a *roche moutonnée*, formed by the powerful cleansing scrape of glacial ice. From many places along our stretch of coast it is possible to mark the position of sunset at both solstices and track their procession throughout the entire calendar year. At this peculiar rock cluster the view is skewed somewhat from the angles and shapes I have come to know so well at the top of the Seaweed Road, tilted somehow, but it covers the same vast sweep of land and sea, from the Red and Black Cuillin of southern Skye to the Point of Ness on Lewis. While there is no archaeological evidence for this site ever being used for anything save sheep-grazing, standing among the stones brings the same sense of passing time and altered perspectives I have felt at many other bigger, greater sites in Britain and Ireland. On a logical, practical day it may be wishful thinking, but when the wonders of the solar system play out over sea and islands it is hard not to wonder if the stones were deliberately placed.

The days washed away, too pale and disappointingly diffuse to see the sun's precise dip and mark its connection to the boulders. I roamed about the great stones anyway while far below the family skittled around on Red Point beach. The thick-pencil horizon lines were rubbed out; the Inner Sound was all smokes and steam, colourless apart from a few stripes of saffron and teal. I leaned against the largest rock and watched the last water-falls of pale-yellow light run dry and the mythical forms of Trotternish smudge to a mantle of jet. By the time we got home the sky was ink-stained and purpled. The heavy quilt of midwinter darkness had begun to fill up the valley. Everything was quiet. Calmness lay deep about the croft.

Each year, we string some small lights on the tree by our main gate where they swing wildly but joyfully in winter gales. In the dark skies of midwinter our own pretty Yuletide illu-minations, tiny though they are, can be seen from high on the hills surrounding the croft. But this time the air was completely still. Rather than thickening, the cloud had dispersed, and as the night deepened it opened wide and the little fairies of coloured light were overwhelmed by the glittering jewel-studded canopy overhead. The solstice had finally moved through me and, as Christmas approached, I could feel the heat of the stars on my face.

(ii) Northern Lights shine

Two great supermoons bookended the 2017 winter solstice and a severe white calm extended through Hogmanay into a swathe of spectacular blue. An unusual pile of northeasterly air seared our skies with a thick glaze of sapphire and turquoise. A sequence of hard frosts crisped the turf. The acute cold was most welcome after months of autumn rain. An old crofter grumbled that he had never experienced such prolonged wetness nor seen the ground so waterlogged and we agreed the 'great wet' of 2017's autumn felt apocalyptic. But in January, with all the swift suddenness often accompanying shifting wind direction, the hills were sheathed in snow and the field ditches and pools of standing water froze to glass. The river grew fringes of ice, some curled and tasselled, others as straight and stiff as fence wire. Meadow turf, so flattened by the months of rain, shone; rushes grew ice-hair; and the tight-furled buds on trees and shrubs, stuck hard and fast against the wind, salt and cold, glared as if some internal cellular shifting and hope of warmth churned within.

Danielle brought fluffy-lined waterproof coats for the old Shetland ponies. Cindy was not impressed and tried to nibble the straps, but as the cold intensified she sneered at us with the grim and resolute resignation old age often requires and accepted her new apparel. Toby merely plodded behind her, ignoring her huffiness and hauteur. They also grudgingly received hay and their small bowl of bran mash and sugar beet in the byre. But apart from feeding time both old ponies, by then aged thirty-eight, continued to refuse the offer of shelter, preferring instead to roam the croft, plinking on the hard frozen ground, scraping at snow and ice so they could nibble at the turf or pick at the rushes. There were many times in near-whiteout conditions when they would be found, as always, shoulder to shoulder, heads down, their manes and tails mingling protectively, snow piled high around their old legs.

When it comes, alongside the first slow return of light, the effect of such intense and extended calm after months of turbulent, wet weather is almost indescribable. Colours feel thicker, denser and stickier, as if oil paints have been applied with a palette knife and not a brush, and the canvas is not flat but three-dimensional and textured. There is earth-glow and rock-gleam. Withered, bleached tussock grasses and dun-coloured crusts of heather pulse with light reflected from their fine coats of rime. Under deeper snows the usual winter motley is white-washed out. The landscape dazzles in chrome; familiar features are reflected in the lochs and lochans and then frozen inside, and each tiny bog pool becomes a polished mirror. Trails and paths vanish until fresh imprints made by booted feet and roaming animals write new letters on the blank page.

One late autumn storm tide had carried the body of a juvenile minke whale onshore. Animals and mild rains stripped away its flesh until only the great bones remained, scattered along the strand-line. Within a few weeks the vertebrae were bleached white as snow and notched with ghost-scripts of the minke's old life, reminders of both the fragility and connectivity of life. The acute, penetrating cold that often follows midwinter can feel coercive and exacting, and, just like the marks on the minke whale bones, etches ghost-shapes into the whitened landscape and pares familiar landmarks from sight and mind. In bitter clear nights the hills seem crafted from highly polished antique silver. Frost sings; ice crystals contort as they grow; starlight plummets into the river and freezes the waterfalls. From time to time there is as much light in the depth of night as at midday. But in the hour or so before the sun lifts above the eastern mountains, the upturned bowl of sky shines with emerald and citrine. At midwinter, more than any other time of year, it feels as though I live at the centre of a great vessel whose base is crafted from ancient rock, whose lid is made of etched and coloured glass.

In the depths of winter there is no orange murk from street lights. Away from an open door we are confronted at first by a solid wall of blackness, but gradually night blooms like a chrysanthemum. Often, if the stars vanish behind a rug of cloud, light emanates from sea, loch and river. The Inner Sound and the Minch glow with spectral green, smeared with gentle biofluorescence as if phytoplankton, angler fish with their strange lamps, eels and glowing jellyfish have swum up from the deeps not knowing where ocean ends and sky begins. The Red River is transformed into a pearl-studded silk ribbon laid out on a dark velvet coat whose nap is lustrous and heavy. But all earthbound lights falter under the fierce alien dancing of the Aurora Borealis. The Northern Lights, created when solar winds encounter our magnetosphere and excite particles in the upper atmosphere into colour and motion, can often be seen from South Erradale and, when sunspot activity is high, auroras of intense neon from green to red come to life.

I admit to being underwhelmed the first time I watched the Northern Lights here. The smudges of green were unexpectedly disappointing. Yet a camera picks up what eyes cannot fathom and thus many images posted on social media show ripples of colour and light. Rob was coached in the dark arts of night-time photography by friend and professional photographer Mark Appleton, and he managed eventually to capture several beautiful auroras. A clear spell of weather in the deep darkness of winter is essential for photographing the night sky but the perfect combination of suitable conditions, sunspot activity and sizeable solar flares does not always occur. One night Rob's phone bleeped with an alert: the Aurora Borealis was not only ongoing but the 'index of activity' suggested a powerful solar storm. The light show would be impressive and vibrant. With greater energy comes more colour; a more powerful solar flare will pour with red, yellow and orange as well as green and white. We wrapped up warmly and stepped out into the frozen dark. At the cliff-top by the Seaweed Road we switched off our head torches and waited until our eyes became accustomed to the dark.

The night was transformed. For the first time I saw the Northern Lights truly, without the aid of technology. Before us, intensified in crystal-sharp air, tall columns of silent colour waved and rippled. Below the coruscating heavens the sea smouldered in livid green, as bright as a spring lawn at midday. Towers and spires of magenta and orange reared over our heads, stretching across the sea to Skye and inland to Baosbheinn and Beinn Alligin. They quivered again and again back into viridescence. To describe these lights as we would church buildings is too formal. I saw no architectural rigidity, only intense fluidity and motion. The colours poured as if paints were running down a canvas, others were billowing pennants and ribbons. The motion was organic and febrile. They are supposed to be silent, these dancing lights, but music accompanied the swirling greens and oranges and reds. To me, it sounded like a Gregorian chant, melodic and haunting, and for months afterwards I assumed it was an illusion, that my mind had conjured the sounds and songs and not those spectral, immense and alien flutterings of colour and light.

The long chain of islands from Skye to Lewis was a narrow shadow caught between the pulsing lights of heaven and the ocean; jade, jasper and ruby sky-fire, jet-black rock, emerald and amethyst seas. All vestiges of earth and ordinary life were lost under the panoply of living light. I thought again about the methane rains on Titan, and of some remote alien authority driving us all forward through the cosmos.

Later, rigid with cold, as the auroral curtain drew back and dimmed into the north, we turned to walk home. But spilling out in the night sky above our house and soaring over our heads was the Milky Way. It had been overcome and diminished by the spectral colours of the Northern Lights. As they vanished it reappeared as a great river made of pale-gold stars, mirroring the shape and direction of Abhain Dearg, sweeping from east to west. 'It's like the Nile,' I said. Ancient Egyptians are thought to have seen the Nile as a mirror image of the Milky Way and sited their major monuments in alignment with its most prominent stars. There are no ancient temples here, and, if they ever existed, are lost under deep peat or hidden among odd piles of stones, moss-covered and silent.

Our breaths flowered loudly in the intense cold and the light of our head torches. Others sounds came up from the river. We turned to look and dozens of red eyes shone back at us, crimson in the reflected torchlight. A group of deer had wandered down to shelter among the riverbank trees. Then the old Shetland ponies came trotting up. Cindy snorted her disgust when she realised there was no feed bucket. She whickered to Toby and he followed meekly. They trotted back towards the river, Cindy shooing the deer away with the same strutting outrage she had shown us.

There is other light too. When the short, compressed dawns of midwinter slowly begin to elongate in cloudless, haze-free conditions, a textbook triplet of twilights opens to greet the days of winter. As a brittle cold night ends, an 'astronomical' twilight is utterly silent yet star-studded, and gradually its outer limits of Prussian blue enfold bands of hot colour, the summer oranges of blooming hawkweed. A 'nautical' twilight of lapis lazuli and sapphire layered with cinnabar and orpiment follows quickly, accompanied by a single line of verse from a solitary robin. And finally a 'civil' twilight of bright egg-yolk yellow and Delft blue bursts open with sparrow- and blackbird-song. Then mountains pale to forget-me-not blue and the whole valley is basted in pale-lavender shadows. The science that defines these triple dawns is of angles and inclinations and decouples us from their raw synergistic beauty. Perhaps in another life I would have been measuring the tides of twilight using an array of numbers – six degrees, twelve degrees, eighteen degrees – to herald each arrival, but in the freezer of a semi-Arctic winter morning here, with my eyes washed in colour and breath dusted with ice, the only thing to do is watch the changing hues of vanishing silence.

(iii) Food becomes scarce as snow squalls blow

When we lived further south I did not think twice about the depth of solstice darkness, its weight and additional colourful substance or astronomical twilights. But here the sensation of returning light is altogether a different phenomenon. A sliver of light is a slight breath of air. It has a sound and scent all of its own, can slip under eyelids and hopscotch across retinas. Although in January the darkness is heavy and dense, thin pale beams creep in to fill the voids left by tidying Christmas clutter. Dust and odd dangling cobwebs are lit by stray wisps of light as they tunnel into a reclusive corner or rest upon a hidden ledge. A beam of light tethered by dust and wafting cobweb is a clear signal; change is coming, the outside world is beginning to stir.

With each added minute of day, the light moves from room to room carefully and precisely. When I first began to record the positions of sunsets and sunrises I would make a tiny pencil mark on walls here or there to record how the year was opening up inside as well as outside. Even when our days were roofed with grey slate and salt-gritted winds, they still flustered with brightness and I could check my pencil marks, counting and measuring.

As January proceeds, sunlight comes earlier each morning and is washed away a few minutes later at day's end. Light begins to flow over, under and into everything. Winter itself waxes and wanes. Snow comes and goes, together with ice and hail, occasional bursts of thunder and lightning, storm-force winds and sub-zero temperatures. Throughout January the battles between glacial airs from the polar north and east and the warmer, wetter and much windier Atlantic westerlies rumble on. It is a hard time of year for wildlife. Nature struggles with the unpredictability of the weather. Up on the mountain tops snow hares are revealed and then vanish. They are bright white against the mahogany and sooty smut of snowless moorland and rock, then invisible again in the marbled whiteouts; prey then not-prey.

Even with all the brutality of wintry weather it is hard to be indoors, for there is so much raw energy outside in winter. A peculiar vivid joy comes from hail-stung skin or fingers frozen by the keening of ice. I sometimes think mountaineers who winter climb have it right. On snow-planed mountains, when rock and scree and alpine turf are buried, climbers ascend the purest realms in those white voids. Once I was caught in a January thunderstorm down by the sea. It had thundered overnight, waking us from sleep with light-flickers and drumming hail. The following morning, I set off for the beach, thinking the worst had passed. Clouds still seethed, moving fast, occasional flashes marking their distant northern edges. The shore path was bedraggled by kelp and rock-cobbles thrown about in haphazard piles. I turned my face away from the first stinging hailstones and was clutched by the buffeting wind, bent double like an old crone; I was Beira yet again. Thunder came with the hail. I crouched in a sheep scrape while lightning struck and momentarily blinded me. Then it all ebbed away, replaced by a curtain of falling snow that muffled everything. I stood up. It was easier to see in the snowstorms whose large flakes, softer than the nails and screws of hail, gentled the spaces around me and quietened the air. The silence was a living being and began to pull my own voice out from my body. I wanted to sing. The thundersnow rushed away. Thick, iced air chased in from the hills. Bands of soot-black and navy-blue cloud dissolved and the sky raised itself up in a silent shell of pearl.

*

With snow, or without it, there is a terrible lowness to January. Meadowland waits for the spring under a tough mat. The hills glower. Tufted grasses are bleached again and again by sub-zero temperatures, heathers gnarl and grizzle from coffee grinds to charcoal, and shrivels of bare earth are baked hard by ice. Under such compressed conditions it is easy to pick a route across the knobbled ground and between the colour-blaze from boulders splashed with centuries-old lichens, and easier to see who has travelled there before me. With each thaw, patches of bare earth turn to soft mud and capture the prints of any passer-by. Then the gales and rain return, hillsides run and flush with water and fields turn into quagmires.

These are hard times for all living things. Food is scarce; insect life all but invisible. Occasionally, when a beam of sunlight dawdles by a field drain, a small eager crowd of insects may start to dance, but they do not last long. I have often wondered if they freeze in mid-flight as the day fails and ice shadows descend and are sprinkled across the ground like edible glitter on a cake. When cold winds thrust up from the sea, small birds are churned and tossed across the fields until they too cascade down in tumbles to find shelter among the hedges and rushes. These are also hard times for crofters and their animals. When the weather is severe, sheep and cattle need additional feeding. Extra hay, silage and bagged foods are brought via mountain roads from the east and south because in the hard depths of a severe winter the meadows simply do not have enough biomass (the sheer weight of living organisms) left to support even the smaller, twenty-first-century herds of South Erradale and other townships. Crofters who manage their meadows for hay are rare.

Like elderly humans, Cindy and Toby gradually became more and more frail, and Danielle thought it was time for a few extra comforts. In the long dark months of winter the old ponies had to work harder to find food out on the croft. Although they nibbled almost any vegetation as they roamed, there simply was not enough soft and nutritious plant material for old teeth and tummies to manage. Besides their new coats, Danielle hoped they would spend more time in the byre. The plan was simple – we were to encourage them inside, as the afternoon wore away, with their bucket of bran and sugar beet, and close the door. 'Hopefully they will get the hang of sleeping indoors,' whispered Danielle. But even in the face of bitter cold or hurricane-force winds the two old ponies objected. Cindy shouted out her fury and kicked the old door until the hinge fell off, while Toby watched in stoic silence. She created such a fuss that we came to a mutual agreement. The two 'oldies' would come into the warm, dry byre at feeding times but the door would remain propped open so they could go out onto the croft once they had finished. No amount of sweet crooning or tempting treats worked. Cindy continued her protests and kicked over the water bucket, preferring instead to drink from the river as she had always done. She was a storm-lover, like me.

The plan worked for two successive very harsh winters, but in 2020 Danielle thought Cindy, by then aged forty, was losing too much weight and condition. Worryingly, on a few occasions the old pony had also become disoriented. The vet called by to check them over. The heart-breaking decision was made to put them both to sleep. Toby had never been separated from Cindy;

he would grieve if left without his lifelong companion. Cindy and Toby came trotting up as usual for their breakfast feed and we stroked and hugged and sang to them, debating whether we were mistaken, and wondering if the two old ponies could have just one more year. But the thought of Cindy potentially collapsing in the middle of a freezing night with Toby alone and upset, was too much to bear. 'Better to have them together, warm and comfortable in the barn,' said Danielle. 'We can cuddle them as they go.' At that moment a high and mournful cry echoed around the valley. A sea eagle swirled above my head in a sky now leafed with pale gold. In that moment of distress and sadness, he had brought the light.

*

Cathma rarely brought her cattle into her large byre in winter. They roamed the hillsides, finding sheltered spots and turning over the ground as they browsed. We would know a bad storm was brewing because the sensible 'ladies' would make their way down from the hills and along the track to Cathma's gate, where they would announce their arrival by bellowing loudly. Occasionally she would guide them onto her croft when winds were particularly fierce and, from time to time, they would come onto Red River Croft. Even through the depths of winter, both cattle and ponies helped us as they moved around – their dung added organic matter and would provide homes for insects, their feet scuffed at the ground and mat of vegetation, breaking it up when it froze hard, and they neatly trimmed the rushes and gorse bushes. Several times the tall wire fence around the garden and vegetable patch was snapped, and not by cattle or sheep. The tell-tale imprints of cloven feet in the soft mounded earth betrayed the identity of the raiders. I only got cross once, when the deer snaffled the last of our beautiful brussels sprouts and purple kale.

Eventually, no matter how hard the January freezing and although the high peaks might still glint with ice, here by the sea dapples and splashes of pale-yellow light hint at warmth to come. Daylight continues to swell. Slowly the living world responds. White sheep seem doused in talcum powder, black sheep buffed and shining with boot polish. The cattle gleam. Even the hooded crows, hunting in slow swoops, are finely dressed in khaki waistcoats and capes of black twill. At the river I look for a flicker of silver in the cola-coloured water which might signal the presence of fish, and, down on the shore, rock pipits hop about, ringed plovers run up and down the sands, their feathers flashing as if stippled with war-paint. Light seeps from the heavens to illume the red beaks of oystercatchers, the wet flanks of otters and the pale yellow in a sea eagle's eye. But, even now, I look for the old ponies, seeking out their quiet wisdom, expecting them to tell me the name of the wind.

2. Sunrise over Tom na Gruagaich, sunset beyond the Old Man of Storr, the Isle of Skye, Celtic month of Rowan (January to February), Wolf Moon

(i) Sea eagles fly low in search of food

I first met a sea eagle under a porcelain winter sky high on Maol Ruadh, the great long hill bordering the south side of our valley. In the thin light and bitter cold and squalls of winter sea eagles come closer and closer to Red River Croft in search of food. We had watched them many times flying low and slow over our heads and also filmed them flying parallel to the shore hunting just a few metres above the surface of the sea. But I headed up the hill as quickly as I could after Danielle had telephoned to say she had spotted an enormous bird on the moor inland of the Red Point road. There was a biting wind and not a single shred of cover anywhere taller than my thighs. My wellies squelched in the peaty ooze between winter-brittle clumps of moorland vegetation and my calves burned from the fast walk upslope. Cresting the hill, I spotted him.

The bird was huge and dwarfed the carcass of a sheep. As he

pulled at the body he gazed about with indifference. I moved slowly closer, still breathing heavily, and despite my best efforts to keep quiet, I could only noisily push through the heather. He must have heard my approach. There was a ring of hooded crows about two metres out from the eagle. One bobbed up and down, cawing. The eagle looked up, shaking his head and ruffling his hind neck-feathers. His white tail swivelled and fanned out. His yellow beak was bright against the drabness of the hill and his talons vibrated with match-flame yellow against the dirty wool of the sheep carcass. I tried to steady my breathing and slowly began to raise my camera.

The great bird turned and fixed one extraordinary pale-yellow eye on me. I held my breath, wondering how even prey could resist him. In that moment a familiar feeling of dissonance and displacement, a sensation I had not felt for forty years, not since working in the mountain rainforests of New Guinea, tickled my insides with a lurch of adrenalin. The eagle turned back to the carcass. My eyes were fixed entirely upon him; my body tingled. Nothing changed, one patch of heather looked exactly like another and the crows were still circling and cawing; nevertheless, I felt it – a tangible surging of blood flow and nerve endings, a strange internalised sensation of having moved from one kind of space into another.

I kept as still as possible and watched the eagle for several minutes. The wind began to gust harder and then he spread his wings. He lifted up into the air. The crows cackled and moved forward, their patience rewarded. I watched him fly away. His huge wings have been called 'barn doors' and 'ironing boards', but they reminded me more of Roman *scuta*, the large rectangular battle shields. The end-feathers were splayed like a piano player's fingers practising complicated scales and his white tail was diamond-shaped like my old kite. Sulphur-yellow feet were quickly and neatly tucked under his body. He was so beautiful. I tried to will him back to me but felt only a rush of empty cold air.

I retraced my route to the road, but just before stepping back across the ditch at the edge of the tarmac realised I had not taken a single photograph. Below Maol Ruadh our little valley with its tiny white cottages surrounded by checkerboard fields and patches of trees was laid out like a tablecloth. Smears of cold lemon chased violet and dun-brown cloud. To my left the sea began to crumple in answer to the strengthening gusts and a pearly-green turmoil was already replacing the cobalt blue. To my right the broad undulating sweep of hill looked like a leather saddle in need of polish while above me the silky sky shredded into streamers and tatters of white and mauve. The wind soughed at my back, clicking through the heather and chilling my fingers. I set off downhill, my mind filled only with the light of the gold-rimmed eye.

From time to time we have watched a distant bird swirl and soar with board-walk wings outstretched, diamond-wedged tail catching the light, yellow beak and yellower feet glinting, and with a thrill known it to be a sea eagle, one of several who frequent our local coast and are often seen gliding over the Erradale valley. *Haliaeetus albicilla*, the White-Tailed Eagle or sea eagle, is a magnificent and enormous bird of prey. Here in the Highlands the raptor is sometimes known as *Iolaire Sùil na Gréine*, the 'eagle with the sunlit eye', for good reason: close to, and these eyes are the yellow of a golden torc. To some the sea eagle is known as an 'erne'. A mature male's head-feathers are also pale, and with his fierce, hooked mustard-yellow beak he wears the bejewelled chain mail of kings. The mighty creature is larger than the golden eagle, though his yip-yapping call is meeker and more plaintive and belies his grandeur and power. As his English name suggests, the short tail is white and this, rather than the

bright yellow of beak and claws, often helps i~
flight.

In the eighteenth century white-tailed eagles were wi~
in Scotland and Ireland, but by 1900 only a small num~er
remained in the British Isles. Finally, in 1918 on Shetland, the
last, lone male sea eagle was shot and the birds were extinct.
Their demise was precipitated by direct persecution from
farmers, crofters, gamekeepers, fishermen and others. Reports
written in the nineteenth century about wildlife and game on
Highland farms and estates and the intense efforts to eradicate
raptors make sickening reading. Even today there is an ingrained
unwillingness to accept the return of the raptor because of its
supposed impacts upon lamb numbers.

In 1975 a reintroduction programme began. Eighty-two young
eagles were brought over from Norway and released on the Isle
of Rum in the Inner Hebrides from where they eventually spread
to the Isle of Mull. In Wester Ross, sea eagles were released in
the 1990s, nesting at first on islands in Loch Maree and later on
the more remote cliff-tops. Across the whole of Scotland there
are now more than a hundred pairs.

White-tailed sea eagles breed when they reach maturity around
five or six years old and they partner for life, living on average
until they are twenty-two. Their nests, made from twigs and
branches and lined with grasses, bracken and rushes, grow in
size with repeated and continual use. Primarily they are 'fisher-
birds', taking fish from the sea or lochs as they fly low over the
water. Individuals have also been observed mobbing and intimi-
dating large gulls until they release their catch in a form of piracy,
but they are also generalists, their diet species-diverse, and they
will take sea birds, small mammals and carrion depending on the
relative abundance of food supply across the seasons.

Stories from crofters about raptors abound. Most contentious are the allegations about sea eagles taking lambs. Although several scientific studies have shown, despite emotive press reports to the contrary, that the sea eagles on Mull only took lambs in spring months when lambs were either not viable or sick, many crofters remain adamant raptors of any kind harm or kill livestock. Some have insisted for years that sea eagles predate healthy lambs yet deaths by predation must be set against a backdrop of other lamb deaths, notably the phenomenon known as 'black loss'. Every year across the Highlands and Islands between ten and thirty per cent of the annual lamb 'crop' dies. The number appears to be growing, though an explanation is yet to be found other than speculation around mineral content of grazing and its potential impact on breeding ewes and foetal growth.

For crofters whose lives and prosperity once wholly depended on the health of their animals, the need to deter raptors of any kind was understandable. In Wester Ross, records of raptor killing date back to the fifteenth century but it was widely adopted as a necessary practice alongside the rapid expansion of sheep farming much later, only in the late eighteenth century. Raptors were viewed as 'vermin' and a significant threat to successful grouse-rearing as well as to sheep. The killing of birds of prey and the destruction of nesting sites and habitats was so severe that by the early 1900s several species had become extinct, including the white-tailed sea eagle, osprey, goshawk and red kite.

Today there remains a high level of tension between agriculture and conservation, and tagged birds are still being lost. However, sea eagles bring visitors, and their future in the Northwest Highlands is assured for now. Nature tourism generates considerable revenue – according to some sources, more than farming, shooting or hunting, and it may be that in the future a workable balance between tourism and livestock farming, with raptors at its heart, will be found, one that will ultimately also benefit the crofters of Wester Ross.

*

Years ago, on an Orkney holiday, Rob and I clambered after our children into the cliff-top 'Tomb of the Eagles' at Isbister on South Ronaldsay. One by one, we scrambled inside, belly-down on a rickety trolley pulled by ropes. Looking around the chamber, wide-eyed in the darkness, we tried to connect with the stillness of the space, hushed by the overpowering feeling of having crossed a threshold other than stone. Afterwards, in a small brightly lit and busy museum, we inspected the eagle bones and talons, stone jewellery and pots, carefully excavated over many years by the landowners and archaeologists. There was no mistaking the deep sense of connection those ancient Orcadians had with their chosen talisman, for the haul was immense. More than six hundred bones and seventy talons had been found among disarticulated human and other remains, suggesting strong links between the people living at Isbister and the wild birds. Standing before cases filled with objects, and surrounded by pictures of living sea eagles photographed in all their glory, it was easy to understand their passion for the great birds.

Sea eagles are immense and beautiful; they exude power and strength – the very traits prehistoric peoples perhaps would have desired for themselves and their families. They may have expected protection from the birds in return for such reverence. Sensations of wildness and power, just as I had experienced on the moors above South Erradale, might well have accompanied their own encounters and been important to the ancient communities, while gathering remains reinforced physical and spiritual bonds with the birds over many generations and perhaps reaffirmed societal connections to nature and the living world. Although such sentiments are debated by archaeologists and anthropologists, similar associations between human bones and those of specific animals have been revealed by excavations on Orkney. At the Knowe of Yarso, on Rousay, people appear to have been buried with deer bones; some thirty-six deer skeletons were excavated there. And at Cuween, near Finstown on Orkney's mainland, human skeletons were buried with twenty-four dog skulls. The consensus is that such connections with particular animal or bird species not only existed, they were important.

In 1979 I lived in Papua New Guinea as part of my doctoral research. The indigenous communities within the mountain rainforests shared their homes and taught me about their ways of life and about their close connections to the natural world. Like the peoples of ancient Orkney, they also gathered totems: feathers from birds of paradise, talons from cassowaries, crocodiles' teeth and boars' tusks. Each community I met had a totemic animal particular to it imbued with the power they sought. Elders and warriors would create fantastical head-dresses from their ancestors' hair threaded with feathers, bones or tusks from their chosen species in a tradition stretching back millennia into the deepest remoteness of time and memory. Some communities also ate specific fauna in order to obtain the particular characteristics of certain species and extract spiritual power and strength, while others believed the spirits of chosen animals offered protection to villagers. Such traditions and ideas varied across the Highlands of New Guinea but their core beliefs were strongly based on notions of equivalence – all organisms living within the forest exerted the same level of spiritual and physical power as people. I suspect the ancient community at Isbister must have been equally impressed and inspired by these enormous birds. They probably gathered bones and talons, and perhaps in the same way as the 'Stone Age' communities of New Guinea, and although separated in space and time, may well have shared common ideas on spirituality in the natural world.

★

At this time of year the day falls into dusk in mid-afternoon. I stepped outside to stand by the gate, my mind still filled with the images of the great bird I had met on Maol Ruadh. I had thought of little else since returning home: his golden eye, his buttercup-yellow beak and the blaze of white-hot tail-feathers. The air was awash with scents, of cold earth, salt and wet stone. A robin was singing; his verses by increments fading as the light dimmed. Snippets of dark shadow around the hedges were silent and growing quickly. I listened to the absence of human activity: there was no traffic, no tractor chug or chainsaw buzz. But then a shushing sound, like a mother quieting her hungry baby, crept over the fields. From just over a kilometre away the distinctive reverberation of waves breaking and retreating across the shore floated up the cliff and over the bog to me. Every returning swoosh of sea-sound was wrapped in the sweetness of the growing dark and accompanied by an occasional boom, the noise made by larger waves when they thump down on rock or sand. Then the sounds dribbled away in a jet-plane droning until I could no longer hear them. I strained to listen. Once or twice a faint echo of a walloping wave shimmied around the valley. And then a single cry, a raptor's wail.

In the long haul of winter one of the most familiar sounds is the eagle's cry. The valley draws sea and golden eagles and a host of smaller birds of prey. Despite crofters' traditional discomfort with the presence of these great birds, there are signs that some are beginning to lose their prejudices. There is a strange and inconsistent dichotomy here – wildlife thrives here because of crofting practices and because the crofts themselves are filled with life.

In the distance the waters of the Inner Sound appeared to be as polished and smooth as the hand axes and sea eagle jewellery of Isbister. Beyond the Minches and above the Outer Hebrides tomorrow's weather was visible in the deepening, thickening bands of midnight-blue and purple. But over my head the sky-dome was still cloud-free and rapidly filling with stars. Standing there at the gate I felt blessed and secure and filled with awe, not just at the darkening star-sprinkled sky, but because of the sea eagle encounter. The great bird had brought the light with him, and the promise of change. He had evidently been holding it through the deepest days and darkest nights of winter in his wondrous eyes, ready for spring.

(ii) Rough seas bring gifts

One morning I set off across the croft convincing myself that signs of spring were peeking out between sharp grey showers. From the top of the Seaweed Road the sea was a rich deep blue and I could see a large and growing patch of opaque turquoise. The winds were hard, dashing in from the west, and the sea began to respond with a flurry of white horses. Visibility was poor, the outer Minch all smoke and glints of mirrored bright-ness. Close inshore dozens and dozens of gannets were tearing at the spray and skewering slicks of water. Other birds were picking at waves, dipping and swooping over the spreading opacity. Then the sun burst out in a rip-rap of yellow; turquoise became neon, blue sea shone like gloss paint.

Peter Cunningham had telephoned earlier and asked us to keep an eye out for increased bird activity offshore and I told him of the milky pastel colour of the sea. 'At this time of year diving gannets might indicate fish shoals rather than a plankton bloom,' Peter had explained. Looking out across the water all I could see was fierce colour and a sea that was increasingly becoming tangled with fast-moving clouds. The smooth glossy surface had gone, replaced by shreds and tatters, foam and noise. But I used the binoculars anyway, until they and my glasses became too salted to see through.

Many in the local community, including Peter, began to hope that fish would return to spawn. Local scallop divers had photographed herring roe covering large areas of seabed off the coast of South Erradale and excitement was growing – could the herring be returning? The stretch of inshore water is potentially quite productive partly because it receives a regular supply of nutrients – minerals derived from the mountains and organic detritus from the peats – and for as long as anyone can remember, scallop divers and lobster pots have been a fixture here. When the divers shared images of the spawning and roe with the media, it was 'big news'. Film footage was broadcast on the BBC's *Springwatch*. Eggs had been laid in such great quantities they almost completely smothered the maerl beds, scallop fields and seagrass meadows. There was considerable excitement, not least because herring shoals had not been seen in the area for decades; they had vanished long ago, taking the herring industry and people with them.

All along the Scottish west coast, areas of inshore waters and seabed are protected by law. In 2014 Marine Protected Areas were created by the Scottish Government to safeguard the

A special place. The old post at the cliff top.

A late summer evening on Red River Croft and the Torridon mountains.

Abhain Dearg (the River Erradale), low flow.

The river rises and floods the lower meadows.

Peter in the river, carrying the electrofishing gear, net ready to scoop up fish or eels for the survey.

Deer crossing the old path from South Erradale to Badachro.

Late autumn squall passes along the Minch and approaches Opinan beach.

Winter squall crossing the Minch at sunset.

The winter solstice sun rises over Maol Ruadh.

Snowstorms approaching.

When the pickings are thin, Cathma's sheep come for treats.

Winter descends.

Storms bring snow and other gifts to the beach.

The sea-log seat.

Bog myrtle, *Myrica gale*, in flower.

Muirburn in the upper Erradale valley.

wildlife and habitats in inshore waters with the long-term aim of shielding fish nurseries. The growing consensus from scientific and fishing communities was that without such protections there would be marine ecosystem collapse taking the fishing with it. How effective such zones of protection may prove to be will take years of research and monitoring, but at the very least they can be annually assessed in terms of species diversity. More data means more information. Looking after these areas would, it is argued, ultimately help fish stocks. The kelp forests close to our shore, and other marine habitats such as maerl beds and seagrass meadows, are vital to the health of Scottish seas and wildlife populations.

In recent years there have been reports of large fishing vessels in the Minch, and on several occasions they had been seen – and photographed – operating inside the no-fishing zones. When scallop divers and conservationists returned again to the potential spawning sites to film, they discovered broad swathes of the seabed had been dredged bare. The scallop beds and fragile maerl had suffered badly. The seafloor had effectively been reduced to an underwater desert. For those trying hard to protect our marine environments, and for many of our local shell-fishermen, it was a terrible shock; while some, also trying to carve a living from the sea, called the zones of protection unnecessary and intrusive.

Discussions about the efficacy of Marine Protected Areas and their potential impacts, and about the effects of different types of fishing, have continued apace. The community has been engaged and vocal. Opinions have differed, but overall there is more optimism than not. Where herring swim, other fish and cetaceans follow, and, as many other regions report, these can boost the local tourist industry.

During the latter half of the twentieth century and the early twenty-first, modern fishing techniques trying to meet large-scale demands for cheap produce have led to significant deterioration in environmental quality and to the sickening of marine livestock. Fish numbers have plummeted. Many organisations and individuals have tried and continue to raise awareness. Here in the coastal waters of Wester Ross local fishermen, in particular the scallop divers and creel men, continue the fight to save and restore fish stocks. Although it will take more than the strategic placing of *èit* stones to restore wild salmon in our rivers, the presence of herring along our coast has generated a lot of interest and hope. In a future set within the context of a warming world and rapidly rising sea temperatures, somehow we must try to figure out how we can best help.

*

A few days after Peter's call I walked to the cliff-top to take a few more pictures. Towards the islands of Rona and Raasay patches of the Inner Sound were once again opaque and turquoise against the pale cloudless sky. The air was filled with moisture; the horizons blurred. Under my feet the croft-ground remained colourless, still crusted stiff with winter and waiting for spring. The waves below were made of pale gold, a shiny version of the pale meadows. The light was coruscating; every minute drop of water seemed to dazzle and flare-flash. Overhead the sky brightened further and clouds galloped in from the west. Shards of silver and white began to drop from the sky – once again gannets were diving at great speed, able to see fish even through the turbulence and stramash. Squinting hard, I scanned the sea, determined to help Peter if I could. If that cloudy stretch of water was a result of spawning fish, then once again there would be great excitement. With a lurch of hope and expectation

I felt sure herring had indeed returned in spite of all the recent problems with trawlers in the protected areas. The mysterious turquoise patch was still there and growing. As I prepared to take photographs, a sea eagle swooped low to claim a fish.

The wind began to run more powerfully up the steep edge of the cliff, and I held my arms out to feel its full force. I felt like a sea bird, born of the wind. Gravity was powerless. Gusts swept straight through my body. Below, the sea turned emerald, the sky a bright sapphire blue. Further out the Minch turned dark olive-green against an indigo wall of cloud. My eyes streamed. I gulped in the fierce air and felt cold enter deep into my body, sharply and painfully. Noise flowed through me too; then light and colour. Everything seemed to be moving and singing and breathing; rock churned beneath my feet and waves pounded the beach. The sheer volume and amount of life and energy were staggering. As the wall of indigo grew, the Inner Sound flared as brightly as a neon sign on a dark street. In a few breaths it reversed again, waters darkening under brilliances of sky. Over the Hebrides, I could see fickle and mean-spirited break-away squalls rushing towards me with steel-rod showers. I could guess their speed and feel their cold even from here. I turned for home to beat the hail.

★

In the same way that the sea fills with colour, light unspools in hints and whispers and the days soon begin to swell and yellow. February the first, the Celtic festival of Imbolc, marks the midpoint between the winter solstice and spring equinox, when light is supposed to grow perceptibly. But in reality, from mid-January onwards, light slices at the nights. Living at the coast means that even the smallest glimpse of returning light is magnified by the sea, and by the interchangeability of waves and winds. Imbolc is also the festival of Brìghde, goddess of fire and fertility, who was transformed into Saint Brigid as the Celtic world was Christianised. In the complicated histories of Christianity the older festival of Imbolc, celebrating the start of spring and the return of light and renewal of life, was appropriated, becoming Candlemas. To both Christian and non-Christian the affirmation of life brought by the longer hours of daylight were so critical that some form of celebration was entirely justified. There is no doubt that Brìghde's day marks a turning point. Even away from the churning waves, I can see it on the croft. There are signs that life as well as light stirs below the flattened turf in the meadows and under the bark of our trees or in the piles of blackened leaves. The almost colourless land begins to fill with hints of colour.

In Gaelic an oystercatcher is often known as *Gille Brìghde*, or 'guide of Saint Brigid'. Legends explain that she would send out the feisty birds to guide ships to safety and it is easy to understand her choice. Any sailor worth his salt would recognise their piercing, distinctive calls and know a safe shore was near. For me, the plaintive songs of oystercatchers frame memories of wild isolation, of having scrambled to a hidden blot of sand, children in tow, accompanied by nothing more than each other and sea-bird voices. As winter swims slowly towards spring their piping perforates the air and heralds the oncoming light and I am transported to those joyous days.

*

Intermittent storms bring gifts to our ruffled coast: great logs and tree branches, thick hemp hawsers, brightly coloured ropes and twine, boxes, pipes and rigging, as well as uncountable smaller fragments of other people's lives: shoes, toys and plastic fragments of many kinds. The detritus of the Anthropocene. A former colleague once grumbled that the term 'Anthropocene' was far too polite. 'It's the Dustbinian,' he said.

A few years ago a long straight log sailed into Opinan's bay on the crest of a late winter storm, a gift from Brìghde. It was foam-coated and colourless and tumbled back and forth as great white wave-roars pounded and shook the shore. Eventually the sea gave it up and left it high on the sands, almost hidden under hills of foam. Together Rob and I dragged and rolled it higher still, to where machair and marram crimp the beach margins. We added rock-cobbles to lock it into place and left it to the rains to wash away the salt, grit and foam. Log became seat, sea-, storm- and saint-gifted.

There was no clue to the log's original home or purpose. With similar diameter and length to a deer-fence strainer-post it may well have once been intended for a coastal paddock, though it could never have been used, for there were no nails or tacks or embedded slivers of fencing wire. I suspected it had not been at sea for very long because there were no worm burrows either. A thick rope and curling branches of silver birch and Scots pine were added, and over time it has been decorated with shells, feathers and small, colourful pebbles. The spot is sheltered from the strongest gales, except those from the north. The view extends across the small bay of Opinan and its patterned sands, out to the Inner Sound and Trotternish peninsula, and over the Minches to the Outer Hebrides. From the log it is possible to see surface-water currents flowing back and forth in tune with the winds and tides, responding to both, and crimping in sweeps and shears of colour. It quickly became a place of contemplation and a wonderful spot to watch sea and sky. Gradually, as our wilder neighbours grew used to the sea-log seat's presence, and me sitting there, they became bolder. Deer leapt over it, small birds gossiped beside it, otters left their spraint on it.

Each early morning visit, whether in rain, cold, sunshine or shadow, storm winds or complete stillness, was another opportunity to gather up thoughts, calm anxieties and, best of all, watch the wilder comings and goings. The log straddles the edge of a narrow band of dune grassland and machair close to a small burn and old, rarely used fields. It is positioned, accidentally yet fortuitously, in a transitional space, not simply the physical coastal edgeland but a place where wildlife regularly moves between rocky and sandy shore, between dunes and beach, between sea and crofts. The seat is one small fixed point along trails used by people, domesticated animals and wild creatures; sheep and cattle, deer, otters, birds, lizards, insects. A resting point on the Seaweed Road, it became my go-to spot to gather the wilder news of the day and later, when illness all but consumed me and when the wind was my much-needed companion, a place of recovery and restoration.

Very early one morning, in a dawn wrapped in mauve shadows and iced stillness, I saw a full moon hanging low over Cathma's house. The air was clear, the dome of sky fuchsia-pink and violet, the moon made of clotted cream. I set off along the Seaweed Road to Opinan. By the time I reached the sea-log seat the moon was beginning to set between the hills of Harris and Lewis. Dram sat close, leaning against my legs. The heat from his body was both comfort blanket and hot-water bottle. Our breaths mingled and frosted. The rising sun had not yet breached the dunes behind me but somehow the beach seemed caught by two great forces of light slowly trying to pull it apart. This is the essence of edgelands. Caught between sun and moon, earth, air and water, they are powerful and bounteous. Life-givers and protectors.

The narrow intertidal space was being impossibly stretched, its red sands paling and thinning. I could feel my own body extending too, drawn between moon-tides and sunrise. When the sun rose up at last to crest the sand hills, the day began to bloom in blue. Where the sky had been lilac and mauve, now it was turquoise. Smokes and vapours smeared the horizon into peach and rose. For a sliver of time I became a rainbow made of nothing but colour, until the moon vanished completely with a silent pop.

(iii) Moss mounds, lichens and ancient rocks glow

In late January and early February snow comes and goes, blowing in from the north and west in fast-moving squalls. The mountains around us fluctuate between dazzling wedding-dress white and funereal black. Weather is fickle and fierce. Yet walkers and climbers are tempted into the hills, lured by the prospect of sharp clear air and crystalline light. Height is intoxicating. The lengthening of daylight hours is tangible now, so the temptation grows and grows.

A walk at this time of year is water-filled and cold. Snow showers brush at the edges of spring. Beira, goddess of winter and bringer of winds, continues to smite the ground with her hammer and raise the eddying wind known as *an sgudal*, 'the sweeper'. Gusting winds are cruel and iced but it is a good time to roam. Burns and rivers run noisily and joyously in full spate, the coast bounces with energetic waves and intermittent brilliance. While the croft waits patiently for warmth, the mountains are whittled by piercing lights. Skiffs and smothers of snow exaggerate space. Bare rock glows as meltwaters pulse downhill, glassy and glinting even in the briefest moment of brightness. The land shines and glowers at the same time. Long hikes are curtailed by the still-short days but there is a clarity now between snow-patch, rock and plant life which makes walking and climbing a pleasure. Mountain air in late winter can be fine, gin-clear and deeply refreshing. In our early years here, we went to the hills as often as possible.

In between clumps of snow-hatted heathers, lichen-covered stones shine vividly – silver, white, copper, blue, rusty red, orange and black – the colours of winter. These micro-landscapes are as enchanting as the peaks. They are maps of age and time; their colours outline and define the battlegrounds between different varieties of lichen; they are evidence of life's ability to withstand extreme conditions, and of longevity and resilience. Some patches can be more than a century old.

Gradually more and more spots of colour daub the slopes. Moss-covered mounds are scattered everywhere. From the valley sides, up onto moorlands and throughout the mountain ranges, boulders, tree stumps, old walls and rocky crags provide foundations and footing for mosses. Beginning as small cushions, like lichens they take years to grow and, as they do, create micro-habitats, small areas which suit the growing needs of a range of species. Eventually the boulder or stump may vanish completely under a spreading quilt. Mosses grow by increment, slowly and steadily building up cover and depth until only the original shape of host boulder or tree stump is visible. Throughout winter the mounds are as pale as our croft meadows and as bleached as montane grasses. When days begin to lengthen and light intensity increases, they change colour, becoming starkly green and vibrantly lime, in contrast to the subdued drabness of heathers and grasses. The mossy cushions defy seasonal gales and deep snow. They fend off ice and frost in their dense, low-growing miniature communities. Mosses with names such as 'woolly fringe', 'common haircap', 'slender mouse-tail' and 'golden-head' grow together in warm, cosy, brightly lit, tiny forests. Before anything else changes, their brighter colour is one of the clearest signs that winter is relinquishing its hold on the hills.

★

This is a time of rapid freezing and thawing. The mosses have the right strategy – keep close to keep warm. But it is also a time of motion and flux. Freeze-thaw fractures rock, part of the aeons-old cycle of weathering. Beyond human timescales, physical processes gradually reduce great summits into fragments and carry them down to the sea.

The mountains of Wester Ross and the islands beyond the Minch are formed from some of the oldest rock strata on the planet. They lie in an area geologists call the 'Hebridean Terrane', a huge region stretching along the westernmost strip of mainland Scotland from Sutherland to the Sleat peninsula of Skye and over the Minches to the Outer Hebrides. The shallow tip of Loch Maree and the village of Kinlochewe mark its easternmost reaches, where younger rock strata were pushed up and over the much older ones. It creates a great basin, one crafted out of a non-human early Earth over imaginable expanses of time, but now filled as much with stories, songs, poems and human conflicts as with water, air and light.

Stand anywhere on the Wester Ross coast facing east and it is possible to trace the scribbled edges of summit ridges and sharp peaks. To a degree these mountain ranges have determined the westering outlook of almost all the villages here. When we watch sunsets our thoughts and dreams are propped up by the rock walls at our backs. They are so tightly folded and knitted together they produce light and shade in scattered edge lines impossible to disentangle. 'Landskein' is too short a word to describe the lengths of these twining horizons.

Today large inland swathes are empty of human voices and many areas bereft of birdsong, yet there is no true silence, for history and time lie deeply in the glens and hills. There are mountains made from three-billion-year-old rocks, peat bogs filled with ten thousand years of climate history and ruins containing remnants of a turbulent human past. The sense of great age and deep time can be felt in all the pinnacles, corries and U-shaped valleys chiselled by glacial ice, in the river-carved gorges, waterfalls and gullies, and in the cliffs and beaches, geos and caves sculpted by the sea. And overlying everything, the languages of Celt and Gael speak of vanished landscapes and habitats, and of lost communities. Landforms are myriad, people are few. Yet prehistory and history reside profoundly here, in every crevice, on each lichen-covered stone, exposed tree root and wandering hill trail.

Two great rock types dominate the landforms of the west – Lewisian gneiss and Torridonian sandstone. Forged by heat, pressure and immense power from earth's original granitic rocks, Lewisian gneiss is extremely tough and resistant to weathering but elegant in colour and form. Bands of deep charcoal grey or olive green are interspersed with white or cream bands of quartz, and are convoluted and folded like ripples of fabric in a ball gown. The sandstones occur in various shades of rose, red and brown but when exposed to weathering they turn purple and grey. Open up a piece of sandstone and it will reveal its true colours – the peach and lavender pastels of winter sunsets.

★

Most of the peaks here are formed by sandstones and much younger creamy-white quartzites sitting on great beds of gneiss. Every walk into the hills generates the same sense of awe. Their overwhelming age, the often bewildering scientific explanations of their formation and their unutterable beauty draw us back, and for the first few years living in South Erradale we succumbed to the pull of the summits, again and again and again.

A late winter walk in the fierce beauty of hill country in volatile weather and dramatic light is a journey into deep time. Fragments of freshly ice-fractured rock reveal the light of early earth, captured in grains of quartz and laid down billions of years ago. That thought alone, of such tremendous age caught inside the rock, can drive me back to the mountains almost as much as the views. The sandstones of these magnificent peaks are themselves the by-product of aeons of weathering and the erosion of long-vanished mountain ranges so big as to be almost inconceivable. It is simply mind-boggling. Sands and gravels, accumulated to enormous depths, were compressed until they turned to stone. The depth and length and breadth of such forces in space and time are beyond description but are wondrous and unsettling. I place my feet on such rock with reverence and awe. Here and there, in small pieces of peach-coloured rock, the ancient light is exposed again, after two billion years. On every descent from a mountain I feel the tug of its deep-time story, as if it is almost reluctant to let me go.

★

But in the spring of 2016 I was suddenly and unexpectedly hamstrung by a few days of debilitating viral fever. My lungs were attacked, joints inflamed, muscles seized up. I could barely stand, let alone walk. What followed burned into weeks and then years of strange, repeating painful attacks on my immune system. I was reduced to relying on medicines and walking with sticks. The crisped and bleached tufts of grass, brittle grey husks of heather and feeble strands of smoky sunlight that riddle a mountain in winter described me perfectly. I tried again and again to be strong. At first doctors implied the symptoms were in my mind. More exercise is the answer, they said, but I fell off a metaphorical cliff. I learned new words – myalgic encephalo-myelitis – and I needed help for contorting muscles, spasms, severe pain and lack of mobility. The shock to my body from the first bout of fever was immediate. Any new infection caused an even greater response from my immune system. Storms raged inside my body. To go from mountain readiness to a prolonged state of reduced confinement was devastating.

When illness struck, I was bereft. Long walks and climbs were beyond me. My husband is tall, six foot four, long and lean, with legs able to make one stride for every three of mine. He is a gentle man who was only very rarely impatient with me when I trailed behind him on an upland path. He knew how much I loved mountains; he felt the same way about high places and remote hill country. It was a struggle for him to see his walking partner so reduced. It was painful for him merely to look at the summits of Torridon from home, especially when the weather was good. Rob longed to climb the peaks and I could sense his sadness and frustration; his loyalty and desire not to cause me additional upset kept him in South Erradale. He had a small boat, but at times I could not even struggle into that, so he had lost his water-buddy too. Friends came to his rescue. Photographer Mark Appleton – another gentle man and mountain-lover – called to ask if Rob would climb with him. My husband hesitated, as I knew he would, and I yelled at him, 'Go, go, go. For goodness' sake, GO!'

I bought Rob new crampons. He and Mark headed into the snow for photography as much as the joy of the climbing. Yes, we would all say, the hills are quiet, no biting insects, and the air tastes so good. There were maps to be studied, names whispered – Slioch, An Teallach, Beinn Eighe. I knew he would be happy. My long-legged husband would not need to worry or alter his pace because I failed to keep up, or listen to my grumbling about slipping and sliding while he strode on ahead with ease. Even though mountain paths can be treacherous in changeable weather, the men would delight in the challenge, and in the late winter light. Their photographs were full of shared joy and magnificent peaks. I asked them to take pictures of moss mounds and lichen but they forgot, their heads lost to the clouds and shining summits.

I watched the days playing out across Baosbheinn, Beinn Dearg and Beinn Alligin. I caught glimpses of Beinn Eighe and Liathach. Again and again, my mind filled up with thoughts of crisp cold air and the scent of bare rock. I would hear an eagle's high cry and instead of looking over my head to see where he soared would look to the distant crags, filled with longing. There were times when I was certain the eagle had come to bring news of the highest spaces just for me. At night my dreams teemed with the silhouetted shapes of these great mountains billowing with blue smokes and iced wrinkles, the men smiling and encouraging me to hurry.

During one of their winter expeditions, I walked through unusual snowy slush to the shore. I dared not look at the mountains but instead answered the call of the sea. On either side of the old trail, amid the melting snow, moss mounds and patches of lichen were revealed. The Seaweed Road was dappled with bright beads of spring green, and like lamps they lit the way home.

3. Sunrise over Beinn Alligin, sunset between Ben Edra and the Bealach Uige, Trotternish, Isle of Skye, Celtic month of Ash (February to March), Ice Moon

(i) Myrtle buds and muirburn

Away from the sea and mountains, in the relative shelter of the Erradale valley, the winter turf remains bleached and thinned, yet it still reflects pockets of light, especially as a day dwindles. We begin to think life will never spring up from the dead, shrink-wrapped ground. But as the sun sinks, for just a few short breaths the ground flushes to a rosy hue. There is a sudden sense of intention, expectation and anticipation. Trees are waiting too. Many have already set buds with a range of defences against the cold. They are tight, sticky, colourful, vibrant. Some are large, others tiny. Buds of black, red, purple, brown, grey and yellow wait to unravel and burst open, and in the interim fleck the woodland with small baubles of gentle colour and hope.

In small wet smothers here and there in our fields, and out across the peatlands that surround us, buds of bog myrtle (*Myrica gale*) begin to plump. Where the drabness of late winter was lit up by moss-glow, colour now comes from swathes of myrtle. Our senses are prickled not merely by the sensation of colour spreading but also from wafts of beautiful scent. When the buds are on the cusp of opening, I like to gather a few, crush them between my fingers and inhale deeply. This is the first real scent of change, of spring, of winter's ending. Fresh myrtle buds contain the very essence of light. If I could fill my house with their scent, I would. If I could gather up enough to fill boxes or sachets to send to everyone, I would. If I could have impregnated these pages with its aromas, I would. The incense of *Myrica* is calming and invigorating, sweet and clear, cleansing and refreshing, and as close to frankincense and myrrh as is possible in this cold, wet country.

Myrtle is embedded deeply in my memory banks, both as salve and elixir. It is so redolent of clean, clear air it almost makes me weep. I remember the filthy atmosphere of my childhood and our rush to Borth on the west coast of Wales, to the great aromatic and ancient bog of the King of Cors Fochno. Myrtle perfume contains the memories of those happy days. Even now it remains the antidote to loss, and my mother's dying.

Years ago, in south Cumbria, I worked with students as they learned about remarkable peatland environments and their specialist flora on a lowland bog known as a 'raised mire'. With each new group I would pass around a few buds and leaves for them to examine. At first sight myrtle seems rather ordinary and uninteresting, with tough winter-darkened dun-brown stems. With gentle encouragement, the students crushed their bits of myrtle to release the aromas, and sniffed. Their reactions were spontaneous and wonderful. 'Breathe it all in. Imbibe the very essence of the wild,' I would say to the smiling faces.

Myrica gale buds swell from brown to sandy orange with the lengthening days, triggered by the returning light, and from February onwards the scent spreads over bogland, fields, hills and homes. Even in a hard, icebound winter a leafless sprig can be scratched to release the perfume. For centuries it was widely used in Britain and Ireland for multiple purposes – its scented oils have been mixed with tallow for candles, and to add flavour to beer and gin; its leaves, buds and flowers have garnished food, and been gathered in sachets and laid in drawers to maintain fresh linen and keep moths out from clothes. And, like me, many people tuck a sprig into a hat or buttonhole to ward off midges and other biting flies.

Of all the plants growing on croft, peatland or hill, it is bog myrtle that resonates most deeply with me. Inhaling molecules of myrtle perfume generates a profound sense of connection, not only to this place and childhood holidays, but to a much older family heritage among the peatlands of Ireland. Like many in Scotland, my ancestral story was one of forced eviction and clearance. Myrtle generates an intense longing for the ancient, myth-filled and musical landscapes of Eire. Yet living here, accompanied by the rich scents of a very particular type of landscape, my mind and body flood with a sense of shared history, of recognition, and of belonging.

Soon myrtle buds burst open into millions of bright orange flowers. They swarm like stars on peatland still draped in the burnt umber of winter. When sunlight warms the bog surface the perfume of bog myrtle, now sensuous and spicy, spreads out like custard poured over a pudding. Scent-cells in my nose and throat test the air for its presence. Its molecules hold a strange sense of restoration and a powerful sense of well-being. I pick a few bunches of woody stems, each with a cascade of open flowers already shedding bright yellow pollen, and place them around the house. What began in late winter and early spring as a sweet and lively scent becomes cathedral-scale frank-incense. Once, when we were young, Rob pushed open the great door of Notre-Dame de Paris and we stepped into the middle of high mass. The great windows drenched the congregation in rainbows, iridescent colours swirled in the mist of incense. In a sudden rush of nostalgia, the coloured perfumes were the same rainbows and mists and thick scents of wild peatlands I had explored as a child with my mother.

Myrtle, to me, is almost holy. It is the essence of memories of exploring wilderness, and of the wilds themselves, and a way-maker to both. Wherever I go the aroma is my companion. On Red River Croft it grows in the enclosure of peats known as the *pàirc*, in damp hollows across the Red River and in one or two places along the riverbank. But on either side of the crofts of South Erradale there are thick, dense, aromatic heaps of it strewn across the peat bogs. Its perfumes soften the fierce grandeur of the mountains and enrich the bareness of moor-lands. It fills the places made empty over millennia by tree-felling, burning and grazing with its intensity and sweetness, compen-sation for the loss of forest and people.

*

There is an almost continuous blanket of moorland over the hills around Erradale and bog myrtle occurs widely, especially in damper hollows. But the valley sides are dominated by heathers, especially common ling (*Calluna vulgaris*), whose purple-blossomed sprigs are almost always associated with the Scottish Highlands. There are others, too, whose late summer flowering is so beloved – the pale blooms of cross-leaved heath (*Erica tetralix*) and the gaudy pinks of bell heather (*Erica cinerea*). But, if left to grow, the heather community matures into tall woody shrubs which produce little in the way of new green growth as they age.

For millennia fire has been used to control the nature and type of vegetation, especially in moor and hill country. Today 'muirburn', the traditional way of encouraging fresh sprouting of heather and grass by setting fire to the moors, usually takes place between October and April. Crofters have used muirburn to enhance the grazing potential of an area for livestock because it prevents heather from becoming too woody and leggy. Fire also removes very tough and unpalatable tussock grasses such as *Molinea caerulea* (purple moor grass). After a small, well-controlled fire, a patch of moorland recovers quickly and the regrowth is often advantageous for other species, including insects such as the heather beetle, as well as providing fresh greenery for sheep, cattle and grouse. Here, as in much of upland Britain, the modern Highland landscape of moorland and heather-covered hills has a long history, one that is intimately entwined with burning and grazing in systems of subsistence agriculture that began long before the establishment of permanent settlements.

Burning in Scotland is supposed to take place under the strict guidelines of the Muirburn Code, but recently many uncontrolled fires have been growing into wildfires. Occasionally they have caused great environmental damage and distress. Ultimately, such fires can lead to peat degradation, soil loss, the death of wildlife and the release of carbon into the atmosphere, but in late winter, especially when a cold spell has dried out the moorland a little, crofters and estate managers continue to set fire to areas of older heather or where tussock grasses have overwhelmed the species animals prefer to eat. Smoke fills the air. At first it tastes sweet and resinous, the perfumes mingling with sootiness. But as a fire progresses, and becomes hotter, sparks fly high, the smokes turn acrid and brown and the fight to regain control begins.

There is no doubt: by setting fire to old heath and rank, acidic, tussock grassland, new green growth is prompted and sweet grasses swiftly fill in the charcoaled spaces. But there are major problems with this practice. Carbon is lost directly into the atmosphere and if a burn is too hot or uncontrolled, too extensive or on very steep slopes, soil and peat may also be ignited. Then organic content is drastically reduced, which in turn increases the relative abundance of mineral content, ultimately to the detriment of soil structure and quality. What remains can easily be washed downslope in heavy rains or is simply blown away by the wind.

Thousands of years of burning have led to considerable soil loss. Increasing numbers of sheep and deer have led to deterioration in the quality of heathland regrowth. Thus, over time – and especially over the last few hundred years – the quality of grazing land in general has fallen and become more acidic, or 'sour'. In many areas today the material underlying the growing turf consists only of remnant basal horizons of once rich, deep soils, or, worse, little more than glacial till. It is estimated that many metres of humus-rich soil developed under mature ancient forests may have been lost as land was cleared, burned and grazed. Soils take millennia to accumulate under thick living biomass. Peat grows only one centimetre every ten to twenty years. It would therefore take two hundred lifetimes to culture deep soil again. Living, working and moving through places emptied of forest and soil is a journey through losses that match the clearances of people from this land. It is almost impossible to walk here without wondering what the valleys and hillsides must have looked like in their prehistoric state. We breathe in the absences every day.

Myrtle and heather are two of the shrubby staple components of moors and peatlands in the Highlands. Vegetation communities dominated by these species are a product of thousands of years of management. While they may represent the long slow degradation of historic landscapes artificially maintained by traditional practices, they also remain iconic, sought after and much loved, and imprinted upon the national psyche as being wholly natural, part of the innate character of upland Scotland.

★

In 2021 a prolonged spell of bitterly cold dry weather was due to end with a rush of gales and rain from the west. The easterlies had freeze-dried everything – heathers, grasses, mosses, bog pools, lochs and burns, even the peat and soil. The land was tinder-dry and desiccated, every molecule of water either frozen hard or blown away in the wind. An hour before sunrise in mid-February we saw flames upriver from the crofting township. What may well have begun as a small burn erupted into large fires that extended upslope and moved faster through the heather than a person could walk. As the day progressed, fire crews came and went, helping the community to beat the flames with brushes and spades, in an effort to encourage them away from homes, trees and byres.

All day, lavender-blue smoke flashed with orange flame, turning again and again to rusty brown and purple. As night fell, the fires had moved away from South Erradale, running over the top of Maol Ruadh, and everyone relaxed. Then, in the early hours of the following day, the wind changed direction and sent the flames back downslope towards the township. Fire crews, by now exhausted from two days and two nights of fire-fighting up and down the west coast, returned to help crofters who had already worked through the night. By noon the following day the fires were out. The skies eventually cleared. The soot and bitter smoke settled. 'It must have been started by sun on broken glass,' was the common explanation. 'It's what crofters have always done,' said others. No one stepped forward to say it was uncontrolled muirburn.

Tales of wildfires ran as swiftly as the flames along the west coast. In the darkness, we could see fires burning along the Trotternish peninsula of Skye, and multiple fires on the Outer Hebrides, great long ribbons of red like flowing lava. There were dozens of fire sites and some of them were large enough to be seen from space. Satellites picked up plumes of smoke running west from the Highlands and Islands far out across the Atlantic. The west was alight.

Reports of large uncontrollable wildfires rushed just as swiftly through the news and social media. Writers lamented the loss of wildlife and nesting sites. Holidaymakers, wild campers and rogue landowners were blamed. Climate change, it was said, exacerbated the conditions that led to so many fires and to their rapid expansion. A complex melee of causes, with different relative importance at the various sites, were undoubtedly to blame. The silence on muirburn activity was deafening. What the fires did do was highlight, in bright red flames, the urgent need to rethink land management and landownership. Yet even in the face of global climate change and environmental crisis, the future still looks smoky.

(ii) Intermittent storms and skylarks rising

In spite of the smokes and flames of muirburn and intermittent snow and ice, in spite of squalls and storm-force winds, more and more bird voices begin to greet the days. Eventually the dawn chorus builds and strengthens. Birdsong fades in and out as storms come and go, rising and falling in time with the gales. But every year, whether summits are snow-capped or not, there is one special warm spring day, rapturous with sunlight and salty breezes, when I throw the windows wide open to let the songs and fresh air in. Plaited and twined with the singing and crystal-clear air are rich aromatic scents. As sea breezes pass over bog and croft they pick up essential oils released by plants, pools, peat and soil, and in those essences of resin and sugar my brain registers colour and music, and a deep longing for wild open spaces.

In spite of the joy open windows may bring, all around us the land's recovery from winter and muirburn can still seem slow. Spring gales and rain may blow the muirburn's residual ash away or wash it downslope and into the rivers. What little potential mineral or nutrient benefit that may have come from the burning vanishes. Yet somehow, even in these thin parched spots, life responds to the trickles of warmth. Heathers slowly begin to grow, dark green at first and then thickening to olive. Where swathes of moorland have escaped the fires, lengthening days spark fresh colour and light. On the bogland, great mounds of *Sphagnum* moss glow; what was once winter-bleached is painted with carmine red and viridian.

Sudden storms and squalls can be almost apoplectic, yet, as they rage and confound, they are magnificent. The battle between winter and spring is retold again and again in varying cloud types, wind speeds and precipitation. As Beira, Queen of Winter, tries to regain control of the world, we are swept up in cloudbursts, snowfall, hard ice, thunder and torrents of wind and water. Each time she is pushed back by spring she is weakened and her next effort has less bite. Checkerboard skies, of light, dark, sun, snow, light, dark, sun, snow, coupled with storm force ten then freezing calm of minus seven, create a tickertape parade of seasons, one following swiftly after the other.

Many early spring storms produce sensational vistas of sky, sea and land, often more spectacular than those of autumn and winter. They catch the light of day and throw it back down to us. Updrafting clouds, towering snowstorms and galloping hail showers can dwarf our highest mountains. Seen from South Erradale, a thousand-metre summit is made small by the seven thousand metres of turbulence above it. Such tumultuous cloud formations recraft landscapes and reduce crofts, homes, river and people to mere scraps and fragments. Light pours out of them. We are humbled and unsettled and insignificant under such power.

Yet storms are participatory. Standing at the cliff-top I do not simply watch a storm, I am interacting. I do not merely feel its power; there is an energy exchange, an almost recognisable communication between the storm and me. We are made of the same stuff. Together we are emotional, physical, chemical, fundamental. In the swirling noise of the blizzards or sharp gusts that rush upslope from the sea I have found solace. The winds know my name; I hear their calls and listen to their stories, have found healing by storm-watching and experiencing their extremes. In the great Covid-19 pandemic, comfort came from the powerful and elemental, losses and longings were given succour. And as I shouted into the gales, my messages of love to my family and friends flew south faster than ever before.

But storm winds fade away and Beira at last succumbs to the spring warmth and light. With renewed hope we search for the signs of spring – myrtle buds opening, frogspawn, solitary bees emerging from the drying earth. The aromas of winter – scents of cold, wet rock and ice – are exchanged for perfumes of spring

– damp soil, myrtle and gorse. Soon the air is filled with the scent of spring, and with sound and motion as well as light. Everywhere and everything seems alert, ready to move, swell and bloom. In the onrush of such sensory overload, birdsong, flower-bloom and green sap rising eventually ignite us all.

*

One melon-yellow and pearl-blue morning I walked to the beach and for a while sat on the sea-log seat and watched two pied wagtails. The sun had yet to crest the back-dunes and the wind blew hard and cold from the northeast but the birds danced on regardless. Singing to each other they flicked up vertically a metre or two, dropping down almost immediately. Between every swift rise they flew back and forth across the sands, landing on boulders or loose stones. Each spiral ascent was accompanied by song as first one bird then the other repeated the tune. Then they would move a few metres north and begin again. Their evident delight at returning to a familiar patch of shore was displayed in a dance I had not witnessed before. They are attracted to this small and quiet northwest-facing coast because of its great variety of fringing habitat – wet and dry dune grasslands, old stone walls, machair and rocky outcrops leading to cliffs. The wagtails' most favoured spot is the southern end of the beach, close to the sea-log seat, where an assortment of carrot-coloured sands and gravels is mixed with a confusion of rusty-red boulders, and a steep bank of old dunes covered with marram grass and fescues and a carpet of herbs.

The wind began to fret, the waves began to bounce. Then above the growing clamour came a single rising thrill of song – the first skylark of the year, pitching his lungs, heart, mind and voice against the boom of sea and the bitter cold. A few ounces of pure wild joy, he only rose about five metres above the ground before descending again and disappearing from view. But his excitement was contagious. Others caught the fervour in his tune and, within minutes, more larks rose up from the machair. Soon the air was electrified and throbbing with skylarks. The sun lifted in a sudden flare of magnesium and the sands flushed with the colours of butternut squash and pumpkin. In the hollowed curve of beach, clusters of birds played about in the spreading sunlight as if enjoying the unusual shelter provided by the dunes and the gentle touch of sun-warmth: oystercatchers, ringed plovers, gulls of many kinds, herons, the wagtails and a pair of curlews. In those few moments there seemed to be more and more buoyancy, a lifting and bounding of life energy in reply to the exuberance of larks. These margins, these hinter-lands between land and sea were awakening. At last this living place was rising up to the sun just as the crofts were. I turned my face to the day to savour the sound of returning life after the long darkness.

The lark-rise song-burst is the open gate to spring, and with a sea breeze the songs flow everywhere. Even though spells of severe weather can still sweep in from the North Atlantic, and although snows may return to the high mountains and even occasionally to the coast, there is no turning back – Beira is well and truly banished. The soils and peats rarely freeze once the larks have begun singing. On the peat bogs nearby, over small black pools sheltered from the wind, tiny flies emerge to dance. They catch the pale spring light in their wings and flicker over the ditches or where tall rushes slow the breezes. They provide much-needed food for meadow birds. Bog and moorland plants sparkle and brighten in the showers. Soon many more species on the croft and riverbanks begin to emerge from the crust of winter dead. Where the mat of vegetation was broken up by ponies' hooves and scuff marks, narrow needles of growth appear in earnest as dense fine brushes of green.

★

When I returned from the beach, I helped Cathma move her ewes across the river. We grumbled about the weather and the lateness of spring but heading back through the top field we noticed hundreds of wormcasts scattered across the grassy turf. Low beams of sunlight picked out the tiny curls of soil. 'Here is spring, right here under our feet,' I laughed. Worms had felt the change through the earth and headed up to find the light. The ground was waking up, nature responding to the sun at last. 'Let's go and see if there's frogspawn in the bog pools,' said Cathma, 'Then we'll really know for sure.'

Most of the springs in our early years in South Erradale were busy with hillwalking, exploring, learning about the land and chores on the croft, working in the garden and, for me, wildlife watching. Rob and I enjoyed long days in the mountains inter-spersed with early morning walks to the beach and sea-log seat followed by fence-mending, helping move sheep across the river from one croft to another or caring for the Shetlands. Chickens came to live with us. Six bright-orange bold ladies who were afraid of absolutely nothing.

When I became ill, spells of healing came from short walks around the croft to investigate the smaller things – the colours of lichen and tiny cushions of moss on exposed rocks and boul-ders and fence posts – or to watch the wildlife activity – beetles in dung piles, birds flying from hedges to meadow to river and back again, flies dancing over ditches – or to try to identify plant species I had not seen before. The chickens followed, curious. Solace came from listening to the breeze play through the rushes, or seeing the first kiss of moonlight on the river. Acceptance came from time spent learning new things – the dung beetle's life cycle, the differences between greenfinches and goldfinches, the newest and most recent names for different cloud types.

I walked slowly about the croft layered in warm clothes and wrapped by spring breezes, willing my muscles to work, to remember how to walk. I perched on riverbank boulders and let gentle river-songs soothe my head. I leaned on the gate and listened to wind whisking through the rushes. On good days and able to walk a little further, I sat by the waterfall at Port na Sgotha, deafened by the sounds of cascading water until my mind cleared of crags and precipices. As I slowly accepted the mountains must wait, I turned to the sea. More and more I was lured by perfumes of salt, kelp and sand mingling with wave-song and sea-bird cries. Soon my unsteady trail cleaved through the meadows, slowly braiding with the tracks of deer and otters. Signposts and symbols greeted me everywhere – otter spraint pointed the way to the sea, oystercatcher voices funnelled up from the shore in welcome, thrift grew on the walls of the byre to remind me of the waves and once, just as I was about to set out with my sticks, a starfish landed at my feet on the doorstep, dropped from height by a passing sea bird. The sea was calling.

Illness changed the way I walked. Light, sound, air, water vapour, scent, heat, cold, the taste of sea spray and earth roamed through my body as I slowly wandered. And I welcomed them in. On one spring day, when the sea was beaten silver, its edges made of peppermint ruffles, and the sky was a cobalt-blue stained-glass window, the light stole my voice, wind-sound swept away layers of thought, and what little remained drifted in the air. I was not walking on the earth and through a place but inside a living space. I walked to the old post at the edge of the cliff and leaned against its weathered wood. I passed old walls and other fence posts covered with the same cushions and small pillows of moss-forest as those found in the mountains. I ran my fingers along their gently undulating greens, remembering what it is like to walk among the tundra-like vegetation on the high peaks. Here were the same moss lights in miniature guiding my way.

My mother called the act of slowly walking that permits such gradual shrugging off of self 'pathering'. Apparently it was an old word used by her family for generations. As a girl I found it hard to grasp what she meant because there were always hills to climb. But as I pathered through the croft and down to the sea my feet slowly and cumulatively wrote a foil and left a scent, just as other creatures do. My footprints were latticed across the landscape with those of other animals, the filaments of our passing all but invisible as they spilled and shimmered through the fields and down to the beach. Trails made by feet were twinned by trails made by my mind. Their gyrating curlicues of colour reached into the Inner Sound and up into the air, augmenting thoughts and writing stories in a language only the wind could carry and waves could read.

My daily goal became a walk by the river and, if possible, along the Seaweed Road as far as the sea-log seat. There I saw that friends had passed by and left messages of comfort in spraint, shell, seaweed and fragments of ancient rock. New log seats appeared, sea-gifted and hauled into place by Rob. Pathering from seat to seat, from rest stop to rest stop, enabled a different way of seeing and new ways of using my senses. Rock, sand and wave were my new companions, birds, deer and insects my news gatherers. And best of all, otters became family.

(iii) Otters seen more frequently

In our first spring we brought a Border Collie pup from Glen Feshie in the Cairngorms to the croft. He was the last of his litter to find a home. All his siblings went to working farms but Dram came to us without any of the pedigree guile and desire to chase so apparent in his brothers and sisters. Rather than persist in trying to train him to override his evidently docile character, I worked with him and Cathma's sheep to teach him how to be quiet and still. He would become a wildlife watcher, I thought. And because animals belonging to others would be roaming the croft, he needed to know how to behave among sheep, cows, ponies, pigs and chickens. Then he would have to learn about deer, otters, pine martens, sea eagles and other wild animals.

Dram was with me when I saw otters for the very first time. He was then just a few months old and I a few years away from illness. It was an exuberant and joyful encounter and occurred one boisterous morning on the beach at Opinan. Breezes shouted along the shore. Heaps of kelp hived with activity. Clamours of oystercatchers, scatters of rock pipits and squabbles of gulls busied about from machair to shingle to sand. Overhead, crows harried a large bird of prey. The emerald sea churned in the windy blusters and pleats of large waves slowly crumpled into champagne lather. Once on the sands I released Dram from his training lead and he chased his ball as we meandered along. As if by sudden magic, two small brown shapes dashed out of the marram-dressed dunes behind us. They sprinted across the sand and shingle and into the foam. Shocked at their boldness both dog and I stopped and stood completely still, watching. Otters! I cannot remember seeing such unfettered seaside joy, unless I count the squealing, splashing delight of my children at play in the surf. They appeared to be playing 'tag', diving again and again into the oncoming waves and skimming out of the water like dolphins, then surfing the breaking crests back towards the shore. For more than ten minutes we stood as still as statues, watching them at play.

The otters rushed out of the water, shook their fur, and dashed up the sands and across the shingle. They twined and twisted, tails curling around each other, and in a fervent display of companionship, nipped at each other's bodies. Then they separated; one ran straight back into the sea, while the other scooted behind us in a long arc to re-enter the foam further along the shore. I watched them both head out past the breakers, still exuberantly diving and resurfacing until they disappeared from view, one swimming north, the other south. Thinking the bold and joyous encounter was done, I stroked my young dog's patient but quivering head, and turned around. But then another otter, much smaller but no less vivacious, a female I think, came gallivanting down from the dunes; she too scampered across the sand and into the sea.

Since then, Rob, Dram and I have watched otters many times. Once, as a marigold sun dipped into the iceberg-turquoise air of a cooling evening, a large male otter whiskered past us as we sat on the sea-log seat. He chattered and whistled as he ran across the still-warm red rocks. The water was like cooling custard, yellow-wrinkled and thick. The otter scored the skin of the sea with his sinuous dive and disappeared. He emerged holding a fish and turned over to float on his back. Languorous and relaxed he devoured the fish swiftly and then delved down for another. Again and again he dived, and every time he went down, in his moment of disappearance, the molten surface closed over his tail, smoothly and silently.

★

There were many days when we did not head up into the hills and, after that first ottery encounter, every time I walked to the sea on 'stay-at-home' mornings I would search for otters or evidence of their passing. There are plenty of habitats they are supposed to prefer, and long sections of rocky shore where kelp beds are deepest, so I was always optimistic.

Otters are abundant in the Northwest Highlands and about fifty per cent of the total Scottish population lives along the coast, where food is abundant. An otter (*Lutra lutra*) living here has a much smaller range than those living inland by loch and rivers, mostly because of the abundance of prey. They take the majority of their food from the sea, but after every seaside swim they need to remove salt from their fur by washing in fresh water. This means they favour stretches of coastline plentiful not only in kelp beds and rock pools, but also with an abundance of rivers and burns. Here on Overside countless small streams and rivulets carve their way from the low hills to the shore. Along the one-kilometre stretch of Seaweed Road between South Erradale and Opinan there are dozens. Although this coast is more exposed than others where otter activity is well known, I regularly found lots of evidence in the form of spraint mounds and slipways to suggest numbers here are thriving. Our wild and ragged shores provide plenty of resources and micro-habitats offering a variety of food – kelp forests, abundant shellfish, freshwater burns, rivers with good populations of trout and eels, dry ground for holts and untouched, people-free shorelines. The otters' success here is a direct result of these abundances but also the relative quiet. These rough-edged marginal spaces of transition, from croft to shore to sea are rich in species diversity, and as I came to learn more and more about our otter neighbours I began to think of the shallow marine environments as our last truly wild spaces.

Some say coastal-dwelling otters may be more active during daylight hours than their inland counterparts, yet they can still be elusive. Spotting them can be difficult, especially if beaches are busy with people and dogs. I began to follow their journeying by looking for footprints in sand and mud and searching for spraint mounds. Spraint is very distinctive in the low turf of winter and early spring; against pale grasses the dark mucus and bright pink-and-white remains of shellfish stand out clearly. Dropped in fairly prominent places as markers or messages to other individuals, spraint helps otters identify potential mates as well as warn of competitors. The droppings are usually left in the same spots and they gradually build up into large mounds.

Shellfish-enriched green mounds stand out like stone mono-liths on Salisbury Plain. Otter spraint heaps are at their most visible when the turf is still winter-pale. They stand out, brightly, because the distinctive combination of shells, bones and tarry mucus adds nutrients and alkalis to the growing heaps. Over many years, as the mounds are regularly used, different grass species and herbs grow on them. I once found an academic paper describing otter movements in western Scotland. In their discussions the authors concluded otter activity is at its greatest in autumn and early winter, and they neatly provided a list of explanations about why this should be so. But there was a problem. They had collected field data about spraint mounds between late October and early December, when ground-cover vegetation blanches and shrivels. It was possible their results may have reflected the distinctiveness of the spraints they recorded, mounds that were so much easier to spot because of their bright 'look-at-me' emerald-greenness in a sea of titian, copper and ash blonde.

Here coastal spraint mounds are numerous. They occur all along the Seaweed Road from croft to beaches, along the cliffs, by gates, ditches and large stones, wherever my path crosses those of the otters, and are evidence of a healthy and growing population. In fact a coast and cliff walk from South Erradale to Opinan crosses or passes by a great number, one roughly every twenty metres. One particularly large spraint mound stands close to the rock steps of the Red River waterfall at Port na Sgotha. Year upon heaped year of scented boundary-marking by countless generations of otters has been layered precisely in this one place. The spraint heap, with its enriched grassy slopes, is over a metre wide and about seventy centimetres high, far larger than any others yet found along this stretch of coast. It is so well defined it stands as tall and clear to an otter as a henge-stone does to us. I have come to think of it as marking a special boundary, perhaps between 'tribes' of otters, rather than individuals or small family groups. Whether that is the case or not would need more research and evidence gathering, but it is a nice idea. What is remarkable, and mysteriously magical, is that the mound lies next to the Erradale river, which may also mark an ancient border.

In this part of Wester Ross there is a North as well as a South Erradale. Each township sits in a river valley which may identify the former and outermost edges of an ancient, most likely Norse, fiefdom. The old Gaelic words *earr* ('boundary') and *dal* ('meadow' or 'field') imply Erradale may refer to ancient boundary fields rather than the sandy ground as some have suggested. There are certainly collapsed relic-walls in our valley which delineate pre-crofting parcels of ground so it is tempting to imagine the layout of Viking territory, or perhaps an even older one. Whatever the truth of walls, settlements and human history, having found the sprainted and mounded evidence by the waterfall, the notion otters have been marking out and remembering their greater and most ancient boundaries is not only enchanting but feasible. They appear to have expressed their own geographical sense of place over time and in doing so have mirrored and overlapped ours. Otter-science might say otherwise but I have come to think we live in an otter kingdom by the sea where these beautiful animals have used the same landscape features as humans for hundreds of generations.

*

When illness forced my mind seawards and away from the summits, the spraint mounds, footprints, hovers, holts and slides were my go-to pick-me-ups. Knowing that if I could just walk a little further, take a few more steps, I might see what the otters had been up to and ascertain if they had visited recently. The idea I might see them from one of Rob's carefully placed log seats helped keep my mind in focus and, at the same time, offered healing. Before my health was compromised I was sure-footed and swift and I spent a long time training young Dram to sit or walk stealthily, so as not to disturb wildlife. When I became too ill for the kind of energetic walks he needed, he kept me company, off-lead but walking close by my side, or lying still while I sat observing the to-ing and fro-ing of otters and other wildlife. He became both friend and fellow watcher.

In 2015 we discovered a resident otter on Red River Croft. On one calm, bright morning I had Dram, then fifteen months old, on his training lead, learning how to move slowly and care-fully among Cathma's ewes and their lambs, picking his way cautiously between the grazing mothers and their new-borns. All of us, sheep, dog and I, were suddenly startled by an otter who ran straight past us and through the flock. He flowed between rushes and vanished in a clump of bog myrtle. For some time afterwards I found bright-pink, toothpaste-white and tarry-black spraint in small spots here and there, in new mounds at the edges of ditches or droppings splashed on boulders and gravel along the river, but there were no more sightings of the otter or otters responsible. I wondered if the individual who had surprised us had a holt on the croft or whether he was simply passing through. Then late one afternoon, as I leaned on the top gate, I spotted him, running fast across the low meadow in the silky sinuous flowing way otters do. He was a large male and ran swiftly past the Shetland ponies before disappearing into the gorse-covered high bank at the top of the field to my left. After a few minutes, certain he must be safely stowed in his den, I walked back and forth around the croft looking for footprints and droppings, followed eagerly by Cindy and Toby. It soon became clear that his long dash to the gorse-bank holt and back to the river had crafted a new desire-path across the fields. And in one place on the riverbank, a smooth, slick channel made by otter-belly slithering resembled an old, well-used children's slide in a city park.

This otter had chosen the croft and adopted us as neighbours. He had selected this place where a tall, dense patch of gorse grew on the steep sides of the high and ancient embankment and where the spiny shrubs merged into the garden hedge and Scots pine. Common gorse is a fierce defence against grazing and disturbance because it has such tough, sharp thorns, though all animals, even the oldest ponies, seem to love nibbling at the soft new spring growth and flowers. On this early spring day, the gorse was brightly yellow and heavy with sweet perfume, swelling with birdsong and insect drone. The gorse was the otter's safe haven. The thicket had become otter-blessed, and when the wind blew through the richly scented blooms, I wondered if he too turned yellow or licked his lips at the sweetness.

Part Three

Spring Equinox to Summer Solstice

1. Sunrise northeast of Creag an Fhithich on Baosbheinn, sunset beyond Ben Volovaig on north Trotternish, Isle of Skye, Celtic month of Alder (March to April), Wind or Plough Moon

(i) Frogspawn in the bog pools

The equinoctial sun sets over the low northern hills of the Trotternish peninsula on the Isle of Skye. From the cliff-top vantage point by the Seaweed Road when the weather is good, the sun becomes a great hot orange orb. It appears to roll down the mountain crags of the western Quiraing, picking up speed until it dips away behind the gentle, crofted slopes of Kilmaluag and Balmaqueen. For just a few moments it slows, caught in an embrace, a communion of fire-born ancient rock and celestial heat, before it vanishes. As long as weathermen do not warn of squalls or snow, there is great joy at the spring equinox sunset, with its promise of longer days, brighter light, energising warmth and busyness.

Spring weather can be fickle and volatile. We are prodded into wakefulness, shaken out of our winter wrappings. The hard work of coping with deep-dark days is largely behind us. But the stutter-starting of warmth and cold, light and gloom, is unpredictable. By the spring equinox, melon-yellow and pearl-blue light can be strong enough to rip through banks of grey cloud; but just as we breathe in and relax, sharp showers and biting cold return. Through it all, and despite the volatility, music and song erupt from every corner of the croft, from the river and along the coast. Woodlands and scrub bounce with activity and birdsong.

In small pools in the croft peat banks and surrounding bogland, heaps of frogspawn appear. During one strangely ultra-dry spring, water levels dropped so severely that even the bog pools were drying out. I spent an afternoon scuttling about and scooping as much of the jelly mounds as possible into buckets and bowls filled with river water. Later, Cathma telephoned to say she had done the very same thing that morning. From then on we kept a close eye on all our 'tadpole nurseries' until the rains returned and the pools were recharged with water. Sharp showers are often interspersed with sharper drying under a bright, fierce, spring sun. Shelter provided by bog pools comes and goes, with tadpole lives dependent upon water table height and amount of rainfall, and intermittent human help. It might seem precarious, yet frogs and toads seem to flourish here, sheltered and shielded by the living, breathing, functioning of the wild peat bogs surrounding the crofts.

As spring deepens around the equinox, Red River Croft thickens in green and yellow while the peatlands sift out the dead colours of winter and warm to russet and ruby. On some days the open ground appears to shudder when wind-squalls rush over it. Every time I walk down the track to Cathma's, or onwards to the cliff-top and Seaweed Road, I pause to check one particular bog pool. It sits right next to the fence. Cathma told me she and her brother went frogspawn hunting when they were children and this pool has been home to spawn and tadpoles for as long as she could remember, so almost eighty years. We use it just as a nurse would use a thermometer. Instead of checking temperature, we assess water depth. If this spot is full of water and frogspawn then other sites across the peatlands will be filled too. In good years the pool is more jelly than water. In low-angled morning brightness the masses are silvery, each egg holding a single black comma; at sunset they are red and slippery like the shiny intestines of some enormous organism. A pool brimming with frogspawn assures me the spring bog is alive with possibilities and hope for the future. The bond between living organism and inorganic processes and materials then feels powerful, twinned and interdependent.

*

In the early years we watched and learned about how the croft's character changed from winter to spring and into summer. I delved into scientific articles assessing carbon sequestration under different grazing regimes. Such subjects had been outside my own academic specialisms and it quickly became apparent the topic raised strong emotions and counter-arguments among real farmers, especially larger landowners and in modern agronomy. One discussion caught my eye. Farmers around the world had been trying out various ways to protect their grass-lands from overgrazing and maintain soil carbon, and after years of experimentation many concluded their measures of soil health, biodiversity and levels of biomass all improved with a particular type of management – grazing rotation. I could not understand why so many media reports and academic articles described the intense rotation of grazing as new. My maternal grandfather ran his small mixed farm in this way for decades, as had his father, and his before. Grandpa's grasslands were species rich, their soils deep. I wondered at first whether my puzzlement and ideas about grazing management were triggered by deep-seated, rose-tinted memories of helping him move his small herd of cows and only later by the science. But slowly these ideas began to assimilate and coalesce. Old memories were rekindled as I watched the year-on-year changes arising from different patterns and types of grazing on the croft, differences instigated because we wanted to help our neighbours.

Whatever my conclusions about the science of grazing practices, Rob and I had instinctively wanted to reduce grazing intensity from the very first. So much of the Highlands has suffered from overgrazing by sheep and deer. To counter this we would need to restrict the time animals spent in the fields as well as reduce overall numbers. In addition, we wanted different species to come and graze at different times. Of course only patience and time would reveal what levels of grazing might offer the greatest benefit in terms of biodiversity and satisfy our obligations both to crofting and the environment.

Decades earlier I lived with an indigenous community in Papua New Guinea. A wise elder said that in order to learn anything about land you need to have an open mind and your feet in the earth. He made me take off my boots. 'Watch, wait and listen,' he had said. 'The land speaks to you but you must be patient and careful. Don't rush, until you have received the answers to your questions.' I was young, adventure ruled my thoughts and the work I was there to undertake had specific aims and objectives. My goal was to figure out how the high mountain landscapes had changed over the last few millennia. The Highlands of Papua New Guinea were then covered mostly by rainforest with small pockets of traditional cultivation around village sites. With guidance from one tiny community the methods of land management were revealed. My research eventually showed that over thousands of years, despite the altitude, severity of the mountain environments, steepness of slopes and torrential tropical rainfall, these methods of agriculture resulted in little or no soil loss, something unheard of in the UK and especially its uplands. Years later, watching a sparrowhawk quarrel with a hooded crow above two old Shetland ponies as they grazed among the rushes, with a sudden pang of shock I remembered the words of the gentle elder who had been my teacher and guide, and a spark of understanding was reignited.

In a Wester Ross spring, small herds of sheep are moved from croft to croft around the township and between South Erradale and other townships. The 'common grazing' area for this part of Overside includes South Erradale, Opinan and Port Henderson, so the narrow single-track road that connects us is busy with the comings and goings of sheep as they pass between areas of open common. Because the ewes are preparing for lambing, they need food supplements to complement the grazing. The mat of vegetation bleached into toughness over winter provides little in the way of nutrients to expectant mothers, so they are provided with mineral licks and given a breakfast of special feed. On Red River Croft Cathma's ewes and cattle came for short spells to graze, followed by groups of ponies belonging to Danielle. Periodically deer ventured back and forth, instinctively following their old trails in search of food, leaping the fences, and crossing the river at the ford as usual. Effectively this new regime was 'mob rule' by rapid bursts of grazing with periods of resting in between. Within two years the croft appeared to be slowly changing. New plant species began to appear – spring gifts in a revitalising space. The reduction in grazing intensity gave many seeds, long held within the soil, the opportunity they had been waiting for. It was an exciting time, but just as my grandfather had done and in the same way the New Guinea elders had taught, I watched the meadows to see who or what would appear next and tried to read the messages from the fields.

For a few years this regime was repeated – animals came and went in short bursts of grazing. The land was rested, then churned by hooves, or by floods. Over time, nutrients were both added and carried off by the river. When old crofters continued to ask what we intended to do with the land, my reply about learning and waiting and watching was met with approval and the nodding of wiser heads than mine. In those early years, in between work and crofting jobs, Rob and I continued to head into the hills, walking and clambering among the higher places. We adventured north and south, learning more and more about Wester Ross, about the land and nature, and about ourselves. Our family came to visit often and, alongside the flourishing croft, it too grew quickly. In the same interim period, almost in tandem with the increasing biodiversity, grandchildren began to arrive, one by one, swelling our little family with three boys and five girls. We were pulled from crofting to midwifery to mountain wandering. We were fit, strong and able, and, like frogspawn in the bog pools, filled with optimism about the future.

(ii) Beaches become busy

As the croft in its small sheltered bowl begins to flush with new growth, the birdsong in the fields, hedges and trees outcompetes wind noise and wave sound from the shore. This exposed coast responds more slowly to the warming days, but gradually it too fills with song. There is a distinct layering in the expanding spring choruses to match the zones of colour in plants and rocks – meadow pipits give way to rock pipits, skylarks to dunlins and ringed plovers. The drive for new life, so redolent with avian voices, appears in the rocky crevices, cliffs, sand dunes and beaches along the short stretch of coast between South Erradale and Opinan, and begins in earnest to herald the arrival of spring.

A walk along the Seaweed Road is greeted by full-on rowdi-ness and a cacophony of joy, from the knobbles of ancient sandstone and gneiss, mounds of boulders, rock cobbles and gravels to the patches of red and gold sands. From the cliff-top viewing point all the way to Opinan, a complex range of micro-habitats now comes to life.

In the pre-holiday season of early spring, the beach is very good at revealing information about how well wildlife is doing. It is easy to spot footprints in the sand and relatively easy to identify the print-makers. Here, when walking was easier, I would spend as much time as possible following bird tracks up and down the sands, trying to figure out who was going where and for what purpose. Besides keeping an eye on local spraint mounds I tracked otters along the sandy shore. And if Dram and I were quiet and patient they would scoot past, darting from the nearby burn, across the sands and into the waves. Depending on tide times and sea state, otters would regularly dash from holt to sea and back again, ignoring our presence. Gradually they became as comfortable with us as we were delighted with them.

★

For years I lived and worked near the Sefton Coast, nineteen kilometres of sand dunes between the Mersey and Ribble, two great rivers of Northwest England both draining into the Irish

Sea. The landscape is famous for its enormous intertidal range, vast sand flats, pinewoods and red squirrels. As a result, Sefton's beaches and dunes are always busy with tourists. Because of its size, even regular research visits over more than a decade revealed little change had occurred. It took extensive studies of maps, aerial photographs and an array of survey methods to determine the extent and rates of coastal transformation there.

Coastal science, like most research, is collaborative, and I worked with a wonderful gentleman called Gordon Roberts at Formby, a part of the Sefton dune system gradually being eroded by the sea, where each high tide uncovered a little more of other types of deposit once hidden by the sands. During his daily beach walks Gordon had discovered that newly exposed silts and clays contained preserved human and animal footprints. Each successive tide revealed more prints and washed away others. Over the course of two decades he meticulously recorded these ephemeral features in photographs and thousands of measurements. Specialists in osteoarchaeology used the data to unravel information about the physical characteristics and gender of people who had once roamed the intertidal zone. There were males running and jumping, pregnant women and children among the trails of deer and aurochs. Everyone who worked on the footprints came to the same conclusion – between five and eight thousand years ago, people were hunting large animals as well as fishing and gathering plants, and, as they did, left imprints in the muds of ancient estuaries, salt marshes and coastal lagoons. On warm windy days, as people and animals passed through the ancient landscape, their footprints dried out and firmed up. When the next tide crept in, any hollows and dimples left by human feet or animals were filled by new layers of mud. In the intervening millennia more sediments accumulated and the footprint-bearing layers were eventually buried and compressed until they were finally hidden underneath the great sand-dune system of Sefton.

Gordon and I regularly wandered along the shore, taking pictures and measuring the footprints. We speculated about the people who had made them and wondered about their lives. And we came to the conclusion they must have had a profound sense of place. Deeply knowledgeable and entwined with their local environments, they would have been firmly tethered to the natural world. For my part I examined sands and muds for the microscopic remains of plants and charcoal from fires to try to determine more about the landscape characteristics of those ancient times. Science was able to recreate the environments in which these people lived and travelled but Gordon's work enabled us to connect with the people themselves. We became friends and time travellers, trying to step between worlds and walk with the ghosts of the past, developing our own shared sense of belonging, as deep as those of the footprint-makers.

*

The Seaweed Road continued to lead me to Opinan where change is the norm and as regular as breathing. The turnover of sand and shingle, the building and then destructive carving of sand banks and fore-dunes, the sheer volume and mass of sediment shunted back and forth, are mind-boggling. All sandy coasts are dynamic but Opinan is particularly responsive to changes in wind direction and force, to wave type and strength, and to tides and storms. It is the most reactive and energetic stretch of coastline I have ever known. Enormous volumes of sand can be removed in a single storm tide, exposing boulders and shingle below, and within twenty-four hours sand banks are rebuilt and the beach configuration restored. As someone used to measuring change on larger and longer timescales in coastal Northwest England, the daily shifting of sand and debris is astonishing. Each day brings new delights and surprises. Storms scour sands away within hours and return them just as quickly. They also deliver great wave-heaps of seaweed. Insects and crustaceans and birds quickly move in to rummage among the bounty, and as the accumulated debris decomposes it enhances fertility, enabling new plant growth and providing food and shelter for wildlife.

The sands of all soft sediment beaches are made of multi-coloured minuscule fragments of rocks, shells and other materials. Under an ordinary magnifying glass, a pinch of Opinan sand is kaleidoscopically colourful – charcoal, olive and russet gneiss; sandstones of apricot, crimson and cochineal; white and cream quartz; minerals that shine like silver or steel; grains of blue, ginger and buttercup-yellow, others of ebony and aubergine. A scoop of sand is a geological portrait of deep time and slow processes, of rocks plucked from the mountains and moved seawards by ice and water over countless millennia and eventually miniaturised by motion and wave action. All sandy beaches have their own distinctive character and unique geological signature, their sand grains made from a particular combination of nearby rock type and eroded sediments. They also contain microscopic remains produced by human activity – waste materials such as fragments of plastic, clothing, glass and polystyrene. Together these tiny pieces create a portrait of the Anthropocene as well as the Archaean earth.

Although there are no preserved ancient footprints, at low tide Opinan's sands are spread out in a large canvas of opportunity. Bird prints, otter tracks and deer trails embroider arcs and knots across the smooth intertidal zone. A receding fair-weather tide scribbles other mysterious shapes – interwoven

A sunburst sunrise over Baosbheinn.

Opinan beach and the sea-log seat.

Otter footprints on Opinan Beach.

Wave drawn landscapes of a remoter past.

The croft and hills come to life.

Sunset beyond An Cliseam, Isle of Harris.

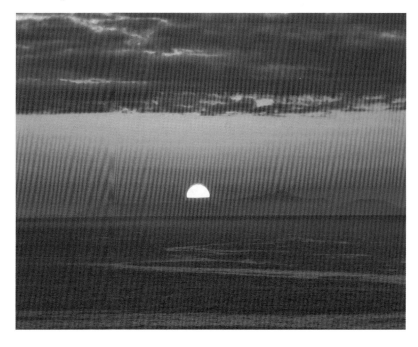

Orchids in flower. Dram waits patiently.

Bog cottons bloom in opulent summer light.

Summer solstice sunset.

The peat bogs and lochans of Overside and the great mountains of Torridon.

Midsummer shower over a jade sea.

Summer haze – made of mists, midges and warm rains.

Tedding the riverside meadows into windrows.

The autumn equinoctial sun descends beyond the northern tip of the Trotternish peninsula on Skye.

After sunset sea colours.

Grandmother trees and natural rewilding in the hills.

curves, arcs and doodles, each crisp line made by a single wave. Together they braid into landscapes. An individual wave unfolds and pencils a fine line, three maybe four sand grains high, and draws a mountain; another brushes a hill overlapping the first, and so it goes on until the whole length of beach is a portraiture, a landskein. There are landforms – mountains and valleys, gullies and cliffs. I have come to think of the wave-drawn sand-landscapes as images of an Archaean or Proterozoic earth. Immeasurably ancient and unknowable stories of deep time so well crafted anyone could understand them, and any geomorphologist could interpret those familiar structures. Perhaps some minute residue of lost, unimaginably old worlds is held inside each single grain of sand and every molecule of seawater and, driven by wind, current and tide, the residues coalesce to create memories of a pre-human earth.

The sea, as artist, thus arranges grains of sand with a watercolourist's precision into sweeps and sways of hills and valleys, reminiscent of paintings created a thousand years ago during the 'Great Age' of Chinese landscapes, when rolling hills and towering peaks were drawn in black ink and shaded with washes of pale colour. On other days the sea foams and spits with waves so full of sediment they too are orange, until the entire beach is washed smooth and there is no evidence of the day's visitors, never mind stories from the remote past.

*

All the beaches and embayments fringing this rocky coast are safe havens for migrating birds. For some it is their summer breeding place, for others an opportunity to refuel and rest. The coast becomes more and more busy – gangs of travelling birds passing through, families of summer residents returning. When northwesterlies blow, the sound of their singing rises up over the cliff and across the peat bog to our front door in a chorus – songs of spring determination and purpose.

Fish spawn in the shallow waters and kelp forests, fry fill the waves and larger animals and birds come to feed. Birds rise up and fall, dip to feed and then sweep along, calling out to each other – here, here, here! It is not uncommon to see a single seal floating vertically in these waters early in the morning, head back and whiskers shining, but when the winds and tides swing around to the north and east, flattening the wave crests yet churning the sea, large family groups come from the more sheltered coves around the Gair Loch or Loch Torridon to visit and play in the supercharged jacuzzi-like conditions.

Opinan is a sheltered nursery and school for youngsters. Clutches of ringed plovers' eggs are often laid in small, sandy hollows or in between the sea-worn rocks. The pale-grey fluffy hatchlings quickly learn to lie still, and hunker down to mimic the random scatter of small weathered stones, silent and still. Many times, my careless step on the shore has brought a few heart-pounding moments and a teeth-sucking flinch at the thought of what damage could have been done.

In January 2021 I was called by a neighbour concerned about a change to drainage through the marram grass and machair which had apparently occurred after an old culvert was restored and redirected. The technological skills and digging equipment of a local crofter had modified the natural flow of water through one of the beachside crofts. The result was a sudden alteration to the hydrology of almost the entire sand-dune system. As the water table rose, the back-dunes flooded and the fore- and embryo-dunes – those closest to the high-water mark – started to sink and collapse. Sand and vegetation slumped onto the beach and was moved by subsequent high tides. Slowly but surely the frontal dunes were being lost to the sea. It was clear that something had to be done about the drainage problem but I was also concerned about an otter holt I knew was hidden in the field. It belonged to the family of otters who regularly passed by the sea-log seat. And the small burn was their highway to and from the sea. I worried both were irredeemably and completely buried.

Concerned locals met at Opinan to discuss how to protect the site. Eventually a new gully was engineered to carry off excess water. We all agreed to watch and wait. Spring growth helped to stabilise the gully sides and the flooded areas began to dry out. I hoped to see otter trails in the sands but none appeared. I checked local spraint mounds and it became clear that the scale of the sand engineering had forced them out of their nearby holt and unsettled their daily feeding patterns. The otters had gone.

But, since then, footprints have reappeared and I have once again watched them feed, surf and play, but I have yet to figure out where their new holt is. One crisp, mauve morning, realising they were somewhere close by, I sat down on the sea-log seat and there by my backpack, on one of the large stones, was a beautiful, fresh, sparkling pink-and-white spraint.

(iii) Yellow light and yellow flowers

There comes a moment, as the sounds of life and growth slowly replace the low emptiness of winter, when yellow light, like lemon juice squeezed on pancakes, trickles all around. Spring snow may still fleetingly coat the mountain tops but the first tentative blooms of gorse suggest any late blast of wintry weather will not interrupt the steadily expanding flow of life. Trees misted with long, pale flower-buds hint at lengthening hours of daylight and gentling of the air. At times birdsong may seem extravagant, foolish even. There is always a risk of a snappy return to ice and severe cold, and yet the singing goes on.

Spring in the Highlands can be a Madeira sponge cake, light, soft and fragile, easily cut by the steel knives of winter. But even with intermittent interludes of brutal grey cold a slow, persistent yellowness continues to spread everywhere, just as butter melts on toast. Patches of gorse burst with hot-yellow flames and rich, thick-scented exuberance. Some think of their perfume as coconut sun cream, of a Mediterranean beach in full summer, but mixed with essence of myrtle it becomes freshly made, newly rolled marzipan, ready for a simnel cake. There are gold-breasted song birds and creamy catkins in the old riverbank trees, and primroses and cowslips speckling the upper fields like lemon zest. Sea mists feather with canary yellow.

Days lengthen, the ground warms. Small holes appear in heaps of soil left when ditches were cleared out in our first autumn. I was uncertain at first about how much or how little they should be dug, but seeing a solitary bee emerge from a pencil-wide hole to taste the air, I could not contain my delight. I plonked myself down to watch as more emerged along the row.

Several lines of old ditches run from the foot of the ancient high terrace on which our house is built down to the river, evidence of long, hard efforts at draining wet ground. They are marked by rows of rushes and other tangles of old growth and, before digging out, were badly infilled, their sides partially collapsed after decades of trampling by cattle and sheep. We debated whether to restore these small drains, especially those that may have been part of some even older, pre-crofting drainage system. Two stone-lined, squared-off long sections, rather like gutters, appeared to be at least two hundred years old. They would be retained to help with carrying off any storm waters and to act as boundary markers to areas of croft we intended to keep as 'wet' meadow. There is also one large natural burn that drains from the expanse of peatland to our north under the track, through a culvert built more than forty years ago and across Red River Croft. We sought Cathma's advice – she and her husband had built the culvert and maintained the track since the 1970s. We would need to keep the burn clear to prevent flooding and erosion of the track with occasional vegetation removal, she advised. Crofters once would set fire to the burn-sides to remove bracken and rushes, but after a few years of reduced grazing intensity ferns began to appear – polypody fern, hart's-tongue and the royal fern, *Osmunda regalis*, remnant signals of a once wooded land.

Around the croft wild cherry trees are soon doused in wedding-white blooms and together with the pale-yellow catkins of birch and alder create an effect more akin to the hop fields of Kent – great blousy blooms of pale yellow that play tricks on the eye. Fritillaries nod in the wet meadow, early bursts of hot-orange hawkbit appear in dry, sheltered sunny spots and the very first flowering orchids begin to flush the top field. Melodies weave with mist, light braids with scent. The earth flickers with ribbons of glinting steam. In rough grassland and drier areas of bog, larks swell upwards with song. What began intermittently in late February over the dunes of Opinan is now a sky-field of joyful trilling and lemon light above Red River Croft.

There is a patch of riverbank close by an old birch tree and surrounded by stipples of furze where tiny bass-clef curls of bracken emerge from the warming sandy soils. Sprinkled among them are bluebells. They are small and pale, unlike the tall, grand blues often seen in parks, gardens and woodlands further south, and much less flamboyant than the invasive Spanish bluebell, yet together they create a mist of powder blue all along the riverbank until they are overwhelmed by the bracken. More surprising are several clusters of wood anemone and lesser celandine that peep shyly from tufts of grass, reminders of woodlands that once grew here.

*

Our little patch of woodland is often reluctant to waken, held fast by the fickleness of wind. But when yellow light prods at the leaf-buds on oak, ash and birch, their readiness to froth open becomes tangible. Further inland, ancient and protected oak woodlands sheltered from the worst of the winds and salt spray bloom much more swiftly. Many of the tall oaks there are set among groves of birch, hazel, alder and holly and tangled with bramble, heather, honeysuckle and ivy, and because of their great age the long, outstretched branches of these grandfather trees spread like protective arms, as if ministering to the young. Soon the royal-purple winter finery of silver birches is replaced by lime brightness, larch branches appear to be covered in tiny crumples of jade tissue paper as they foam with needles, and, at last, the solemn brown buds of oaks start to open, crimping and burnishing branch tips with copper. Although full leaf is some weeks away, these old trees are glorious; they brindle with colour and shudder with birdsong.

The high river terrace close to the house is almost at the same level as the tree tops of our small wood. Rob wedged an old plank of wood between two tree stumps to make a small seat right at the edge of the terrace. He figured that if I was not able to get to the shore then at least from this seat I would be able to see both croft and sea. The effect is of sitting among the high branches of the pines, perched like a song bird. On cold blustery days it is a sheltered spot, hidden from everyone and everything. When the gorse bushes of the embankment come into flower, the little plank seat is wrapped in the heady sweetness of coconut. In the midday sun, when every single bloom becomes a furnace of yellow, it is hard to distinguish the shape and form of each individual flower. I cannot help wondering whether the otter slumbering in his holt below the gorse dreams in yellow or sneezes in his sleep. Knowing he is so close is as delicious as the perfume.

In the lower meadows of the croft, where the ditches are left untouched and around the old croft springs, there is a flood, not of water, but of the luminous mustard-yellow flowers of marsh marigolds. *Caltha palustris* is also known as 'kingcup'. As April broadens towards May, close to the 'Yellow Day of Beltane' (*Latha Buidhe Bealltainn*), when fairies are supposed to dance around the wellsprings, the flowers' yellowness feels cram-full of life, their bright-green leaves filled with energy.

With marigolds as the signal, the ponies who stayed with us for a few weeks in late winter are moved as the grass begins to come through. The fields are ruffled using a borrowed quad bike and an old set of harrows. This helps to aerate the ground and scratch up any remaining hard winter crust. There are many jobs to do: fences to be checked – especially where they have been used as rubbing spots by the ponies or cattle – seeds to be planted, willow whips to be cut and stored ready for hurdle-making. Once the ground has warmed, and where the seaweed gathered the previous autumn has decomposed, the small paddock used for growing hardy vegetables is slowly dug over. In the warmth and wind, the harrowed strips dry quickly; they attract large numbers of birds – meadow pipits, skylarks, song thrushes, and many others I cannot identify. The crofts of Erradale are busy with hope and renewal. After a few weeks of overwintering, when the croft was rested, Cathma's sheep come back, followed by ponies or cows, for short, intense bursts of grazing. Nutrients are cycled and recycled. But with the arrival of blooming kingcups, the animals are moved on and Red River Croft opens itself to the promise of summer.

*

In the yellowness of spring, evenings begin to stretch out too. Moisture-laden skies flush with new colours – smoked salmon and sweet potato. Sunrises and sunsets may pour with cinnabar and henna; dawn and dusk can ripple with crimson and purple. These gentle shades and hues extend the hours of daylight and reach out to the stars. One evening we walked through strange, lavender mists to sit by the shore and watch mysterious fogs slide over a sea of mercury. Cold kissed our faces. As the sun set quickly, banks of haar the colour of sea-asters glided over a slate sea, its chromic shine gone. There was a hint of sunlight, a thin, pale, silvery sheen marked the surface of the water, although no boundaries or horizons were visible. By the log seat we gathered driftwood and lit a small fire. Though its flames were small, the fire seemed strangely vivid and luminous and almost inappropriate in the near-glacial calm. There was no sound apart from an occasional shoosh of water on boulders and a crackle from burning bark. Then a head appeared, nose first from the quicksilver. A seal. We sat quite still, the water's edge at high tide only a few metres from the fire, and watched as it gazed at us, hints of yellow in its large luminous eyes. The seal dived and resurfaced, turning to look at us one more time before it disappeared. To our left there was another, smaller flash of sable. This time an otter, swimming along, head up, then diving with a high loop of its back and flick of tail, resurfacing seconds later. The actions were repeated as the otter came close. Then it clambered out onto a large flat rock. We watched for almost half an hour as the otter repeatedly returned to the rock with crab or fish, the noise of eating matched only by the crackling of the fire. The otter finally disappeared just as the tide turned and a gentle breeze began to shear the mists. Waves began to rise up to meet the smoke. The entire world was coloured with woad and indigo as we fell into night and all the yellows of the day were gathered up by the stars.

2. Sunrise over Glac Gheal, upper Erradale valley, sunset beyond An Cliseam on the Isle of Harris, Celtic month of Willow (April to May), Budding Moon

(i) Orchids bloom

Now and again, even in deep spring, the days bubble and fret with wet windy greys and intermittent brightness and fleeting spells of rainbow-coloured warmth. We are powerfully, noisily barcoded by light and dark, and bitterly, relentlessly flayed by cold, salted gusts and icy gales rushing up from the shore. And then we sweat in a yellow-scented blue-sky heatwave. Spring weather is untrustworthy and lively – there are days when all seasons run swiftly past in just a few hours. Sharp showers try to sift out the birdsong but they fail – even in the worst conditions, birds sing. Over the shrillest, loudest squalls sparrow gangs maintain a crescendo of noise from hedge to hedge, out-singing the charged hubbub of gales and hard rain. Light and birdsong reach meaningfully into the days, wriggling into any cold and wet, working their magic.

It is a busy time for raptors too. The hunt is on for food.

A lone sea eagle is often seen, cruising the higher airs now as he flies over the valley and crofts. Buzzards roam and golden eagles soar over the hills on either side of Erradale. Hooded crows and ravens arrive in loud-mouthed gangs. As I walked the lower meadow I once watched a female sparrowhawk lifting up and down as she followed the river. She looped along in shallow arcs, each one a few metres in length, oblivious to my presence. At least a dozen times she rose up then vanished below the level of riverbank vegetation.

*

There are several patches on the croft where orchids bloom. They first appear on the high embankments overlooking the flood meadows, in the *pàirc* and in the large sheltered corner across the river. Small, shy individuals followed by rank upon rank of bold spears. Together their flowers create a pale, dusky, rose-pink flush above newly awakening earth. Orchids flourish in ground left unploughed and uncut by spade or blade. Since grazing intensity has been reduced, they have spread out further across the croft. Old soils contain larger populations of fungi with dense networks of hyphae, and it is these the orchids rely on. In a symbiotic partnership, fungi provide nutrients to the tiny, almost dust-like orchid seeds. The seeds, blown around the croft in late summer, have little in the way of energy resources. What they do have is quickly used in germination and so they rely on their partnership with fungi in order to survive. In return, fungi receive sugars from the maturing orchids' root tips. The presence of orchids is joyous, not least because of their delicate beauty, colour and fragrance, but also because they indicate the presence of old, undisturbed soils. In the same way as celandines, bluebells and anemones remind us of the presence of woodland, orchids reveal yet more about the long natural history of these few acres.

*

For crofters with herds of sheep, lambing begins with a frenzy of sleepless nights and midwifery when interventions are necessary. Cathma's ewes deliver their lambs in the paddock closest to her house. But during our first few years here, the *pàirc* acted as a nursery. The little paddock adjacent to Cathma's croft was sectioned off decades ago, and is part of the peat banks that straddle the track to the sea and extend across the crofts and onto the large area of common grazing to the north. It was once cut for peats, so is an uneven and unusual area of ground, but it is sheltered from the prevailing winds. There are large mounds of *Sphagnum* moss, a swathe of bog myrtle, stands of dwarf willow, tiny scraps of bare peat crammed full of sundews in the summer, and numerous small pools. And in between the patches of bog, countless small pockets of sweet grasses and herbs. The ewes came into this scented, soft and comfortable place almost as soon as they had given birth. And whether it was the deliciously perfumed air, the aromatic plants or gentle, sponge-like ground, both mothers and lambs thrived.

Later, once the ear tags and necessary health checks were completed, the sheep came onto the main fields. For a week or two they played and gambolled up and down the embankments and along the river, sheltered from the worst weather, until Cathma was satisfied they were robust enough to begin roaming the hills. In both the *pàirc* and upper fields lambs would gain strength, play games and nibble at the sward. But they never ate the orchids. No matter how many sheep or how close-cropped the grasses and herbs, the orchids bloomed defiantly.

For a time this was sheep country, and to some extent it still is. Twenty-first-century herds are much reduced from the many thousands that once roamed open country. Birch woodland, scrub, heather moor and rushes are spreading, and some crofters are unhappy about this perceived degeneration in land quality. Many traditions deemed sensible in the past, such as cutting back whin, burning heather and tidying riverbanks and ditches, continue to be practised today despite the growing debate about the need to enable natural regrowth for conservation purposes and although some species are known to act as refuges for rare birds and insects. Plants like marsh marigolds, bog myrtle, thistles, broom and gorse are regularly removed to 'improve' the land and increase the area available for grant aid. Yet new research reports how gorse and broom contain between fifteen and twenty per cent protein; both species would make very good animal fodder. In the past, during times of great need – perhaps when crops failed – both gorse and broom were once fed to livestock, so it would be entirely feasible to use them again as animal food. In the spring, as gorse almost appears to burst into flame with yellow blossom and new tender green needles, the wise old Shetland ponies, sheep and cattle graze on what they instinctively know is nutritious and nibble the coconut-scented and flourishing flowers.

*

For the last few years on Red River Croft, as soon as the kingcups flower sometime in late April or early May, the whole croft is free of animals. If Cathma needs help, the ewes and new-borns may still spend a few days on the *pàirc* but they are soon moved on to other crofts. The early pink orchids rise when lambing begins and continue for several weeks. From the first emergence of spotted leaves and pink flower-buds right through to midsummer, different parts of the croft flood with the flower spikes of orchids, waves of pink, white, fuchsia and dark purple.

In 2018 the delicate cream blooms of the lesser butterfly orchid appeared in one old patch of meadow. That year I counted eight individuals. The following spring there were dozens – they had spread out across the croft into a variety of micro-habitats, clearly flourishing. Again, as with other orchid species, their seedlings employ a symbiotic relationship with fungi in order to germinate and flourish. Their appearance and increasing numbers reflected a new phase in the restoration of the croft. Underground, underland, things were changing. Above ground too – butterfly orchids are pollinated by hawk moths, including the elephant hawk moth, and their appearance meant more positive news for insect populations.

One evening, as I stood at the main gate to the top field watching the sunset, I became aware of a new scent rising up from the darkening meadow below. It was as sweet as vanilla essence. Puzzled, I tried to pinpoint its source. I opened the gate and began to search. Kneeling down in the damp grasses, I breathed in deeply. These beautiful butterfly orchids, ones I had thought scentless, were releasing their perfume, adding their blessing to the ending of the day.

(ii) Cuckoos and swallows return

With spring deepening towards summer, the days are rampant and joyous, filled with the scents of myrtle and citrus earth. The voices of animals and people twine around each other – crofters checking on livestock, children playing after school, the tumbling river, and the distant shushing of waves breaking on Opinan's shore. This is a heady time, full of promise. The sounds evoke deep memories of a childhood contoured by nature despite growing up in a town filled with smoke – such different experiences compared to the children of South Erradale. While Cathma ran barefoot around the Erradale valley, I wore a scarf over my mouth as I climbed trees whose bark was drenched in black soot.

Among the hubbub of skylarks come the two-tone notes of cuckoos as they begin to arrive from their long transcontinental journeys. This small remote valley, shielded by the great arc of mountains and by the sea, contains a mixture of rough grazing, hay meadows, trees and scrub. The land here is managed without pesticides and herbicides and with little fertiliser, apart from animal dung, seaweeds and organic mulches, and by the slow, natural accumulation of organic matter. The net result is a series of vibrant and complex habitats providing space and resources for a great range of wildlife and large numbers of birds such as the meadow pipit. Many of the smaller birds living here are 'hosts' to cuckoo young. Without these semi-wilded natural habitats with their singular geographical character and complex history, shielded and protected by remote and empty mountain ranges, there would be no cuckoos in Erradale.

When I was young, larks were the soundtrack to spring's arrival and the promise of summer in spite of the smokes of air pollution. They sang brightly on the low hills above my home town and over the salt marshes and fields that bordered the River Mersey, but cuckoos were the rare voices of countryside far beyond the confines of the industrial landscapes of northern England. They were birds of stories, reference books and distant places. Yet in Wester Ross cuckoos are common. Here in Erradale the calm, smoothly measured cuckoo calls brush through the frenetic hullabaloo of other voices and darting flight. They are mobbed and chased by feisty gangs of small birds. I once watched a female cuckoo, sitting on a telegraph pole near our main gate, being repeatedly harassed. She merely shrugged and continued to chortle.

Cuculus canorus is known as the 'gowk' here in Scotland, a term thought to have Viking origins, a strange connection between the word, the bird and our valley's history and historically documented names. Across northern Britain Viking settlers sought out sandy, gravelly soils. Their own agricultural systems had developed on such substrates and, as a result, they were drawn to valleys like Erradale – gently sloped, mountain-backed, riverine, packed full of rich, free-draining cultivable land.

The cuckoos arrive just as meadow pipits are building their nests. Once an opportunity is spotted, the female lays a single egg and, because of a clever quirk of nature, the chick will hatch out a day or so earlier than those of the pipits. What follows is well known. Adult cuckoos remain in South Erradale for a few weeks, ignoring the surrounding coast and higher hills in favour of the crofts, gardens and little patches of woodland. Over the heads of sheep and their lambs, competing cuckoo voices, subtly different in tone and musicality and very much not in unison, become joyful choruses of Andean panpipes echoing around the valley. The rearing of young is left entirely to the hosts when the parents leave for Africa at the end of June. Only when able to fly will the juvenile cuckoos make the incredible journey by themselves.

*

As spring moves towards summer, walking is easier. The ground is less wet, the days are longer and lighter. The daily walks back to health continued. If I felt well, I would go two or even three times a day, rain or shine. Around the croft and by the riverbank, down to the Seaweed Road and along the shore to Opinan, accompanied by Dram. A rest on the sea-log seat or one of the other wood or rock seats spaced at regular intervals, and a return by the same route. In all, the circuit was little more than three kilometres, though I would extend it by going up onto the cliffs at the northern end of the beach or south to Port na Sgotha and the mouth of the Red River. There were other days when I could barely reach the cliff-top viewing point without help. But when feeling able, hours would be spent pathering, sitting, watching, writing, sketching or taking photographs. If I close my eyes, I can retrace every step and map the route or draw features of interest and the views from the 'seats' Rob had created. During the first year of illness he found three more logs, each one brought in on a storm tide. And then three very good spots among the rocks of South Erradale's shore – large boulder-seats with perfect, bottom-shaped hollows. All in all, there were seven special places to aim for, and when walking became more difficult each became a specific target, then the next one and the one after.

Though the route is identical, no walk is ever the same. Weather, meetings with wildlife, river-flow, tides and waves – they run through the seasons in a gift book of colour and sound, and pass right through me. Once, sitting on seat number three, the whole space around me turned to silver. Damp grassland, wet rock, shining sea, sunburst from scudding clouds – all physical structures, including my own body, dissolved in the flux and motion and in the darkness and soul-uplifting light.

The more I walked and watched and waited, the more I seemed to become part of the living edgelands, the spaces between tides and meadows. Cuckoo songs were interchangeable with oystercatcher voices. Often it was impossible to discern where one song became another. There was an invisible boundary between croft and coast. What at first were separate sections of a landscape, clearly identifiable in my geographer's mind by their living characteristics and component parts, began to gather together. My daily walk, a route repeated again and again, was binding these distinctive places and habitats together as one. To me, they were coalescing, organic and fluid. Then one day, as I sat by the sea, a cuckoo landed on the stones by the water's edge. He was as complexly blue as the curling waves. He rippled with the fierce grey-blue so redolent of incoming storms. Later, when I returned through the fields, a family of oystercatchers grazed among the orchids.

★

Soon after the first cuckoo choruses, chitter-chattering whoops of swallows and sand martins add to the music. Over the last few years the order of their arrival has been topsy-turvy, determined to some extent by the enormous changes to global weather patterns. These remarkable avian travellers are storm-blown, jet-stream riders and desert-skimmers, in possession of astonishing mind maps, world patterns and inherited cartography which lead them to South Erradale. In 2020 the sand martins arrived a full week before the cuckoos and two weeks before the first lone swallow. It would be another two weeks of concerned watching before swallows were diving through the byre door to check out their old nests. Many of us discussed the strange timings, their synchronicity with the global pandemic, the meaning of this and other worrying events in the natural world. Global upheavals were affecting everything and everyone.

Once here, swallows and martins swoop and dive in

exhilarating flashes of cream and jet, swimming on wavelets of wind. They always seem so pleased to be back. Bubbles of joy well up at their furious loud chatter. They are impossible to ignore, and in the unusual spring of 2020 our collective happiness at their return was greater than ever. Like swifts in the cities, swallows are smile-makers. They cavort in and out of the byre and settle briefly on wires, before soaring and sweeping over the meadows. Sand martins return to their nesting holes in the old river terrace and surf with the swallows through growing waves of insects.

In Wester Ross, as in so many parts of the UK, there is a long association between *Hirundinidae* and the agricultural landscape. Their annual return predates crofting, and families of both species will have been returning to Erradale and the surrounding valleys of Overside for centuries. The origins of agriculture and pastoralism here stretch back into prehistory but the modern version, comprising crofts with small-scale sheep- and cattle-grazing and food production, continues a long tradition of largely chemical-free, organic practices. There is no doubt the insect populations flourish because of this and they contribute to the cascade of life in spring and summer.

*

Crofts were allotted to individuals and families who had been removed from other settlements inland or relocated in the reorganisation of coastal communities in order to restructure and repurpose the land of the Gairloch Estate during the nineteenth century. Although some altruistic motives were apparent in the wish to improve soil and productivity, the main purpose of crofting was to rehome people cleared from inland settlements and manage the estate's financial outputs in the form of deer, sheep and other produce in order to deliver sustainable profit. The establishment of crofts enhanced the long tradition of controlling land and people seen across whole swathes of Britain and Ireland.

Today the purpose of crofting is very different. The rules and obligations laid out by the Crofting Commission are clear – we must live on the croft or no more than thirty-two kilometres away, and must not misuse or neglect it; we must cultivate and maintain the land or put it to other purposeful use; we must encourage conservation or enhance ecological status wherever possible and cause no damage or deterioration to the ground. And owners and tenants are obliged to ensure their crofts can be used for cultivation in the future. In theory, modern crofting practices help maintain a landscape that is wildlife-friendly and, since the use of pesticides and fertilisers is limited, insects, small mammals and birds can and should flourish. But over the latter half of the twentieth century consistent grazing pressure especially from deer and sheep, in part encouraged and maintained by EU and government grants, culminated in a cumulative loss of biodiversity, the disappearance of insect species and declining soil quality, and prevented the regeneration of woodland.

Scottish agriculture and crofting await the ultimate outcomes of current debates on land reform, and the impacts of 'Brexit' will unfold over time. It is possible systems of grant aid for remote rural smallholdings, especially those that are deemed less productive, on marginal or hill ground, will disappear. Hopes for greater wildlife and environmental protection are high, however there is widespread concern about potential loss of support for small farms, something that could devastate crofting, and thus the rare crofted landscapes.

From the start our main management strategy for Red River Croft has aimed to enhance biodiversity, restore soil quality and maintain the various habitats for wildlife but at the same time oversee the meadows for the future. Our land boundaries are straight and simple, but unlike most crofts in South Erradale and elsewhere on Overside, they enclose a complex series of micro-habitats that include wet bog, wet flood and dry meadows, dwarf alder and willow scrub, riverbanks and species-rich grassland. The croft is also bisected by the Red River, whose waters add sediments to and carry deposits from the lower meadows, enriching and replenishing mineral content then sweeping soil and vegetation away, changing their character. Mindful of the impact any new planting on the riverbank or interference to its structure might have in the longer term, and recognising our plans for woodland were unlikely, we decided to encourage as many species of plants and animals as possible in the hope they would make their homes here and thrive.

Inherent within our plans was an obligation to preserve the land for heritage purposes so the croft could be handed on to the next generation in a good state. To us that meant – and still means – land with good soils, high biodiversity, shelter belts, species-rich meadows and healthy riparian habitats. Our ideas about trees, hedges and grazing seemed appropriate within a conservation context, but we needed to figure out how our plans would benefit the community as a whole. We did not want the croft simply to be used for grazing, an ecological framework was required.

Even the initial reduction in grazing intensity had a measurable impact on biodiversity. I began to think that at least partial rewilding was a good idea. Rewilding, seen by some as a panacea for countering environmental degradation and species loss, is not viewed with the same enthusiasm by many crofters. Old habits and practices are difficult to argue against without evidence, and hard to undo. Yet because the overall number of grazing animals associated with South Erradale and its surrounding common grazing and wider hill country had fallen considerably, there had already been a certain level of semi-wilding underway around the valley. Trees and patches of scrub containing gorse, alder and hazel were spreading. On Red River Croft the more determined reduction of grazing intensity reaped rewards, quickly and surprisingly. I had assumed that years of resting and careful reseeding would be necessary. Instead, the soil's own 'seed bank' provided enough regenerative power to see an annual incremental increase in plant diversity.

The crofted landscapes are ecosystems in their own right. Without doubt, the arrival of cuckoos, swallows and martins has great significance. They are bio-indicator species, organisms that tell us about the relative health of the crofts and surrounding countryside. Their presence means our fields are insect rich; if the meadows are insect rich then soils and vegetation are in reasonable condition too. I marked the arrival and departure dates of the birds, listening and learning with increasing interest and hope. As I watched, the relationships between croft and cuckoos and swallows, and also the more complex interactions between plants and animals within the broader landscape, began to reveal themselves. People, wildlife and environment in close, interdependent and mutually respectful associations. It was time to figure out what could be given back to the land and our community over and above the limited access to seasonal grazing granted to our neighbours.

*

One spring morning I walked with Dram along the usual riverside trail. We were followed by Cathma's sheep and newest lambs who were drawn by the expectation of food or the prospect of visiting another field. Cathma had asked if her small flock could be let onto the croft for a few hours ahead of being herded across the river and out onto the common grazing. The ewes were restless for the hill. They were bleating their eagerness as well as instructions and encouragement to their lambs. I became aware both dog and flock had stopped behind me. I turned to see why they had halted and laughed at all the upturned faces. Dog, ewes and lambs were looking up at a maelstrom of movement in the air. Our collective feet, trampling through the grass, had disturbed clouds of small flies. And in the rush to feed, gravity-defying swallow-swoops of iridescent jet and clotted cream with hints of flashing turquoise and scraps of cinnamon were tumbling again and again over the woolly backs, the dog and me. For a few minutes the sheep stood still and then separated into two groups. At first I thought they were allowing Dram to pass but he had also moved aside. A dark, undulating shadow was running close to the ground coming through the middle of the sheep. Once again, it was our resident otter, his whistles mingling with the startled bleating of lambs and confusion of birds and insects as he rushed by.

(iii) Spring arrives in the hills

In between mustard-yellow blooms of gorse and pink spears of orchids, the greens of growing grass deepen. Although the sward is still short, bright colours and emerging blossoms frame the backcloth of mountains rather than the other way around. Spring air tends to be brighter and clearer, days are longer, and in the full force of a clear late spring day the mountains appear sharply delineated. They seem closer than ever, more powerful than before, more so than when in winter garb and dressed with snow. Gullies and ridges replace smudges of colour and uncertain shadows. The effect is mesmerising. At this time of year these mountains, whose shapes are so familiar, whose voices I know, call out more loudly than ever. Again and again, unable to walk in the hills and too unwell, I forced myself to turn away and concentrate on what was all around me, on the swallows, and the cuckoo-calling, and the croft flourishing under my feet. Without doubt, the songs and jubilant flying enhanced and magnified the overall sense of renewal, of the burgeoning of life across the croft.

Year on year, the affirmation of life coming from the avian migrants in late spring is no less astonishing. They are the way-markers to summer. The joy they bring, regardless of what else might happen, is unquestionable. In their company I continued to walk around the croft whenever I felt well enough and could manage it. They soared and dived above my head and around my body as I slowly pathered to the river or cliff-top. When I made it down the Seaweed Road and onto the shore, swallows and martins swerved across my route, out across the rocks and sandy beach, accompanied by an occasional echoing cuckoo call.

Yet in spite of their companionship, every now and then I began to feel the nag and pull of ancient rock and mountain heights. It is a sensation that can never be fully shrugged off. For those who have climbed among pinnacles and peaks, the yearning to return can become a compulsion. Even on my lowest days, in the most dreadful weather, I would wonder what conditions were like on the summit of Beinn Alligin. I would gaze up at Baosbheinn for some message, some inkling of how hard the winds were blowing on the tops. I could guess of course, and read mountain weather summaries for the day in question, but nothing seemed to calm the itch for the special scent of rock and grit found in the higher places, or the feel of pulling cold air deeply into lungs burning with effort and joy.

Oftentimes a stinging pang of longing would overwrite the enjoyment I found walking locally. Now and again, neither croft or coast could dampen a growing desire to see the peaks close up and taste mountain air. Rob and Mark had continued with their mountain escapades, returning happy and tired, with tall tales of adventure and their cameras full of pictures. For much of the time I enjoyed hearing their stories and scouring their photographs. But sensing my unhappiness one day, Rob suggested a familiar low-level walk that would take us into the heart of the Torridon mountains. I had begun to recover a little from the debilitating illness; my muscles were remembering what they should be used for, and I agreed, even a short walk in the heart of hill country would do me good. Although the summits I can see every day from home would not be within touching distance, at least I would be able to see their ramparts and crags from the valley below rather than across thirteen kilometres of open country.

Below the scudding cumulus cloud and fiercely blue skies of early morning, shadows chased one another across the hillsides. The trail we had chosen rose very gently into an empty valley that leads into the remote, wilder heart of the Torridon mountains. The valley was bright in its spring coat, its river dazzling downhill to Loch Maree. As the morning passed, the valley sank into a haze, the kind of mistiness that will build into high clouds and thunderstorms in late spring and early summer. When tiredness and pain began to resurface, we found a rocky seat and sat for a while enjoying the view and sipping our drinks. Across the slopes, scattered pockets of Scots pine were dark-green cushions. We were surrounded by low-growing heathers and short tufts of grass mixed with lichens and dark moss. The woody heathers were contorted and prostrate, most did not reach my calves. Either the vegetation here was heavily grazed or the area around us had been burned. But we found no charcoal or blackened heather stems. Most of the rocks and boulders strewn about the hillside were coated by familiar colourful and ancient lichen colonies or topped by rich dense hats of moss. Age sat deeply on the largest. Yet the air all around us and above the shallow blanket of heathered turf and mossy rocks was empty; there was no birdsong of any kind, not a single call or cry; in fact, I could not see a bird anywhere, not even a crow.

Rob felt it too and asked, 'Can you hear it? The silence? No birdsong? No birds! None, none at all.' All we could hear was air, slowly brushing past us and sighing as it went by. We sat for a few minutes listening and thinking about what species should be flying and singing in the hills. 'Do you remember the last walk I was able to do? The slopes were full of birds and insects. Where are they?' Deep into this glorious glen leading all the way to the feet of Beinn Eighe and Liathach, all we could find among the clumps of heather and in between the tussocks of grass were small cobwebs. The more we looked, the more we found. Threads of gossamer were strung between individual leaves. Others floated up as they caught the air currents. Above us the splendid outthrusts of peak and precipice were billowing with shadows, bare rock glinting. Around us the filaments of spider-lives also glistened. The creeping sense of absence, of loss, was deeply unsettling. There was no insect-hum, birdsong or raptor cry. Below us the valley screamed with emptiness, as if every drop of sound had been scraped away. Overhead the sky turned opaque and colourless as moisture continued to build into cloud. We turned to retrace our steps, wearing sadness like a heavy coat.

Back home, the comparison between our mountain walk, with its awful grandeur and staggering beauty, and this area of coast was striking. On the moorland surrounding South Erradale heather grows thick and dense. For much of summer the turf is rich and aromatic, bird-filled and suffused with insects. There are bees everywhere, and hoverflies, wasps, beetles and damsel-flies, and insects I cannot name. The air is full of humming and buzzing. Small meadow birds flit back and forth, swallows and sand martins swoop and the whole place feels brim-full. Compared to that remote glen this narrow band of land between hill and croft and sea seemed buoyantly rich, a space filled with activity and noise. The contrast could not have been greater.

The richness of coastal flora and fauna is in part due to the work of crofters. Grazing intensity is lower than in the past since sheep numbers have declined and deer in significant numbers are by and large kept away from crofting townships by a variety of means. Some crofts have been abandoned and are slowly and naturally rewilding, and the common grazings, though still peri-odically burned on a much smaller scale, are not as intensely managed as they once were. But it is also because there are natural gradients within and between habitats here, variations in species type and biodiversity. From shallow marine environ-ments into the hills, these edgelands – these in-between places where croft merges into machair, riverbank into rock pool and beach, scrub into woodland – are borders and frontiers between competing natural systems, and are richer for that. Margins flourish because they enable greater movement of species between one habitat and another. Complexity of this kind gener-ates richness and enhances resilience in the face of large external stresses and pressures.

*

I was concerned about the perceived absences of wildlife in the mountains and wishing I could go back. For consolation, I returned to counting wildflowers and relearning the half-remembered names of grasses and sedges. And in my notebooks proof of the differences between the glen and the Erradale valley had already begun to emerge in the numbers – more plant species lived here than in the mountains.

It took me a few days to recover from the glen walk but then I returned to the daily round. On the cliff-top one bright and unusually cold late spring day I watched frisks of bone-white cloud being chased down the Minch by a wickedly stiff northerly wind. The fields shivered on the skittish breeze. Swallows dived over the rippling grasses, feeding on insects thrown up by the turbulence. Cuckoo voices followed me to the cliff-top, bounced around by the wind. Yet despite the gusting air, bees were still able to zip from flower to flower as if the wind could not catch them. Again and again I thought of the magnificent but empty mountain valley. There were signs of hope – young trees, self-seeded, among the grandfather pines and deep pillows of moss and lichen – but the disparity between coast and hill country was marked.

When we first came to live in the Highlands, my heart flew among the mountains, my face always turned to the summits. I knew their names, had climbed many, and we planned to climb many more. But as my walking became more problematic, I began to find the particular, the singular and the special in the smaller places – the croft, the Red River, the short stretch of coast, the sea. These edgeland spaces were giving more than I could ever have imagined. I learned what species grew where, the order in which they appeared, how the river behaved, where the deer ran, where the birds nested, where and when the solitary bees emerged. This rich place was my classroom and companion, my solace and healer. Through their generosity, non-human species offered restoration. My awareness of space and place was utterly changed.

I followed the old trail to the sea-log seat. The shore was busy. Dram and I sat down to watch. Crowds of dunlins whizzed from one end of the beach to the other, three separate groups of ringed plovers chased the foaming waves back and forth and skylarks rose up and down through the piercing light. A bonxie flew overhead, his shadow the shape of a stealth fighter jet on the sands. A second one followed a few hundred metres behind. Stonechats clattered in alarm from fence post to fence post and oystercatchers piped furiously from the rocks nearby. It was busy, noisy and brightly life-filled. Waves spilled higher up the beach; spray and spume began to rise. An otter tumbled out of the sea and ran past us into the dune grassland. The day unfolded with joy.

3. Sunrise over Cnoc an Fhuarain, Erradale, sunset over north Lewis, Outer Hebrides, Celtic month of Hawthorn (May to June), Mother's Moon

(i) Flowers bloom and mountains shine in opulent light

Spring light is all motion and trickery and opulence and vigour. It dresses us like royalty. At the same time, it reveals the secrets of mountains and even retells tales of the mythical figures who 'created' these grand landscapes. The last remnants of winter fall from our eyes until we are blinded again and again by the rising or setting sun and accompanying decadent kaleidoscopes of colour. We greedily gulp down the bowlful of extra light each day brings.

In the intense clarity of unpolluted Highland air the finest details of the crags and crevices of Torridon's mountains emerge. As the eagle flies, their summits are thirteen kilometres from my back garden, yet on some days the brightness of late spring and early summer can sharpen their familiar shapes more than the ice-cold of deep winter. Baosbheinn, Beinn Dearg and Beinn Alligin – whose tops include Sgùrr Mhòr and Tom na

Gruagaich – become crystalline and proud in the fierce glare. There are more glimpses too of Ruadh Stac-Mhòr, one of Beinn Eighe's highest outthrusting ramparts.

Close to the summit of Sgùrr Mhòr is a distinctive cleft. Imagine a conical cake with a slice cut out near the top to create a small, flat platform. This is our view of Alligin's grandeur from South Erradale and I repeatedly dream of camping up there. The dream started shortly after I became ill. In it I find a near-summit pitch. Around me is a close sward of green baize studded with tiny blue and even smaller white flowers. From this imaginary platform my dream follows a complete solar year, with sunrises over distant ripples of mountains and sunsets running from island to island.

Since my slow steady recovery began, a climb on Beinn Alligin has become my long-term aim. I yearn to see real sunrises and sunsets from that high place. Yet there is no platform as such. It is merely a trick of the eye crafted from wishful thinking. The notch marks the top of a long defile dropping almost a thousand feet down the other side of the mountain. Seen from Coire Mhic Nobaill and Loch Torridon the feature appears as a dark gash in the mountain's steepest slope. There is no benign camping plat- form, only a great yawning slash in the rockface. The mountainside of Sgùrr Mhòr below the summit collapsed in a great rock avalanche, one almost impossible to imagine. Geologists and geomorphologists studying the mountain's features have concluded it formed almost four thousand years ago during a single event.

The resulting rock debris is distributed all around the foot of the mountain. Scientists who have studied the cleft and materials deposited in the valley below explain how the cascade of rock would have made a strange sound, one heard for miles around, not merely a rumbling as one might expect, but a higher pitched wailing created by the speed of movement, size of rock fragments and sheer steepness of slope. A tale of pure physics at play as well as geology and geography.

In the UK we mostly think of hills and valleys forming slowly and steadily over great rafts of time and not in sudden, catastrophic events. Our mountains seem stable, dependable, their individual shapes and characters are well known. But it is named, this special place. *Eag Dhubh na h-Eigheachd* (the 'black gash of the wailing') or *Leum na Caillich* (the 'hag's leap'). Both names are evocative and, in all likelihood, ancient. It is possible the first refers to the sound acoustic scientists believe was made as the mountainside collapsed. Astonishingly the names have remained in use for four millennia, since the event itself, and they perhaps capture the terror, amazement, shock and disbelief felt by communities living here at the time. The second name may refer to the legends of Beira, Queen of Winter, who raged around the land smiting the hills with her hammer. Across the Celtic world she is the wild and unpredictable Cailleach, credited with creating the mountain landscapes of Wester Ross. To me, she is possibly the first woman to use a geological hammer.

It is tempting to speculate about how many other legends are married to measurable physical, geomorphological and geological events in this way. The naming of Eag Dhubh na h-Eigheachd and Leum na Caillich may also be tied to climate change. Four thousand years ago, the climate was rapidly becoming cooler and wetter. And it is entirely possible intense rainfall, coupled with rapid freezing and thawing, would have weakened the rock along its faultlines until the face came crashing down in one sudden and enormous event. Yet here we are, tantalisingly in touching distance of what people experienced long ago because their reactions remain, described and preserved within the place names and legends of Wester Ross.

*

By late May, Beira has lost her battles. Spring wholly envelops our small valley. Summer approaches. The croft yearns for it; we long for it too, but also do not want the delicious summer days to pass too quickly. Once the solstice is here, days begin to shorten and we can see winter waiting in the dark cleft of Beinn Alligin.

Our late spring days can be multifaceted gemstone bright. Sunsets at this time may be filled with strong, deeply resonating colours, often as rich and thick as melted wax. They suffuse and supercharge the western skies. One evening a squad of showers blustered down the Minch and threatened to wipe away the sunset, but they were exposed as wisp and whimsy by the strong and lavish light pouring through them. They became pale-lavender lace framing hot-orange glass and began to fall apart as the day faded.

When skies are clear the almost-solstice sunsets are also almost nuclear. One evening, as we sat on sea-log seat number one, the setting sun became a great expanding orb, an enormous disc, the yellow of kingcups in full flower. The sky was so thick with colour it appeared to be daubed with undiluted acrylic paint in concentric circles created by a thick brush. It took me back more than twenty-five years to an almost identical sunset.

Following my mother's death at the winter solstice, I drove home to be with my husband and four children, a journey of about three hours over the hills of mid- and north Wales. Since it was almost Christmas some of the drive would inevitably be in the dark but I wanted to get home to the children in plenty of time for the normal routines of evening meal, bath and bedtime stories. When I got to Llandegla Moor, the sun was setting. Here, for some strange reason, I felt compelled to stop. The valley below had all but disappeared in the flaming light. I could see the disc of the sun, but around it halos of treacle-thick colour began to swell. The silhouettes of upland and valley fizzled away and everything was consumed by fierce light until no landforms or earthly shapes remained.

My mother loved to watch the setting sun from her hill farm overlooking the great bog of Cors Fochno and the wide sweep of Cardigan Bay. In summer we would sit together, draped in and wrapped up by the golden light and drinking deeply of the richly scented air. The memory of her voice has burned within every sunset since those happy days.

Just as it had over Llandegla Moor, from the sea-log seat the sun appeared to swallow up the whole world. I had not seen sunset colours so condensed in spring-time before. Then, as it finally fell to earth, the spell was broken by oystercatchers and curlews, whose songs rippled through a strange pale-grey mist thrown up by the waves.

*

At last, in the long warm days of early June, our meadows, hedges and woodlands begin to catch up with the blooming of wildflowers further south, but it is always an impatient and slightly uneasy wait and one that is, for me, tinged with jealousy. I anxiously await the first flowers, jealous of the meadows and frothy flower-filled hedgerows already in bloom in southern England, even though I know we are at least three weeks behind. Nevertheless, I wander the croft, peering into tufts and clumps, hoping and willing the turf into action. It happens suddenly, often after a spell of rain and warm winds, heralded by a burst of insect life synchronous with the rapid greening of crofts, peat bogs and moorland, part of the rich, dense partnership that is our living green envelope. And then, very quickly, the green swards are flecked with flowers.

Wildflowers bloom in a regular sequence. While the turf is still quite short, heath bedstraw, tormentil and heath milkwort prickle the ground with creamy white, yellow and blue. The flowers of milkwort are delicate and tiny, are difficult to see, but when you have found one, the whole place seems sewn together with stitches of deep blue. They emerge on the croft and all across the drier heathery ground of surrounding hills. The yellow flowers of tormentil also flicker on the moorland, among the low-growth young heathers and tufts of grass on peats and crofts. And over long-buried walls or along the edges of paths bedstraw froths with abundances of tiny cream flowers. Some then vanish, subsumed by the growing sward so quickly they are gone before you have had time to enjoy them.

Sunrise is around four o'clock. In the early pre-dawn, an hour before the sun crests the eastern hills, the sky is transformed by translucent yet opulent light. The high cleft of Sgùrr Mhòr on Beinn Alligin sits for a while as a deep-purple streak. I imagine the summit-cold of my campsite and bivouac. Below the peaks, gullies pour with shadows. Cold winds fall down each one, away from the rising sun, perhaps producing a single wail, unheard by no one but the Cailleach. Now the same gloss-paint finish found in sunsets slides over our heads and warmth chases the last cold shadows. The dawn chorus erupts as livid turquoise and peacock-blue turn to polished hesperidium.

(ii) The sea changes colour

From the croft the sea often appears to glow with a galvanic current. Its surface waters glint with mischief. The known becomes unknown, and, with the folding and unfolding of its long canvas of colours, real is recast as allegory. The lure of the sea grows as summer swells, but it also grew as I was forced to subdue the mountains in my mind.

The daily walks to the cliff-top vantage point slowly encouraged a gentle recovery of mind and body, a renewal of sorts, and I put that down to the bracing sea air as much as to time spent on the croft. Alongside the scents and sounds of flourishing meadows and a busy shore, the sea offered another kind of companionship, enabling a new way of looking at the whole world.

Often, in early summer, the sea turns opaque. Downpours send braided currents of sediment-loaded water swirling out into the Minch, adding to the abundant mix of colours and clouding surface waters. Plankton bloom in the less oxygenated conditions, decreasing levels of clarity in sea water. Bright colours become pastel, azure turns to turquoise and mother-of-pearl, aquamarine to peppermint tea. Changes in colour and opacity, cloud density and light diffraction are especially complex and fast-moving here. Some westerlies green the sea, others turn the water to milk. The nature of light and colour is not only driven by the motion of sea and air, it is changed by the life held within the waters. Decades ago James Lovelock wrote his masterpiece on the regulation of climate by the biosphere. In his Gaia hypothesis he described how life within oceans regulates planetary temperatures and how specialist microbes (the phytoplankton) make a molecule called dimethyl sulphide which acts as a seed nucleus for droplets of condensing water. The gas-releasing phytoplankton attract zooplankton and other organisms that feed on them and so the waters become opaque. Opacity is enhanced further, especially on windy days in summer, as bottom sediments are churned up by the increased agitation of waves and currents adding to the mixture, and soon fish come to feed. And so the bloom of light and colour repeatedly revitalises itself and sings with the promise of life. A summer sea throbs – turquoise, azure and jade.

*

The Inner Sound and Minches are busy with people as well as wildlife. Together they form a palaeogeographical region as rich in cultural development and history as natural resources. The ties of history and palaeogeography are powerful and resonate across time from the remote past to the present day. Over millennia, ancient sea paths connecting disparate groups of islands and mainland coasts, from northern Europe down to the Mediterranean, enabled travel by mystics, invaders, religious groups, traders and migrants. Journeys made by water defined communities, culture and heritage and ultimately made the Highlands and Islands what they are today. While overland jour-neys were long and arduous, sea travel was economically and practically prudent. Around the margins of the Inner Sound and Minches archaeological finds suggest people would have moved seasonally, following the blooms of abundant life – plants, shoals of fish and sea birds – then trading and transporting goods. The first and closest, almost symbiotic, associations Mesolithic people had with the sea have long gone, yet even in the twenty-first century the same allure and power of the Minch and Inner Sound are active and resonate with communities here. In our remote past these inshore waters from Skye north to Ullapool and from Gairloch to Stornoway may have been more closely interconnected than any early land routes. But until structures as large as Maes Howe or Callanish are found here on the coastal margins of Wester Ross, the long-held paradigm of sea as a barrier to the diffusion of knowledge and understanding may still hold sway.

Over the millennia, communities would have been deeply intimate with the natural world and its physical characteristics. However, the written word does not stretch back into prehistory so we know little of their thoughts or systems of belief. Yet in a small number of preserved religious texts, created thousands of years later, individuals expressed their deep longing for solitude and for communion with the elements. They wrote about the sense of isolation. They purposefully sought out the unique and dramatic interplay of air and water found in remote rocky places, islands or mountain tops. Such seemingly inaccessible places became centres of religious scholarship and cultural enlightenment. As anyone who visits remote islands today will affirm, the powerful elemental exchanges between sea, land and sky would have provided endless opportunities to examine the wonders of the natural world, and introspectively challenge their relationship to God. Watching drifting curls and crescents of colour written onto water, I wonder if the hermits and religious ascetics, in the splendid isolation of such marginal, liminal places, wrote sea-water orisons as well as in ink.

To imagine a life with the sea at its centre requires an overturning of imagination for someone whose life has been entirely land-based. Yet it happened to me, landlubber and seasickness-sufferer. From my cliff-top leaning post I came to realise I was standing at the centre of an enormous bowl created from ancient rock and wild seas. From here there is a three-hundred-and-sixty-degree view of crofts, peatlands, mountains, sea and islands. I have the feeling of being in the centre of a *mappa mundi*, or of a portolan whose rhumb lines emanate directly from the post, or from me.

The rim, running around the entire compass, is wrinkled and fluted with high peaks to the east, islands to the west and heaped layers of hills north and south. In only one place does it become a flat-edged, smooth horizon of sea, between the Point of Ness on the Isle of Lewis and the mainland. Also from here I can tick off the hilltops and high mountain peaks one by one: Longa to Meall Imireach; Cnoc an Fhuarain to Baosbheinn; the summits of Beinn Eighe, Beinn Dearg, Liathach, the Horns of Alligin, Sgùrr Mhòr and Tom na Gruagaich; from Maol Ruadh to the Cuillin of Skye, Isles Rona and Raasay, and the ridges of Trotternish from the Old Man of Storr to the Quiraing; from the tip of north Trotternish past the Uists to An Cliseam on Harris; and beyond Lewis to the throat of open sea that brings the Atlantic into the Minches. The calendrical year is played out around this enormous amphitheatre of earth, sea and sky, the solar cycle measured by terrestrial crags and notches, its sunrises and sunsets marked by geology and the forces of geomorphology.

The sun's slow passage is matched and magnified by the lustrous colours and music of the Inner Sound and Minches. At times there is no separation between the celestial and earthbound. This inner sea, with its island and mountain boundaries, is whole and alive in its entirety. Westwards, the islands and sea are in partnership with the setting sun; in the east, mountains commune with sunrise. The midsummer sun breaks over the ancient peat bogs and lochs that fill the hollowed hills beyond Erradale. Turn one hundred and eighty degrees as the low sun of the winter solstice slides down behind the Isle of Skye, and the great spine of Trotternish becomes the splayed and sleeping form of a dragon. In high summer the sun sets beyond the tip of Lewis with a cascade of red and gold on the surface of the sea; at the winter solstice the sun rises over the smooth rump of Maol Ruadh, pouring light over the moorland like water running off a deer's back.

The more I walked the short circuit to the cliff, lured to the sea, the more a strong sensation of being at the centre of an enormous natural calendar grew. Every day I took photographs – of the sea, sky and horizon. They became an archive of colour across the solar year, helping to enhance the slow transformational process of healing begun by the croft and by watching wildlife. Where the meadows, their tiny flowers, insects and birds taught me about the minutiae of wild nature, the sea reanimated my relationship with landscape-scale views. It placed the non-solid ahead of solid forms in my mind and completely transformed my understanding of light, colour and sound.

Years ago, I was introduced to the works of the late American painter Jon Schueler, a contemporary of Mark Rothko and Jackson Pollock. Schueler periodically lived further south, at Mallaig in Lochaber, travelling between the United States and Scotland to paint. He worked in a small cottage overlooking the Sound of Sleat, a vibrant stretch of water which runs between the Morar coast and the Isle of Skye, similar to the Inner Sound to the north. Schueler wrote at length of the powerful impact raw oceanic and atmospheric elements had upon him, and his paintings eventually came to consist mostly of sea and sky, at times horizon-less, yet always filled with rich colour and a sense of space. He saw and described these landless lacunae as constructs of raw emotion, concepts of mind and bodily senses, saying that only ocean and atmosphere could teach him to truly understand light and colour and salve his troubled mind. Schueler described the Sound of Sleat paintings as his soul laid bare. He used light, dark, and raw emotions found in the bond and powerful exchanges of energy between sea and atmosphere to express his innermost feelings – dark waves for guilt, anger and sorrow; sumptuous light for joy and love.

Many of my sea and sky pictures, taken from the cliff-top, contain abstract shapes and lines. The swirls and sweeping arcs on the waters of the Minch appear mysterious and enchanting. They can grow and vanish in the shape of a quicksilver half-moon, forget-me-not-blue loop or lavender spiral replete with meanings impossible to fathom and in languages pulled up from the deeps or caught on the winds. They are sea-poems and stories, conversations and histories, and at times they have been prayers.

*

Today the sea lanes in the Minch and Inner Sound are busy with fishing boats, tourists and nuclear submarines as well as whales, mackerel and herring. In summer many tourist boats leave the sheltered harbour at Gairloch and sail out into the Minch. There are wildlife tours which follow cetaceans, seals, basking sharks and sea birds, as well as fishing boats running back and forth along the entire west coast from island to mainland and back again. From the Seaweed Road, summer on the sea appears as lively as it might once have been in the remoter past.

In deep undersea channels known as 'whale roads', researchers have marked the passage of orcas, humpbacks and minke whales as they navigate waters throbbing with the noise of engines and echo sounders. Sadly, marine wildlife must also cope with plastic pollution, discarded rubbish, fishing gear and remnants of our dirtier past. One female orca autopsied in 2013 revealed such extraordinarily high concentrations of poly-chlorinated biphenyls (PCBs) that she would never have been able to conceive and bear young. The 'West Coast Pod' of orcas ranges widely around the Hebrides and is thought to have greater similarity to pods from the Antarctic than to any plying the northern waters from Orkney to the Arctic. But no calves have been seen for twenty-five years and their final songs may vanish from the Inner Sound and Minch within the next two decades.

The lure of the sea was strong in other ways. Soon after moving here, Rob bought an old boat with an inboard engine. He spent months fiddling with nuts and bolts, electric wires, pumps and levers. I helped staple new waterproof covers onto the bedraggled seating in the cabin and privately worried if it would ever sail. We never ventured out into the deeper waters: neither of us possess the seamanship for such an adventure. Instead, we made shorter journeys, of the kind people have done for thousands of years, slowly passing between skerries and small islands, fishing in the shallow, sheltered waters at the edges of the Gair Loch by Badachro and Shieldaig. Although we are separated from the ancient navigators and fisherfolk by millennia, tradition and by skill, each tiny adventure repeated the smaller journeys stretching back into prehistory, those taken by people securing bounty from the sea, providing food for their families, their communities.

To float on a sea the colour of moonstone or molten gold became yet another blessing, especially when accompanied by wildlife unperturbed by our little boat and hapless hunting skills. Trying to read the currents and winds, all I could find were words in the curls and lines of rippling colour. A quiet calm and sense of separation would come with distance from the shore as my internal geographies and perspectives were radically changed. And while Rob carefully navigated the countless tiny skerries and submerged rocks I would dangle my fingers in the water and listen for snippets of sea songs on the waves and in sea birds' voices. When the sea breeze blew brightly and bonxies came to inspect our catches, hints of what life was like long ago skimmed past us over the waves.

(iii) Bog-cottons flower, Sphagnum mounds grow

The countryside around South Erradale is largely moorland. Blankets of peat lie over solid rock. Bog-cottons bloom here, dancing like ballerinas in the sea breezes, snow white by day, red gold at sunset and sunrise, and ghost silver in the short hours of night. In warm weather the peatlands bubble with curlew panpipes, skylarking piccolos and gleeful chattering of swallows. Coloured song-ribbons wave in the breeze. Atoms of air bind with the music of birdsong and in a shimmer of sound blend with molecules of fragrance. The aromatic incense of unique bog flora rises, roams and seeps into everything. There is no separation between bog surface and lower atmosphere; perfumes, sounds and light merge, their essential natures are exchanged.

*

Peat itself is a sensuous material, darkly brown like melted chocolate, soft and moist. It squidges between fingers and oozes rusty-red water when squeezed. And yet it is deceptive, shivering underfoot like blancmange, but with form and substance and strength when completely dried. It is possible to bounce-walk on deep, quaking peat. Now and again a foot will sink into a black, wet, peaty hole, the peat unwilling to let go.

Peat bogs are formidable, singular, preternatural and spell-binding. Peat is an organic substance which incorporates pollen and spores from living plants, and insect and animal remains.

There are no inorganic components other than those falling to the bog surface with rain: minute remnants of human activity such as visible smoke, pollution and dust, the invisible by-products of combustion in power stations and vehicles, metal-liferous and radioactive particles, and naturally produced materials such as tiny rock slivers of volcanic ash. Peat is formed principally from *Sphagnum* moss, a genus of plants with no roots, though with specialist tissues to store water. Everything required for growth and development comes from the atmosphere via precipitation and air movement, so it thrives in the moist, cool temperate climate of Britain, and especially in Scotland, northern England and Ireland. Individual *Sphagnum* plants grow from the tips of their stems, so their lower, older parts become buried and compressed by the weight of growing biomass above. But even in their state of compression they have an incredibly strong internal structure that can still hold water. Any particles deposited on and embraced by the growing tips of plants eventually become subsumed within the bog and are preserved for millennia in the acidic and anaerobic conditions of the deeper peat. As years pass, every single fragment of *Sphagnum*, curling and fragile, compresses and folds up on itself, becoming buried deeper and deeper, carrying with it micro-scopic forensic evidence of our changing environments, climate and human histories. Over time, layers of dead *Sphagnum*, several centimetres below the living surface, gradually accumulate. This new material is peat.

Bogs first form where rainfall is heavy and incessant and where forest cover is absent. As rainwaters pass through soils they leach out nutrients and minerals and eventually the ground becomes waterlogged and infertile. Because *Sphagnum* species can thrive on so little nourishment and make do with the nutrients contained only in rainwater, they are ideally suited to such conditions and become the first colonisers of poor, degraded and wet ground. In the absence of grazing pressure, a *Sphagnum*-moss carpet will develop. Eventually the landscape becomes so radically altered that it begins to function in a wholly different way and a deep moss bog emerges in place of grassland, raised above any movement of ground or surface water. Where this process has been going on for many millennia, large tracts of bogland have developed and buried the original landscape beneath thick blankets of peat, metres deep.

Blanket-bog formation began in Scotland more than nine thousand years ago, with the greatest building phase some five millennia later. It is likely this occurred for two reasons: first, people were clearing the forests at a much greater scale; and second, climate was beginning to deteriorate. As climate became wetter and cooler, communities would have needed more wood for fuel and shelter. That in turn opened up land surfaces and *Sphagnum* growth was instigated. Today much of the north is deforested. Peatland has become the organic beating heart of these landscapes in the same way that mountains are their bones and rivers their blood vessels. Bogs pulse with life; they inhale and exhale, exchanging gases with the atmosphere, just as we do; and very importantly, in the current context of a warming world, they store carbon.

Peat burns with a satisfying red heat and sweet, cloying smoke. For centuries Highland and Island communities have cut peat from bogs into blocks which are then open-air dried, in readiness for cooking and heating. Once the great forests had been largely cleared, and in the absence of coal, the use of peat for burning became widespread. A special implement called a *taisgear*, essentially a long wooden handle with an angled blade, is used to cut peat in late spring or early summer. The rectangular blocks are piled in a small stack known as a *cruach* to dry out during the summer, each stack built according to local traditions, and when the stack has dried it is carried home to the croft. Peat used to be carried by the women in a peat-creel, known locally as a *cliabh moine*, though today most use quad bikes and trailers. Banks of hill or valley peat were allocated to crofters for cutting, but many of the beds around South Erradale are now abandoned.

Where excessive peat-cutting occurred, it radically altered the topography of the moorland. In the Erradale valley and up on Maol Ruadh there are old peat-cuttings everywhere and in some places the peat 'hags' are so tall, ditches so flooded and deep, bog pools so treacherous, they have been fenced off to prevent cattle from floundering and becoming buried. Over time, tonnes of carbon have been emptied into the atmosphere by peat-burning, but communities could have done little else in the absence of woodland to maintain home and hearth, unaware of their contribution to climate change.

Peat is one of nature's miracles. It grows steadily by increments, breathtakingly slowly, roughly one millimetre each year. This means a crofter, cutting down to carve off brick-shaped slabs of peat, is slicing through time and removing decades or centuries of their own history. In some areas, where the cuttings are stepped and deep, as much as four thousand years of history has gone or is exposed at the cut edge. A newly cut face of peat is multi-coloured, with every shade of brown from almost dun to coal black. It oozes with water after rain and pools form at the base of the cutting. Once an area has been harvested, vegetation recolonises the rows and ridges, creating a landscape of steps and heaps where it is possible to decipher how wet an area is by the type of plants growing there. In midsummer an abandoned peat bog becomes an intricate tapestry of whites, yellows and greens, where bog-cottons, asphodels and tormentil, and various grasses and heathers, grow according to their relative tolerances of waterlogging and acidity.

Freshly cut peat is banded with colours; black bands indicating warm climate periods such as Scotland's 'High Middle Ages' when much of the country came under unified rule and the arts flourished, and much paler layers indicating the mid-ninth century 'Dark Ages' when climate had deteriorated and drove Vikings south to establish new settlements across Britain and Ireland. The most recent pale dun-brown layers of peat are contiguous with the Little Ice Age, a period of severe climate cooling that contributed in no small measure to the potato famines, the Clearances and the establishment of crofting communities all across the Highlands and Islands. The whole peat-covered landscape is therefore an historical archive of change, a repository of insect and animal life and plant communities, and a recorder of the lives and impacts of people long gone.

Where bogland is undisturbed, mosses grow in mounds and they can be more than a metre in diameter. A bog's surface can appear flamboyantly quilted in garnet, magenta, sage, emerald and ochre, each cushion with an individual inner glow as if lit from within. If the mounds dry out in summer heat they fade to pink, pale olive and bleached blonde. There are pools of water, some wholly black, others turquoise blue and reflective of light, their margins laced with rare and delicate sedges and sundews. As water passes through a bog it takes on the colour of peat, becoming brown and in some cases almost black when it enters burns and rivers. For years both water and peat have been treasured, especially in the creation of some of Scotland's most famous whiskies. Peat has been used for centuries to heat the pot stills and, more importantly, for drying out the maltings. Many of the west coast, Island and Highland whiskies are characterised by the varied peatiness and differences in water chemistry involved in the production process. When barley grain is dried over a peat fire it takes on a distinctive smoky character, the level of 'smokiness' depending on how long the barley is exposed to peat smoke, and it is this part of the whisky-making process that contributes most significantly to the flavour.

In Dixon's (1886) book, *Gairloch and Guide to Loch Maree*, he wrote that no whisky was produced in the parish of Gairloch before 1880, an assertion somewhat difficult to believe. Production was officially permitted in Kinlochewe that year to be sold at the inn there, but unofficially it is highly likely there were numerous illicit stills across the region. Close to the old road to Badachro, just where it leaves behind the sounds of life in the Erradale valley, there is a small man-made hollow and culvert where it is believed local people used water from the myriad lochans and burns for their own whisky ventures.

On a warm, bright day, the lowest layer of air over the large peat bogs beyond the township appears to quaver and oscillate, a mirage fuelled by the exchange of gases and water vapour and the ebb and flow of sound and light. In a summer heat haze, the peatlands glitter with wing and carapace. Among the undulating hummocks and hollows of the bog surfaces many species of insects find food and shelter and places to breed – dragonflies, damselflies, daddy-long-legs, beetles, bees, hoverflies, spiders and others – and birds find nesting sites. When any of these organisms die, they too become incorporated in the peat.

The bog immediately adjacent to our croft reveals tell-tale signs about the water table. There is a strange trick of light that comes immediately after rain when the mounded bog surface prickles with chalk-white brightness, like a paper doily held up to sunlight, and its iron-black pools swell to pearlescent plashes. In the rain-shimmer of reflected light, mounds of moss silver as they soak up the wetness and then I know the deeper inland mires will be wetter still. In my mind's eye I see individual moss stems, tiny, fragile and delicate, absinthe green and claret red, joyously holding their uppermost fronds to the sky: a million, billion, trillion microscopic hands cupped to catch the falling droplets of rain.

Part Four

Summer Solstice to Autumn Equinox

1. Sunrise over Meall Imireach beyond Gairloch, sunset over the sea north of the Point of Ness, Isle of Lewis, Celtic month of Oak (June to July), Rose Moon

(i) Corncrakes sing in the white nights

In the Northwest Highlands there is a special kind of summer bounty that comes with the long hours of daylight – colours of land, sea and air intensify in a way not seen elsewhere. When June weather is clear, calm and dry, a sunset sky resembles an upturned bowl of turquoise trimmed with orange glaze. When the sun vanishes beyond the northern tip of Lewis, the Minch is brushed with cochineal and crimson. Around the Erradale valley white-walled cottages blush. Green fields radiate and pink sheep wander between ruby clumps of heather on the moorlands and common grazing. Beyond the township, mountains are pincushion soft in rose and salmon pink, their uppermost cragginess tipped with violet. Midnight approaches with a last roaring rush of blood. But then the light stretches out like cellophane. The sea pales to translucence. Nights become thin and watery. This is the 'simmer dim', the high midsummer when night slips away even further north and leaves us all silvered and grey. Shetlanders say 'simmer dim' is theirs, a Norse name for the twilight dimming, but folk in Wester Ross speak it too, another connection to the settlers who made their homes here long ago. We look forward to these short white hours of middle-night bookended by birdsong and batwing.

Every ounce of light and jot of colour sprinkling through the lengthening days is longed for. We have waited all through the deepest darkness and dismal greys of winter for this time of year. We hope the weather will be generous. There is enough age in my bones to register the swift running of the seasons, so each year I relish the measured rolling in of summer, piece by delicious piece. It is a time when all the senses are topsy-turvy. I want to sup and savour the colours of the Inner Sound, catch the tinkling sound of rainbows on my tongue and drink in the pale mists for cuckoo song and swallow dive.

Often on windless evenings, in the last hours of brightness, remnant heat lingers in the ground, warming and releasing a potpourri of perfumes that thrusts and seeps through windows and doors still open to the world. As temperatures drop, the air fills with scent, not the warm headiness of sun-brushed bog myrtle, clover, chamomile and thyme, but a vibrant, sharp, almost resinous smell. It is so strongly redolent of sugar and lemons it could be sipped as a liqueur. This crystal-sharp perfume ushers in the pale nights and laminates the silvers and greys of the simmer dim. At the heart of middle-night it solders the layers together with aromatic platinum and white gold.

At the solstice there is no true darkness. There are no stars, the moon pales to almost nothing and the Northern Lights are banished. For just a few hours everything is drained of colour. The living and non-living become enfolded in metallic magic – mercury, lithium, pewter, steel, tin and chromium. A new world emerges, one in which it is easy to imagine where summer fairies dance, bog sprites gyre and phantoms caper. Rock seems alive. Outside, I am convinced I hear earth sounds as well as the wind. Once again, we see deer roam down from the hills. They move carefully through mist and leaf, breath snorting, tails flicking and bright eyes seeking. They come in the dimming to lie in cool blankets of dew. Threading through the mists is a persistent insect flit and flutter. Night fliers scoop and scour, feeding in the grey, glimmering, crepuscular airs. The simmer dim is a myopic time of otherness, a blurry, indistinct trans-space, and overhead the firmament is little more than a dome made of Pentelic marble.

This is midsummer, these are our most flower-filled days, when the nights are not dark but almost white. The silvery middle-night hours illume the ground enough for us to wander torch-less. It is possible then to feel more open than ever to the existence of a closely interconnected living world, one that operates in quite different time frames to our own. And in the midnight dimming my life seems no more or no less important than the tiny flowers of bog rosemary or glistening sundew. I am just one tiny fragment of a greater whole.

*

Light and scent become stratified in the lower atmosphere and their strength and intensity vary throughout the day. There are bands of perfume, just as there seem to be bands of colour and air temperature. I watch them swish around the crofts and over surrounding bogland until they vanish into the hills. I see them swirl over the sea currents in the Inner Sound and away to the Minch and imagine hidden messages sent between mainland and islands. Summer's light can be intoxicating, disturbing and comforting all at the same time.

In recent years some of our Highland summer days have been stifling. In midsummer 2018, for the first time since we moved here, fierce sunlight and cloudless skies drove me to my bedroom. I drew the curtains, cutting off a peacock-blue sky. My head throbbed. It was almost ten o'clock, and although an evening sea breeze was grating the heaviness and humidity, my room still felt very warm. As always, the window was open wide and the curtains ruffled in the moving air. I lay down and let the blessed darkness soothe my headache caused, I think, by simply too much sunlight. I had been out all day, counting vegetation species and trying to identify grasses coming into flower. In the windless heat, even with sunhat and sunglasses, I had been squinting.

In the lengthy days of summer, the temptation to remain outside for as much as possible is overpowering. Everyone works on their crofts and in their gardens. Children stay up late, and from my darkened cave I could hear them playing down by the bridge. The smell of a late barbeque followed their laughter.

Rob came in with a glass of water. 'Can you hear the kids?' he asked. 'They're having fun with bikes up and down the road. I remember that age. I'd peg a piece of plastic to the fork so it'd catch at the wheel spokes, and I'd pretend to be riding a motor-bike. Well, it sounds a bit like that. Must be the kids.' I sipped the water and listened. For a few moments there were only squeals and shouting, and then another sound seeped through our memories, a sound not made by children. I sat up and, frustrated that only warped snippets of the strange noise were filtering through, went to the lounge. The sound seemed to be coming from below the house. 'Rob! Listen to this!' We stepped out onto the lawn. Imagine running a fingernail along the thin edge of a comb. Click, click, click, click. Ah yes, the bike trick. But then it changed. Crex, crex, crexex, crex – a sound I had not heard since an Irish summer holiday long ago. 'Corncrakes! Oh, my goodness, we have corncrakes!'

Corncrakes are small birds that migrate from wintering grounds in Africa to breed in grassy peat bogs, marshy meadows, and fields with tall crops. They like nettles, long grasses, knapweeds and clumps of irises, vegetation that is not too dense but more than twenty centimetres tall. Land managed more intensively for hay with high grass content or for silage is less attractive; overgrazed meadows not inviting at all. The corncrake has a Latin name that literally sounds like the call of a male, *Crex crex*. The birds were once known as the 'sound of night fields', but their numbers were so reduced by changing and intensifying agricultural practices that they all but vanished from the British mainland. They were once so numerous the sound of their night-time singing must have been as noisy as crickets in the Mediterranean maquis. The decline was so severe that by 1970 their geographical range had contracted disastrously. Breeding pairs could be found only in Orkney, the Outer Hebrides, Mull, Islay and Jura, Coll and Tiree, and, very rarely, along the isolated fringes of the mainland's northwest coast. But with help from conservation agencies, who have encouraged corncrake-friendly farming, their numbers have risen.

For many years, across the country, rising numbers of sheep and changes to the timing and method of cutting hay and other crops meant available ground for nesting was severely reduced. Now that the South Erradale flock sizes have fallen considerably and the acreage of ground left ungrazed or with limited grazing has increased, more favourable habitats have been created. And so the corncrakes have returned to the valley.

That night they sang without ceasing through the dusk and pale shimmer of night and on until boisterous rabbles of sparrows cracked open the morning. The following day we discussed what we had heard. I had hardly slept. With my bedroom window wide open, I had lain on the bed listening to the calling corncrakes, imagining myself in Ireland among small turf-roofed cottages and waist-high fields of hay. But this is the twenty-first century, there are huge tractors and enormous baling machines and lots of livestock. Most farmers and crofters cut early for silage. There was only one possible reason the corncrakes had returned. Our decision to keep animals from the croft had enabled the sward to grow. Now, with vegetation deep and thick and tall, these rare birds had seized the opportunity and, for one night at least, had decided to stay.

The presence of corncrakes was the reinforcement I needed for our plan to leave the croft uncut and ungrazed until late summer or early autumn. The more I thought about it, the more it made sense. As the croft bloomed there would be plenty of food and shelter for these secretive birds. In addition, the wildflower and grass seeds would be spread around the croft, adding to the 'seed bank' in the soils and future-proofing the fields. I discussed the idea of giving the croft a late cut with Cathma. 'It was always done that way in the old days,' she said. 'The animals were kept off the crofts all summer. Some fields were given over to hay, others to food crops or barley.' We chatted some more about the notion of corncrake-friendly hay meadows, about the losses since her childhood, most seemingly unnoticed by people in general. Two big questions planted themselves squarely in front of me – how on earth would Rob and I cut the hay since we did not even possess a tractor, let alone any cutting machinery, and when should the work be done. 'I'll ask the boys from Opinan if they'd be happy to come and cut for hay, at end of August perhaps,' said Cathma, 'You've no need to fret!'

The 'boys' from Opinan, young crofting sons of Donald

'Duck' Mackenzie, sent word back quickly – yes, they would be happy to come with their father later in the summer to assess what could be done. 'For now,' said Cathma, 'You'll have to watch and wait!'

Over the next few weeks, as the croft meadows matured, the corncrakes sang. At first only males calling and calling, crex, crex, crexex, crex, and then a single female, and another. I slipped out into the simmer dim again and again to listen. Crumpled and crackly as their voices were, I could only think of them as a blessing and a validation for the changes we had made. But, try as I might, I did not catch sight of these secretive birds.

Then one evening I wandered slowly around the riverside meadow. The sky was paling from mother-of-pearl into a white night. The sound of my walking sticks click-clacked like yellow rattle. There were still several weeks of growing to come but already the sward reached over my knees. I saw no signs at all of corncrakes. Doubt crept in and I began to wonder whether I had imagined the whole business and everything, literally everything, was a dream – the silver nights, the warm air, the heady aromas, the sound of the river more like bells ringing than water splashing. Then I paused to listen again. Two hinds rose up from their riverbank nest-hollow, spraying droplets of pearl and silver everywhere, and as they dashed towards the sea a small brown bird ran in the opposite direction.

(ii) Midges rise and cuckoos depart

As we slide away from the solstice the weather flickers, in and out, up and down; heat and searing light rapidly give way to cooler days bringing sea fogs or downpours. Rains arrive sharply and leave floodily. The land begins to sweat with insects. On some days the atmosphere seethes with them. They try to fill every space, every tiny corner. They sneak behind my glasses and under my hat. Clouds formed almost entirely of midges swell and swish around the croft.

Cuckoo voices fall silent as these midge hordes arrive. The voids left by their departing songs are filled by curlew-trill, corncrake-crex and midge-mist. Despised and feared by many, the tiny flies – known here as the *meanbh-chuileag* – can arrive any time from late spring until late summer. If spring was warm and wet, midges arrive early, often appearing in May, and by the solstice are rising in such fearsome numbers they appear to coat everything and everybody. In the main, a cold, dry spring prevents early hatching and the midge-armies arrive later – as June passes into July. At the height of their breeding season midges can find their way indoors even if all our windows and doors are kept closed, but on a hot summer's night I will close the bedroom curtains across my open window before turning on a bedside light. This fools them, mostly.

The females bite, taking blood from livestock animals, deer and humans. A single nasty sharp prick from midge mandibles acting like saws leaves a red and extremely itchy lump. Multiple bites bring misery. As they cut into the skin, saliva is secreted to prevent coagulation of blood and our bodies respond by releasing histamines. When we first came to the Highlands, we instantly reacted to bites, persecuted by the need to scratch. Now, they merely raise a few red spots that vanish almost as quickly as they come.

Blood is taken to enable egg-laying in the spongy ground of peat bogs, in wet meadows and in the damp soils of woodland, and if conditions are favourable there may be several phases of hatching. Northwest Scotland, with its high annual rainfall, generally cloudy and humid summers and vast areas of suitably wet and boggy ground, is famous for the seasonal storm clouds of biting midges. They are most active at dawn and sunset, or in the low light and calm conditions of a damp grey day. The Scottish Midge Forecast collects data from midge traps and weather stations, combining the information to give a picture of activity across the country. In South Erradale and along the Wester Ross coast we suffer less than most. On a bright and breezy summer's day the midges stay hidden. And there are so few breeze-less days here by the sea that we are not subject to the same level of persecution that bedevils inland areas where there is more woodland. *Culicoides impunctatus* prefers moist and cloudy conditions, so the birch and oak woodlands and sheltered coves of Badachro and Shieldaig are more suitable than the open and windy salted coastal crofts of South Erradale.

*

The summer solstice is a crest, a summit, a passage. The first half of the year always outpaces me. In the weeks leading into the solstice I dawdle and focus on spring, yet yearn for high summer. I savour every long day of light, and want each and every one of them to slow. But the solar year drives relentlessly onwards, and with a sudden blooming of flowers and joy the solstice passes. A few deep breaths and it is gone. Orchid numbers dwindle and their pink carpet thins, but now flag irises wave from the ditches and cotton grasses nod in accompaniment to the layers upon layers of birdsong, scent and gentle light. Even on the dullest days, light floods in from the sea, bound up in rolling banks of cloud and waves that shove and push each other along the shore. The days begin to incrementally shrink of course, an imperceptible loss at first, but there are weeks of growing before our meadows are mature enough and ready for hay-cutting. There is a lot of summer yet to come, a lot of growth, a lot of sun and hope.

The cuckoos disappear quickly at the end of June. I have never witnessed them leaving. Their departure registers as a sudden gap in the air, an emptiness in the valley. A project run by the British Trust for Ornithology (BTO) followed tagged cuckoos migrating from sub-Saharan Africa to Scotland and identified two main migration routes, one via Italy, the other through Spain. The BTO concluded the most successful birds arriving this far north were more likely to have flown along the spine of Italy. It is fascinating to imagine their flight over Italy's picture-postcard landscapes, over all its ancient Roman glories, to come to our semi-wilded small valley. According to the BTO, cuckoos may spend almost half their year in Africa, more than a third on migration and less than a fifth here. So little summer-time here to achieve so much. En route home, tagged adults have been recorded in Italy's Po Valley, where favourable conditions allow them to restore calorie deficits before the last leg of their journey. With my geographer's hat on, I think of the Po's beautiful fields and woodlands but also the old cities with some of the highest levels of air pollution in Europe. I cannot help but wonder if the pockets of pollution particulates they must fly through are absorbed into their bodies as they were into my mother's.

Quite how the cuckoo young know when it's time to abandon Erradale and fly south is a mystery to me. I watch the small birds in our garden and out on the croft feeding their young as fast and frantically as they can, and look out for outsized 'cuckoo' babies, but I've yet to see one. There are many tiny and bedraggled parents about, likely candidates for the extreme parenting cuckoo young would need. They remind me of myself, exhausted into dish-cloth grey by four small children, born within a year or so of each other.

★

One evening at the cliff-top I watched the sea smooth into aluminium then a peculiar and unsettling pink. Overhead the sky was a strange mixture of purple and grey; the blushing sea seemed lit from below somehow. I puzzled at the change and, as I watched, pink was slowly sifted into the colours of a wolf pelt. It was too cold for midges – they had settled down among the vegetation, sheltering from the sea breeze – but moths flick-ered in and out of sight. As I faced the sea I caught their flickerings in the corner of my eye. I turned around; their small dense clouds in the shelter my body seemed to cast a non-shadow, a drift of ivory and white petals, whispering to each other in ghost-wing murmurs.

I started off for home. There were many voices filtering through the cooling air: night-time singers, corncrakes rasping, and the strange winnowing ululations of snipe gently spreading across the bogland surrounding our croft. The songs of snipe are wistful and strange, more alien to me than those of corn-crakes. My grandfather once told me they sang laments to the lost souls and spirits of the land. He said he did not mean the spirits of humans but those of 'trees and fish and birds and bugs – the ones we should be listening to'. I walked back home wrapped in wistful music and salted myrtle and deep memories of other bogs and other shores.

★

From the solstice onwards, sunsets flip and track back along the spine of islands we can see from home, the solar year marked by the Outer Hebrides and, in the darker half of the year, by the Isle of Skye. As we dance further into July the summer days are often silvery green, wet and mild, perfect midge weather. Thick clouds arrive to dampen and dull the gloss of summer light. But compensation comes in great lungfuls of thick, rich perfume. Bog myrtle scent is ubiquitous – I smell it everywhere I go – but soon other scents rise and swirl about. The aromas of growing grass and wildflowers blooming begin to overwrite everything and everyone.

I remember such summers from camping trips – damp, wet, green. As an undergraduate, I camped on the shore of Loch Awe with friends. We fished, cooked and ate our catch and prepared to spend the evening chatting about where to go next and which mountain would be tackled first. For about an hour, we planned the days to come, and relaxed. Then, as the evening cooled, a mist began to pool on the surface of the loch, growing quickly as we watched. Within minutes the 'mist' enveloped us, becoming a shroud of biting needles. We were driven away. It was a severe lesson, one that has never been forgotten. Twenty years later, Edwin Morgan's poem 'Midge' was published. It described our group of poor student adventurers perfectly, arrogant in youth, naive and inexperienced. Each summer, when the first midge-dense clouds appear in the shaded hollows or under the trees in our little patch of woodland, I think of these lines and remember the shock of Loch Awe.

The loch lies silent, the air is still.
The sun's last rays linger over the water
and there is a faint smirr, almost a smudge
of summer rain . . .

See the innocents, my sisters,
the clumsy ones, the laughing ones,
the rolled-up sleeves and the flapping shorts,
there is even a kilt . . .

(iii) Flag irises bloom

The croft glows. The joyous delicious scent of life is all around, especially in sheltered sunlit spots. Daily growth becomes almost visible. I convince myself it is audible too. This summer surge comes suddenly. The burst of insect life is synchronous with the greening, part of the rich, dense partnership that is the envelope of planetary life. Within the greenery and standing tall are bright yellow flags of iris, crowding in ditches and wet flushes. I enjoy their defiance in the face of tidy crofts, crofting grant require-ments and determined grazers. 'Guerrilla flowering,' I say to Rob. The yellow flowers, untidily folded handkerchiefs, are attractive and soon covered with insects: crowds of tiny bugs peppering every yellow petal.

As days pass, the height of the sward increases swiftly; chamo-mile, mayweed, vetch and yellow rattle seek the sun; grasses nod, myriad forms and colours beginning to outpace the rushes. It is a time of profusion and abundance. While each afternoon lopes along, the growth of green and yellow life is an undertone to the day's work, audible despite the sea breezes. The land swells; it is succulent, fleshy and verdant. Like the wildlife and domesticated animals, we wallow in it all, savouring the juiciness. There is so much growth, every step across the croft squeaks and flickers.

Though richly colourful and noisy, this living landscape of

valley crofts and grazed moorlands is attenuated and somewhat diminished. The ancient extensive forests are long gone, soils are largely thin and acidic. In places there is only a thin covering of blanket peat. On overgrazed crofts only tough nutrient-poor grasses and rushes grow. Too many sheep selectively eating the more nutritious plant species over many generations has reduced biodiversity and impoverished grazing land. Although the legacy of soil loss, woodland clearance and centuries of grazing and burning is apparent all across this place, somehow wildlife finds a way to thrive. There are remarkable and often surprising abundances. I see them threaded through the crofted landscapes like gold woven into tapestry. Without doubt, to me they feel relatively rich and remarkable compared to the once denuded and polluted landscapes around my childhood home. Like so many of us, I measure presence or absence in the light of lived experiences, especially those of youth. My baseline for how I perceive abundance is derived from what I saw and experienced in my younger years, and this phenomenon tends to be the same for all of us. Summers were always warm and sunny, my sister and I caught sticklebacks from the small pond in our local park, and only blackbirds and robins sang in the gardens. There were no cuckoos, swallows or pink ragged robin. In comparison, life on the croft feels dense, richly abundant to those days, but it is a false construct. There has been so much loss here too.

Having made the decision to leave the fields uncut and allow summer to do her work, I began to record the types and number of plant species on the croft using the same few plant identification books I had read for decades, in particular an old battered copy of *The Wild Flowers of Britain and Northern Europe* by Fitter, Fitter and Blamey. Counting and identifying flora needs expertise, patience, time and great care. I am a poor botanist, a novice to the flora of field and meadow, although I know plants of peat bog and hill very well and much, much more about the micro-scopic forms of British flora, the shapes of their pollen and spores, the microtopography of their lives. Yet even to my inex-perienced eye it quickly became apparent that alterations to the level of grazing intensity had begun to influence the floristic composition on the croft. Changing the grazing regime appeared to directly affect the number of plant species growing in the meadows. Furthermore, the species lists grew incrementally year on year. Just as the flowers themselves open in summer sun, their significance to the health of the croft and importance to wildlife began slowly to unfurl.

Identification and counting continued whenever possible throughout the growing season. Bog species grow well on the peat banks in the small *pàirc* but there were many more varieties of grass, sedge and moss in our fields. Even if I could not ascribe a name to a new find it was added to the counts along with a description, a sketch and a photograph. I became more and more convinced the arrival of new species and variations in their numbers (both measures of biodiversity) were a result of the change in management. Different types and levels of grazing across the mixture of micro-habitats, coupled with the range of soil charac-teristics and patterns of drainage, appeared to have encouraged varying heights of sward across the fields and enhanced species diversity. Year on year, I counted more plant species. The croft filled with insects, birds and other wildlife. Everywhere felt busier. Tallies of plant species showed incremental increases in abundance and species richness. In addition, the height of the plants across the croft, a rough guide to biomass, appeared to have improved. After just one season of restricted summer grazing, yellow rattle (*Rhinanthus minor*) appeared in the lower meadow by the river. Rattle is thought to be indicative of positive change and is often introduced by conservationists to benefit wildflower meadows.

Hemiparasitical on grasses, the plant weakens them so other wild-flowers have a greater chance of growing and setting seeds. The strange name comes from the sound made by its seed cases knocking against one another in the wind. It is said that when yellow rattle 'rattles', hay is ready to cut.

In a pesticide-free sward there is a vast unseen near-microscopic underworld inhabited by bugs as well as fungi. I began to hope the resurgence above ground was being matched by similar improvements below the surface. Early clues had come from the piles of dung produced by cattle and horses offering homes to different types of beetles. They were riddled with holes or entirely crumbled by insect and worm activity. It was hard not to be fascinated by the power of dung in attracting all kinds of insects. 'Poo,' I proudly announced, 'properly active poo, is a sure sign that our soils are healthy too.' I was optimistic.

For much of the year the potential for success and survival is reduced to a thin compression of vegetative life; grasses and flowers die back into a blonde thatch which protects the soil surface from heavy rains and provides shelter for hibernating insects over the winter months. But in summer the upward growth of grasses and flowers transforms the mat into a tall, dense ecosystem, like a miniature forest. There is as much vertical variation in the layers created by different plants above ground and in the soil layers below as there is in a jungle. Red River Croft, with its variety and patchwork of micro-habitats, could hold more than a tonne of bug-life in summer. And the more I knelt to peer into these smaller places the more optimistic I became. Even a partially flourishing meadow seemed to me to be a form of rewilding, helped by wildflowers like yellow rattle. 'Guerrilla flowering,' I said out loud again, basking in the cama-raderie of new-found plants and insects.

Wherever possible during spring, using temporary fencing,

we had kept animals away from the river's edge, apart from the ford where they could go to drink. In response, the field margins and riverbanks were reinvigorated with gorse, a number of tree saplings, small shrubs, including dwarf willow and bog myrtle, and a greater array of wildflowers such as flag iris, knapweed, angelica and cow parsley. Where once the banks were tidily maintained by grazing and cutting, they now looked messy, but I was happy to see all the renewed growth. Where a short stretch of river was once straightened for about one hundred and fifty metres, it began to wiggle, trying almost immediately to resume its natural modus operandi. The effect on insect and bird numbers was clear – as the riverbank area transformed, it became a unique habitat in its own right. The close-cropped baize-like turf once bordering the river vanished under an abundance of thick, lush life. Ultimately, in the years to come, the river itself will benefit from the extra shade. Riverside plants provide more habitats for insects and, in return, this encourages more fish; the fish themselves prefer darker, shady places to rest and hide from prying eyes and a full sun. Well-vegetated river margins soak up greater volumes of water and help slow down destructive flow, so the river's capacity to handle storm floods will also eventually improve. It slowly began to dawn on me – on a very small-scale Red River Croft was rewilding. It was almost unnoticeable to anyone beyond the croft fences but I knew, and so did the wild-life.

Over generations of farming sheep, more and more land is needed to rear the same number of animals, because intense grazing pressure results in the loss of 'good' grass species, lowering biomass and detrimentally affecting soil quality. Such effects are cumulative and can be seen across large swathes of upland Britain. To combat this, many farmers supplement with nutritious animal feeds. The traditional pre-Clearance ways of farming, where much smaller numbers of cattle and other animals grazing mixed pasture, woodland, riverbanks and loch-sides, maintained a relatively high level of species-rich habitats. Two hundred years on, and although for many rewilding equates only to tree-planting and forest management, others espouse a return to those methods of land management. While we cannot rewild on the scale of estates such as England's Knepp in West Sussex or Alladale in Sutherland, or refashion our farming way of life to keep wildlife and nature at its heart, as espoused by James Rebanks, the small-scale changes already seen over just a few years on Red River Croft are a good start.

*

Forty years ago I returned home from the tropics utterly changed. My perspectives on the natural world were trans-formed, my eyes opened in high mountain jungles virtually untouched by human activity. New Guinea is an island south of the equator and north of Australia. Lying on the 'Ring of Fire' it is tectonically unstable and in the late 1970s its remote interior remained difficult to access. So topographically extreme and so dense was the montane forest cover of New Guinea it had only been possible to travel to the central mountain ranges since first contact in the late 1950s. For tens of centuries the interior had been deemed inaccessible by outsiders. It was unmapped and unexplored, and for very good reason.

However, people did live there, in small sustainable commu-nities, reliant on the forests for hunting and gathering the materials needed for life. But they also created small spaces they called 'gardens' to grow crops such as sweet potato. For a time, as part of my doctoral research, living with one small commu-nity, I learned how they gardened and hunted, about the sheer profusion of living organisms, about the deep and complex interconnections between people and place, and how living in harmony with the non-human required a wholly different approach to the 'Western' way of life I had been born into.

Four decades on, and each summer in this small place, as insects rise with every step as we walk through the croft, I am reminded of those tropical garden plots. Roaming gangs of small birds hurtle down into the thick meadow growth and then lift up to sit on the wires. Up, down, up and down; they weave and thread themselves through the tumbles of honey-coloured air. Glints of gold and white strike out from their bodies as they twist over and over; up, down, up and down. As often as possible, from a large boulder-seat close to the river, happy in the company of ghosts and unremembered stories of the stones lying behind me, Dram at my side, I watch the wildlife passing by. Despite the lack of trees, but because of the ripening meadows, I am reminded again and again of New Guinea, of the fecundity of that forest long ago and of the interactions between living organisms.

★

I have managed to identify more than seventy flowering meadow plants growing across the croft. The lists do not include grasses, sedges and rushes, for my skills are still too poor, but I have drawn many species in pencil and ink, trying to learn their individual natures. Each one is utterly beautiful. In the structure of the flowering meadow I see a rainforest in miniature and feel blessed. There are distinct bands, from the flowering tops to the layers of soil chock-full of roots and fungi, all of them brimming with insect life.

The abundance of high summer is heady, and by mid-July growth can be almost waist high. Heavy rains are more common now and the meadows become saturated. Water soaks my jeans even above my wellies. It is hard work wading through the thick tangles, especially with my sticks and mistimed steps. I feel I am swimming through wind-whipped waist-high waves of plant life. Gulping in the air is akin to ducking my head under water. It takes me deeper and deeper until I am almost fully assimilated, absorbed by meadow.

But I shake my head clear and carry on, intent on counting plants. Then unseen forces, from the ever-present sea and sky songs of the west to the very ground beneath my feet, tug and pull. I am completely unable to resist their calls or to fight the currents of energy streaming from high mountain peaks to the rippling thicknesses of distant blues. So off I go, slowly and painfully to the sea, always down to the sea, where wind, wave and birdsong coalesce, sewn together by the light.

2. Sunrise over Cnoc an Fhuarain, Erradale, sunset over north Lewis, Outer Hebrides, Celtic month of Holly (July to August), Herb Moon

(i) Warm rains and thunder

In high summer the days slowly begin to contract. The night sky stretches to darkness and ushers in stars that have been missing for a few weeks. Coolness ripples in the midnight air. Our weather changes, becoming more agitated and uncertain. Understandably, by mid-July on Overside and around much of Wester Ross, most farmers and crofters have already cut for silage. As soon as dry spells are needed for haymaking, great gouts of cloud spill in from the Atlantic. Warm low-pressure systems fill with oceanic moisture and create enormous billowing thunderclouds. The threat of rain is ever-present. Summer fills with water.

Often these threats dissipate into mist and greyness but every so often an intense and damaging summer storm blows in from the west or southwest. Usually these unruly weather systems are relatively short lived, but they can be much more damaging than those of winter, with deluges and destructive winds. The reason for this is their sudden arrival. They run in quickly, dump their load of rain, and disappear. Rainstorms in August can be almost equatorial in nature, with torrential downpours, thunder, lightning and flash floods. It is hard, mean weather for a gentle west coast summer. Occasionally a deep North Atlantic low-pressure system will drag in so much rain that the road from Gairloch to Overside becomes flooded at the Kerry River and for a time, with the bridge inaccessible, we are cut off and become an island.

In 2015 one such thunderous summer storm rolled over the valley, ripping branches from the trees. The Red River burst its banks. Where the floodwaters cascaded from the croft to Port na Sgotha, they created a fifteen-metre-wide waterfall which boiled and barged its way through to the sea. Danielle's ponies, on a short respite visit at the time, had to be rescued from a raised bank in the middle of the lower fields. All around them was rushing and rising black floodwater. The Shetlands looked on with disdain, watching the kerfuffle safely from their sensible perch high on the old embankment, while we tempted the silly horses through the hock-deep stramash with treats and buckets of mash. Cindy stared hard at her silly fellow creatures and they stared hard at us with our tempting buckets.

A great branch got caught on one of the meanders and, over the following few hours, gathered a heap of debris. Boulders were shunted into new positions. When the water finally subsided, there was a new structure suspended more than a metre over the river channel, like a sluice gate made of wood, turf, heather, rope and twine; a story in collage.

After the deluge, floodwaters drained quickly, rushing away to the west. The whole valley appeared to be smoking, as if in the aftermath of a huge fire. The croft steamed. The meadows were completely flattened. There were fresh gouges in the riverbanks. Sediment, debris and dead wildlife were strewn everywhere. The whole place had been upended, shaken and reorganised. Hundreds of birds descended to pick at the mess, from small meadow birds to great black-backed gulls. But while the storm had brought death it delivered potential for renewal. Fine sediments added mineral nutrients. Lumps of peat, leaves, dead animals, and turf added organic matter. Together they would eventually enrich the flood meadows. Gradually, over the following days, grasses and rushes perked up and the croft began to return to normal. Clouds of insects took to the air. Gangs of birds sang loudly. One by one, the wildflowers stood to attention.

The heat of that wild stormy day eventually softened into opalescent mistiness. I headed down to the shore with Rob and Dram, hoping to find a cool breeze to counteract the thundery heaviness remaining in the air. The boundaries between sea, sky and earth were blurred and familiar, reliable markers such as gates and fence posts rubbed out. The evening wrapped us in a silent fog the colour of sea-aster while mysterious lavender vapours slid over a slate sea. Large lichen-covered and thrift-tufted boulders were silver tipped, machair gleamed with white gold and the sea was as smooth and motionless as a crucible filled with mercury. The thick, soupy air began to stir. I looked up through the haze to a linger of orange light. Swirls of smoky violet and indigo moved as if watercolour paints were being mixed and the effect was wholly disorientating. Strangely, there was no birdsong, no sounds other than an occasional sploshing of water.

We lit a small fire from driftwood. The growing flames were oddly vivid and luminous and almost inappropriate in the stillness; the smoke rose vertically and merged with the haar. We sat and said nothing, both of us listening now to the sigh of vapours and swish of sea, and the odd crackle of burning bark.

Every so often the air above our heads cleared as the mists began to shrivel upwards into tatters of small pink and purple clouds. Now and again we heard a faint rumble of distant thunder. Here and there on the quicksilver sea were spots of scarlet, like drops of blood.

We heard a splashing sound. Dram was instantly alert, ears raised. There was a flash of sable and a ring of turbulence on the surface. An otter was coming towards us, head up, followed by a high loop of back, then a dive which left an imprint of tail-twitch on the water. The otter clambered onto a large flat-topped boulder just a few metres in front of us. He had something held firmly in his mouth. As he turned, we could see it was an enormous crab whose body seemed larger than the otter's head. He devoured his meal in a staccato percussion of crunching and cracking. All around us it was breath-calm and quiet. We debated in whispers, wondering whether the otter knew he was being watched. We agreed he probably did but the usual rules of engagement did not seem to exist in that misty, spectral space. For days the braids of life had been a funfair of spinning colour and sound, sunlit and filled with motion, culminating in thundery havoc, floods and upheaval. But in that moment by the ottery sea, shrouded in mauve and violet mists, the world quietened with a long deep silver sigh.

★

In 2021 we had one of our warmest Augusts yet. High humidity levels enhanced the cloying, dense, well-heated lower atmosphere. It reminded me of the tropics. One day, after a forecast had predicted thunderstorms for Northeast Scotland but not here, I wandered to the top gate, where I could look out across the croft. There was a long line of late and tattered flowering flag irises in the old ditch that marked the field boundary across the river. It looked like a thin strip of bold yellow paint. The afternoon had grown incrementally tense and began to feel potentially thunderous. To my left, garden birds were squabbling and yelling raucously from the hedge around the house. Gangs of goldfinches fought each other fiercely up and down and around the field. The weather was making them tetchy. Soon the view over the croft garden hedge began to change. Bright cerulean skies were quickly overtaken by high, building clouds. It was hard to judge their height, but in relation to the thousand-metre summits of Torridon along the jagged southeast horizon, they appeared to stretch up for at least ten kilometres. Then the cloud tops disappeared altogether. They were building swiftly into masses of indigo. Beneath the darknesses of the upper atmosphere, bright white cumuli roiled and boiled, merging then separating. From what I could tell, the whole mass of cloud, now the colour of dried mussel shells, was coming our way.

Once indoors I went upstairs to watch from the attic. Silvery-grey shelf clouds began to extend as a storm cell, with textbook structure and definition, slowly emerged from the blue-black inky skies. Cooler outflow winds blew in through the open attic window as the shelf clouds spread over Maol Ruadh. The head of the Erradale valley vanished. At the same time, the sky began to swirl and pedestal clouds appeared, with multiple lightning strikes around the rotating updrafts. The whole mass had developed into an independent system with a well-defined, almost ground-hugging base as it moved rapidly down the valley towards us. The centre came closer and, as it did, more lightning strikes to earth and cloud to cloud stung my eyes.

The change in pressure was powerful and swift enough to induce a quite unpleasant headache and instigate sudden changes in wind direction as various parts of the storm cell passed by.

I watched dozens and dozens of swallows streaming over the croft despite the lightning, feeding whenever the gusting winds came and went. They appeared to be tracking the wind direction and therefore the storm's passage. A combination of downdrafts and changes to air pressure, temperature and humidity was raising clouds of insects; it was these the swallows chased. In the rear-flanking downdraft, sharply delineated shelf clouds formed once again. Then, as if a single great gunmetal-grey blanket had been thrown over us all, torrential rain arrived and obscured any further semblance of form or structure. Lightning struck the river three times, so close I was temporarily blinded. And still the swallows danced.

This was the largest single summer storm to hit South Erradale in recent years. It was violent, aggressive, beautiful and radiant all at the same time. It is rare to see such a tempest develop and display all the classic features and structures so brazenly. I kept thinking of the damage the rains could have caused and what might have happened to the legions of rapidly growing grasses and flowers in our hay meadows.

Later, as the valley steamed, we went to have a look. The entire croft was flattened. But only a few days later, under the brightest azure and sapphire-blue sky, the grasses stood tall, their stems clacking in conversation, their flowers held high to greet the sun.

(ii) Plovers nest again in warm sand

Early one morning I headed out for the beach at Opinan. A day of heat had been forecast but the morning was dew-drenched. Large, fat droplets of water clung to nodding meadow grasses, and even where sunlight had not yet reached the bottom fields, they sparkled. The air was still, but full of vapour. Beyond the cliff edge there was an avalanche of pale blue. In the distance the sea was a smooth and shining mass of opal and moonstone, horizon-less. Shadows of purple were thronging in the coastal moorland and northwards through the haze. Dram ranged back and forth, excited at the prospect of the beach, impatient at my slow pace. I called him to my side. This morning's pather had a purpose. According to a neighbour's friend, ringed plovers had begun to nest again. Although a late brood, eggs were sitting in the sands close to the sea-log seat. I badly wanted to see them for myself. The beach had become holiday-busy and I wondered if the story was true. Of course Dram and I would both have to be patient and as stealthy as possible.

My face and lips were catching spiders' webs as I walked, single strands of dewy filigree that were lifting in the warming air. I could not tell whether the tickling sensation was web or condensing moisture, and as I brushed them away I was reminded of the empty spider realms in the mountains. The Seaweed Road to Opinan was busy with birds. Dunlins, sanderlings, rock pipits and oystercatchers ran about the rocks to my left, wheatears and stonechats flitted from fence post to fence post on my right. For them all, the day was well underway.

Approaching the sands, beyond the gangs of ringed plovers running back and forth to the sea, I could see wreckage. The sea-log seat had somehow been dismantled. Various bits and pieces were strewn about, but the log itself had vanished, along with the branches of silver birch and Scots pine Rob had used to make a backrest. Only an empty and bedraggled space, scattered with a few remnant shells and stones, remained. Hot anger welled up; I strode forward furiously. My change of speed and body language disturbed Dram, he had grown used to my slow pace. The resident ringed plovers scattered so I slowed down, anxious not to upset them any further. I spotted the log about fifty metres along the beach, above the high tide's strandline. This was most definitely not the work of the sea; in any case the previous night had been calm, with only a four-metre high tide.

Whoever had tried to take the great log must have given up. Standing over it in that moment I felt as if the damage had been done not to the sea-log seat but to me and to *my* body, to the plovers and all the other wildlife living here. It was a childish, unreasonable response, yet this near destruction of the seat and space around it felt intensely personal. The log was more than a seat. It had become a sanctuary, a refuge for reflection and thought, and for recovery, where I could watch the waves, scribble in my notebook or converse with the wind. When I was first taken ill, the sea-log seat became an objective to be reached each day, somewhere I could pause to rest before walking home again. The seat was somewhere to turn to when mountain summits were impossible, a place where the wilder world came to me and where I felt part of a much broader wilderness. It was here I watched otters scurry past, ringed plovers run back and forth to feed and, on several occasions, encourage their young to venture out from nests made of sand. And the seat was not just mine, it belonged to our community of people and wildlife.

I roamed the beach for other bits and pieces and tried to figure out why anyone would want to demolish a deliberately placed and well-used construction. At the bay's northern end is a relatively flat but small area of dune grassland. The main path to the shore weaves through the dunes there and follows a small burn fringed by watercress and irises; it leads to the machair and a good place to camp. It is a pretty place and, to many visitors, a wild one. Approaching the 'campsite' from the beach, I could see a large stone-ringed firepit dug into the turf. In it were remnants of the curved pine, reduced to dislocated and shrivelled charcoal stumps. The long, curling silver-birch branch lay nearby, unburnt but pitted by dozens of marks, probably made by a small camping axe.

I picked up the branch and tried to balance it on my shoulder but it kept slipping off as I staggered along the sand. Slowly and painfully I half carried and half dragged it back to the seat's original site. Then I returned for the log. It was too heavy to lift so I rocked it back and forth to free it from the grip of sand. Searching about for solutions I found a length of rope and looped it around one end. With every muscle straining and with much tugging and cursing, I slowly managed to haul the log through the soft sand and up the gentle slope of the upper beach. Eventually I managed to shove it back into place. To this day I have no idea where the strength to reconstruct the sea-log seat came from. For a while I lay flat in the sand, sweating and breathing hard, looking up at the sky. It was a quilt of cream lace embroidered with pink rosebuds, so I hid under it and cried until my anger and pain had subsided. Dram brought a few small stones and dropped them by my head, licked my face and my salty tears, lay down and waited. The plovers gathered and came closer.

Over the next few days, small gifts appeared: colourful stones, a few shells, feathers and wrinkles of dried seaweed. Where or who they came from, I will never know. I added a small chunk of polished driftwood as pale as ice, and fragments of birch bark that had been sliced off during the seat's dismantling. A long hawser was left by a high tide. Rob helped me wrap it around the log and birch branch to secure the seat.

A week later, feeling pleased with my handiwork and enjoying the afternoon peace, certain there would be no more attempts to cause damage, I sat watching the shore birds come and go. Two plovers came up close, little more than a metre away, gently whistling and piping and unafraid. At the other end of the bay a lady appeared through the dunes and began to meander along the beach. She eventually came up from the water's edge and asked if she could join me, saying how she loved the spot and took every opportunity to sit there and while away a comfortable hour or so, bird spotting.

The woman introduced herself as a 'transient', and I was puzzled. She had a Highlander's accent, and although we had not met before it was evident she was very familiar with Opinan and the surrounding countryside. I asked about her transience, wondering what she meant. 'Ach, I'm someone with a holiday home and deep connections – decades of family holidays here,' she explained. 'But I've no permanent foothold, I just keep coming back, like the tide,' she continued, 'and I do like to come and sit here.' We talked some more about the wildlife and weather and the apparent boldness of ringed plovers. Then she asked if I knew the history of the log and who had created the seat. Who, she mused, had chosen this spot? Laughing, I confessed, and told her the history of the log, about how it was storm-gifted by the winter sea. Then I relayed my story of the seat's near destruction and how furious anger had been converted into kinetic energy and enabled me to rebuild the sea-log seat alone, when it had originally taken two of us. We laughed at my outrage, she with empathy, me with embarrassment.

We chatted for a while longer about our individual sense of belonging, she a Scot but not of this place, I the real transient and migrant, now rooted. 'I think that because you come here so often, and because you created this space and the seat, you've made an impression here,' she said. 'And there is no greater achievement than to have breathed additional life and form into a place. That's real belonging, the giving of your energy and love. It is a powerful thing to do, it's reciprocal, an exchange of everyday life between you and this spot.'

For the first time I saw myself through the eyes of another. This gentle and insightful lady was seeing me as a creature of this space, living within it and not on it. A peculiar tugging sensation ran from my feet into the sand and back up again, accompanied by a subtle, internal shifting. We sat for a while longer, easy in each other's company, doing nothing more than enjoying the warm sun and glinting sea, and occasionally commenting on the birds passing by. The afternoon began to ooze away when we finally said farewell.

I returned much later, just as the sun was setting. In summer a sunset is often still very warm as the residue of heat is exuded from the ground in colourful flags of apricot, cochineal and ruby. The log, branch and rope arrangement had suffered no further damage and was bathed in red-orange light. Shells and feathers gleamed in copper. In front of the seat the sand was crimson, behind it the machair was no longer green but a rich amber, and the grasses flickered with evening zephyrs. Westwards, the horizon was diffuse; there were no sharp edges; the islands and sea were smudged with humidity, and the sky overhead was smeared in a rainbow of colour.

The sunset deepened further. The ringed plovers ran back and forth, their orange legs blurring and voices gently piping, their delicate footprints overwriting the jumble of others left during the day. As usual they did not seem alarmed by my presence or by Dram. One plover paused and, for a fleeting moment, caught my eye before disappearing between clumps of lyme grass at the very edge of the dunes. When the adults stopped dashing up and down and settled to feed by the water's edge, I got up and crept slowly along the machair until I could see what they had been running to and from. There, secreted safely in a sandy hollow between three large stones, on this little beach littered with the evidence of a busy summer's day, were three fluffy chicks, the result of a second or possibly third attempt to raise a family. In that small, quiet moment I was no longer an observer but an accepted presence, a fragment of a wilder space, woven into it, braided with the moving lives and elementals that made it.

Strangely, though many people come and go and clearly use the seat, I have not met the lady there again. Gifts from the seashore are left as decorations from time to time, others are rearranged, and some of the gifts may indeed be hers, but each small change is a reminder that this tiny place is used and enjoyed. I have been told it is known as the 'contemplation seat', pictures of it have appeared on social media, taken by others who have visited Opinan, and a kind neighbour painted a scallop shell with the words 'our seat' and attached it to the backrest.

I add my own small beachcombing finds from time to time. Extra layers of stones have been built around it which are periodically reworked by storm waves and winds. Through these small acts of placing, finding, moving and resiting – a footprint here, a shell there, a stone here, a sprig of heather there – fragments of consciousness are added to the space, to its visual and aural energy, and to its wild spirit. Early one morning, an otter spraint appeared in the middle of the log; on another occasion, a long thick remnant of fleece. Holidaymakers have left painted stones, and eight painted lady butterflies once settled in a row on the backrest as if contemplating the view. I think about the people who have come to sit here, the creatures that have passed by, and wonder if they too realise how our lives are inextricably yet invisibly connected through space and time. Their abundant stories are added to mine and fill the air; they grow like layers in peat, or annual rings in trees.

*

On a beautiful silver-dazzle evening I walked once again to Opinan. At the beach, scouring gusts of warm wind by the water's edge prickled my bare arms and legs with millions of tiny silver needles. The air was alive with salt and water droplets, iodine and microscopic life. I was aware of my body soaking up light, sound, colour and energy. In tune with wave-rhythm, sun-pulse and wind-buffet came a sensation of sky-diving through clouds of purist white. The waves were brightly turquoise, topped with crests of royal icing. Dram danced in and out of the sea, birds rushed back and forth. We were alone on the shore and my mind drifted in and out of flickering gold and silver memories of childhood holidays.

I spotted others coming onto the beach and turned away from the glinting water. I sat on the sea-log seat at the edge of the machair and Dram lay down in the warm sand, his eyes closed. A family walked slowly along; a small child, parents and another adult with a walking stick, a grandparent perhaps. This little scene could have been a replay of my own family; happy days, fleeting and bright, captured in old cine films. The small child tottered back and forth, picking up shells, seaweed and handfuls of sand. There is a picture of me with my own mother doing exactly the same thing on a long-ago beach. It could be laid alongside photographs of our children and now our grandchildren, and with others of my grandparents – sepia glitter-children themselves – and I would be able to trace an instinctive love of the sea and shore in them all.

I realised the family of holidaymakers had gone and I had

missed them leaving. Dram and I had the beach to ourselves. The light was pearlescent and opaque, the beach sands dimpled and puckered by the passage of many feet and decorated with scraps of crisping seaweed, shells and small stones. The sand held the remnants of the day's meetings and glowed with radiating warmth, and among the divots, criss-crossing over our human footprints, were deer and otter tracks. Dram came close to sit at my feet, sensing my mood. Together we watched the plovers run about, their orange legs blurring, voices gently piping, adding their delicate footprints to the jumble of others. Once again, they did not seem alarmed by our presence. One pair came very close. Back and forth they ran to precisely the same spot – where, little more than a metre away, several large cobbles of pale-purple weathered sandstone sat proud of the peachy sands. When one bird ran to the sea, the other rushed back to the cluster of stones, and I realised this was where another late summer nest lay hidden. The sun began to sink, and gradually the sands turned from ash blonde to ochre and dun, the colours of a lioness. Returning from the sea once more, one of the plovers paused. For a fleeting moment he caught my eye, and then he vanished.

(iii) Wildflowers fade, grasses bloom

One summer holiday, more than fifty-five years ago, I gathered wildflowers and pressed them between the rough-grained pages of a large book, a practice frowned upon today. My mother taught me their 'secret' names. Much later, I learned their Latin ones. The book still exists, its contents crisp and faded. Whispers of my mother's voice are held within. Every time I open it, a little bit of dust and a few sweet memories fall out. Most of the contents are the remains of dried flowers and leaves, but on one page a few grasses are held fast to the paper with yellow Sellotape. To this day I can remember gathering them. With my mother and sister, I walked along a narrow path leading inland from the railway station at Borth in mid-Wales. Only the sound of jackdaws and a blustering wind accompanied us. We were heading for the banks of the River Leri, where a path would take us through tall bulrushes and reeds up onto a levee, from where we would be able to see the enormous stretch of Cors Fochno bog. The field had been ploughed but along its rim, between the black soil and footpath, in a strip no wider than my outstretched arms, tall grasses nodded in the breeze. One by distinctive one, I picked a dozen or more flowering grass stalks. There were pale-yellow trees, and tightly furled clusters, purple dangling bells and pointed green nodules. Each so different, so distinctive. They had strange and funny names – foxtail, cocksfoot, fescue, bent, rye – but the architecture of their flowering was beautiful to me. I gathered a bunch, tied them together with a long thin green leaf and later stuck them in my book.

There are other meadow-memories. Deep-seated images of my grandfather's hay meadows, whose blooming grasses were almost as tall as me. I must have been very young, for he was forced to give up his tenant farm when I was a small child. But one particular memory is clear, rich and colourful, and filled with the aromas of hot, dry grasses in a hot, dry meadow under a deep-blue sky. Grass seed fell from their stalks and stuck to my bare legs and arms and my clothes as I followed my grandfather through the field. He talked as he walked. 'Listen to the land; it whispers to us.' The memory is pale and golden and almost spiritual, a tiny remnant of a lost world and time that I, as a child, only brushed past. Now the world has changed almost beyond recognition.

Thoughts of those happy days returned with each traverse of the croft as I tried to identify the grasses and flowers growing through spring and summer, from the first upstart orchid blooms in April to the last flowering grasses before autumn. Grass names to be checked, pictures compared, flower spikelets gathered for reference. I could name the species tied in my old book but there seemed to be so many more out there on the croft.

Eventually my untidy records and notes about the sequence of flowering, number of species and height of the sward had yielded a numerical surprise. Year on year, what I perceived to be steady yet distinct and delightful increases in the abundance of plant species and in the height of mature meadow were confirmed. Flowers, many new to the croft, had appeared everywhere. By the end of 2017 the way forward became clear. Rob and I were certain the flatter riverside parts of the croft would be managed into the future as species-rich hay meadows.

The traditions of the scientific method and ecology – of identifying and counting plants – are well known. My early, mother-led learning culminated in familiarity with the mountain, coast and peat-bog floras of Britain, and later with those of the rainforests of Papua New Guinea; but on the croft, with only my trusty old and battered flora, and without the specialists of field and meadow to guide me, I would be sure to miss species and misidentify others. Field botanists are valuable. Without them we would know little about the magical world of plants and even less about what has been lost. Yet even a novice like me can see the differences between an overgrazed meadow and one left to flourish. Collectively, cumulatively, stealthily, across the generations, the losses in terms of biodiversity have been creeping up on us all for years.

In his book *Gairloch and Guide to Loch Maree*, Dixon implored the 'searchers of wildflowers' to resist picking or destroying plants. Many of the species found in this part of the world 'have become rare', he wrote, or have disappeared entirely, mostly since the introduction of sheep farming. Dixon also referred to a much earlier voice, Dr John Mackenzie, factor of the Gairloch Estate, who in a brief essay in the early nineteenth century – some two decades before he instigated new agricultural practices and laid out the crofting townships including South Erradale – described the abundances of shrubs and wildflowers as 'a perfect jungle'. Mackenzie waxed lyrical about varieties of *Epipactis* (helleborine), calling them 'a lovely drug'. But in 1883 Dixon found only one or two during his wanderings. Yet even as he expressed concerns about the loss of species once thought common and his anxiety about collectors, Dixon nonetheless recorded more than three hundred and sixty flowering plants. He included them in a list accompanying his essay. To me, this archive is a treasure against which I can measure my own counts. I might well rejoice in the rising numbers of flowering species on Red River Croft, but comparing my totals to Dixon's, we still fall a long way short. Even in the light of hope, generated by what was happening to floristic diversity on the croft, I must face up to and somehow address what has been lost. Although the meadows are recovering through a form of almost accidental, partial rewilding, the differences between my twenty-first-century counts and those of one hundred and forty years ago are stark.

Time and time again we use our own childhood memories and their store of information as the baseline against which we compare what we see, hear and feel in our adult lives. It is no different when thinking about plants and animals. I remember the bounty on my grandfather's farm, or the banks of the River

Leri, but blank out the dark minimalism of the chemical town where I grew up. Blackbirds and robins sang in trees darkened by pollution and grime, but I could escape to the fields behind our road to play in the stubble or seek for treasures in the hedgerows. The 'countryside' was still there, close by, but it was diminished and reduced by polluted air. The wildflowers, trees and shrubs, grasses and sedges growing on the croft, and the different species on the bogland and hill country all around us today, are bountiful in comparison to my old home town, but substantially attenuated compared to Dixon's accounts.

Having read the list of flowering plants in the book about Gairloch, my mind was filled with thoughts of loss. I lamented what seemed to have vanished since Dr Mackenzie wrote about the perfect Highland jungle. He used that word specifically. 'Jungle', with its implied abundance, fecundity, cornucopia, profuseness, its thriving, plentiful, rich, lush densities of life. He was talking about rainforests, the cool temperate rainforests of Northwest Scotland, in the same way I had written about the forests of Papua New Guinea in my thesis.

*

There is a sequence to growth and blooming in the croft meadows that begins with orchids. They herald the start of a continual flowering which culminates with the tallest grasses in late August. During long summer days, wildflowers grow steadily up through the grasses, sedges and rushes, stretching upwards to the sun, offering their blooms to insects and birds. The density of growth is mutually supportive: thin, delicate filigree twists and twines up, through and around, in purple, pink, white, yellow and blue – paint-splashes of colour across the canvas of greens. Many plants, such as vetches, clovers and mayflowers, grow faster and produce their blooms long before the grasses flower. This height advantage allows their colourful heads to stand out in a sea of green, and thus attract the pollinators.

As summer progresses and the wildflowers begin to set seed, the grasses produce their flowers in an array of shapes and forms. Their colours are much more subtle – pale peach, russet, cream and yellow – but their delicate nodding heads, or bracts like zippers or tufts and braids, are beautiful and distinctive. The perfume is delicious and overpowers the scent of myrtle from surrounding bogland or saltiness and ozone from the sea. And when the wind blows, the meadows whisper in gentle sounds made by dozens of different types of stem and leaf all moving together. In drier areas the last patches of yellow rattle live up to the name. Its seed pods are percussion instruments played by the breezes. The whole croft fills with drumming and tapping and humming and shushing. Each plant has a unique way of dancing to the wind – some sway or gently wave, others click and jerk. The overall effect is of one great organism rippling and oscillating and singing. There is a phrase, 'a sea of grass'. It describes almost what a mature meadow feels like: a living organic entity, a single inland sea ruled by the same physical laws as the ocean. The meadow-sea is compensation for Dr Mackenzie's missing jungle.

Inside, the structure of the meadow is reminiscent of a rain-forest. There are tall stems that resemble tree trunks; creepers and climbers; there are big leaves and decomposing vegetable matter; there are seeds dropping and insects leaping or flitting from plant to plant. It is warm, moist, dark and fecund. The canopy is bright and colourful, flickering with emerging insects. There is an internal sound too, almost out of reach yet definitely present, one that can only be heard by kneeling or lying down among the blooms, a strange crackling overriding the sounds of seeds and clicking stems. Together, all these sounds are the tunes of life and earth, light and scent in miniature, the interconnectedness of living things made manifest.

The importance and significance of healthy grasslands becomes apparent when the meadow is in full bloom. The sward is thick and dense with chamomile, knapweeds, hogweed, meadowsweet, purple and yellow vetches, scentless mayweeds. The fields become variegated with colours and forms – sedges, rushes, grasses – their delicate flowers already set with seed and bobbing gently as the air wafts between them. There is as much below ground as above. The roots of dandelion and red clover can delve down more than a metre, common knapweed and great burnet more than two. Even the roots of the diminutive bird's-foot trefoil may extend a metre below the surface. Other species have dense sprays of fine roots able to bind the upper surface of the soil together – meadow grass, timothy grass, common sedge, tormentil. Together they create an interactive and powerful bond with fungi, microbes, insects and invertebrates, an underland rich in potential.

Insects throng. One day there were so many I was afraid of trampling and crushing them. I bent down and counted thirty craneflies in one tiny square of meadow. They are short-lived – every delicate dance could be their last. Dozens of white butterflies with blue-black bodies were threading themselves together as if stitched by invisible hands. There were browns and smaller blues, hundreds of tiny moths, some white, some cream, others, smaller still, were yellow and beige. There were bees and hoverflies, beetles and hopping insects whose names I did not know. I still have no idea about the best way to count them.

The variety of insect life is enormous. There are so many different wing and body shapes, colours, leg lengths and see-through wing patterns. The first time I saw grasshoppers on the croft I could only make out three types. The largest was mottled brown, even its eyes were dun-coloured. Another appeared to have green leg stripes and a green face, while the smallest was entirely bright, spring green. I was not even sure it was a grasshopper. All I could think was how much I did not know or understand or had forgotten. But one thing was certain – if the fields had been cut in July, most of this insect life would have been lost.

The presence of so many types of insects was reassuring. They lifted up in small clouds whenever a whisper of wind passed through the valley and followed me as I walked along. Birds swooped in low loops and ripples that matched the waves passing through the grasses. They swept around my head and filled the spaces between the river and woodland. Above the stratification seen inside the meadows were more layers of activity – small birds feeding on insects disturbed by my passage or by the wind; over them, larger birds, gulls, crows, twisting and turning; and higher still, a raptor circling. Above them all, the haze of a summer's day and high cloud reaching beyond the limits of sight. From the soil beneath my feet to birds circling high above, the complexity of life seemed bound together by the maturing meadow.

In 2021 the late summer sward reached to my thighs, almost ready for harvest. Once again, I struggled to wade through the tangles even at the fields' margins, even if I used my two sticks to push a way through. To prevent damage, we had kept close to the edges all summer long. But even from the fence I could see all kinds of late flowers – species like knapweed, parsley and angelica were busy again. The sheer volume and variety this year was greater than ever before. In that moment I decided I would ask for expert help in future. I felt stupid and ignorant and reminded myself of all those who rightly lament the losses and cry out in frustration and warning. If we cannot name organisms who live alongside us in these precious spaces they will be truly lost for good.

As I watched the rippling waves of grass, the scent of myrtle found me, even there at the heart of all this abundant meadow growth. The air was mostly filled with perfumes of chamomile, sweet grasses and, from the edge of the little patch of woodland, lemony pine. It was clear some species had returned with a second flowering – yellow and purple vetches in tangles as deep as jungle vines, bright-red clover and white mayweed – while others were heavy with seed. I could see sorrels standing tall on stems of crimson, their seeded tops pointing skywards like rusted spears left to mark the fallen on an ancient battlefield. The last pale, dry remnants of midsummer blooms rattled and whispered messages of hope for the future even as their seeds scattered.

I paused to lean back on the fence post close to the embankments. A dragonfly danced past. Behind me and higher than the post, where the bank rises steeply, the blue and purple flowers of devil's-bit scabious nodded and danced. Higher still I could see the first fuchsia and pink and mauve blooms of bell heather and common ling. Together the flowers swayed in the breeze and hummed with bees, their purples, pinks and blues a sure sign of autumn.

3. Sunrise over Glac Gheal, upper Erradale valley, sunset between the Isle of Harris and northern tip of the Isle of Skye, Celtic month of Hazel (August to September), Grain Moon

(i) The croft fills with gold and the sounds of haymaking

With warm weather in late August come the first real hints of autumnal light, all pale gold and shimmering like grasses in flower. Gone are the crisp pastel hues of early summer dawns and evenings. The air is thick, redolent of dripping honey and mead, somnolent and heady. In clear weather the blue-bright middle hours of day return to full summer, the colours of June, and we may have a few hours of bling, when everything glitters and shines, crystalline and vivid. But now the mornings whisper of autumn. By increments summer fails just as the hay meadows reach their best.

★

Full of hope and uncertainty about whether there was to be any hay at all, the call went out. Cathma rang Donald 'Duck'

Mackenzie in Opinan and, as we had all agreed earlier in the summer, yes, he would come and have a look at the croft. He arrived as amber light washed over the whole valley, the air filled with midges and dragonflies. Duck's three boys, affectionately known as 'the Ducklings', strong young men with a deep, shared love of crofting and animal husbandry, came too. Together they paced back and forth, picking at seed heads and examining the dimensions of the field. Cathma and I showed them where the springs and ditches were hidden by tall grasses and dense summer growth, where the tractor could get safely and where the old ruins lay. 'Good. Aha,' they agreed. 'It's bigger than we thought. We'll come and cut and see how well it does.'

We discussed using this first trial harvest for silage because Duck thought it might not dry out enough to bale as hay. But when a few consecutive days of warm dry weather were predicted, he rang to say they would begin as soon as possible. The preceding weeks had been very wet. Large patches of meadow had been flattened by winds and rain. Rain can break stems and cause enough damage to make a hay harvest very difficult and the unusually heavy and persistent downpours had left a broken and tangled mess that would not be easy to cut. August can be a volatile month, its summer storms short but powerful, but the boys were undeterred – they would come after work, they said.

Most local crofts are cut in early summer for silage. In general, they are made up of large square fields, as originally laid out under the direction of Dr Mackenzie some one hundred and seventy years ago. Although the boundaries to Red River Croft are also linear, they hold within them a complex mosaic of habitats and complicated topography, making the use of large machinery almost impossible. Today, few crofts in this area grow grass for traditional hay. Where once the dried grasses were cut by scythe and drawn by hand into hay stooks or ricks, or later mechanically gathered into small rectangular bales, now they are rolled into great round bales and wrapped in plastic. Several crofters own large-scale tractors and cutting machinery and, mostly in July, they harvest silage up and down Wester Ross, moving from croft to larger farm to croft as swiftly as possible.

However, these enormous vehicles cannot cope with the small, convoluted areas of Red River Croft. And so, with an old Ford tractor and cutting machine, the Mackenzie boys came to cut the lower meadows. The evening was once again made of liquid gold. Where the river flowed past the areas to be harvested, the air was hazy, filled with moisture and insects. Just a few days later, the cuttings were parcelled up by a baler even older than the tractor and the traditional rectangular bales hauled away. Although our very first hay-cut seemed small, it was species rich and full of promise. Duck thought the quality was good and said he and the boys would keep several bales as hay to see how well the harvest overwintered and whether their cows would eat them. In the end, the whole Red River Croft harvest was kept as hay because their cattle preferred it to their own silage. In future years, we agreed, weather permitting, they would come again to cut for hay. I fizzed with excitement at the prospect. I was overwhelmed with the feeling that at last we knew what we were supposed to do. Our partnership with the croft was being underwritten by a new bond of understanding between us and the land. Of course a hay harvest would not pay the bills, but some rewards do not come with coin.

The meadows are so flower rich and diverse we collectively felt good, nutritious hay could be produced as long as the weather played its part. Everything would hinge on that, just as it had in my grandfather's day. This older, traditional method of harvesting animal food for the winter months depends upon warm dry days, whereas fields used for silage can be cut in damp weather. There are benefits and hazards with both methods. Traditional hay-cutting ultimately supports the longevity of insect and bird populations, helping to maintain and promote biodiversity. It uses no plastics or other chemical products. And it ensures the maturing herbage has time to set and then drop seeds to the ground, where they become part of the natural 'seed bank' for years to come. Silage is not weather dependent and therefore offers a large measure of security for the winter ahead. There can even be a second cut in late September, if conditions are right. And there are economies of scale for the crofters who share their machinery, time, skill and effort.

*

The weather in the following summer was much kinder. August was windy, warm and dry. Plants grew taller than ever. Again, I waded hip-height through the meadows. Dram completely disappeared from view. This time the Ducklings would cut, dry and bale over about a week. They began after work at the end of one long, hot day. The air was swirling with insects and steamy heat, the sound of droning almost as loud as the tractor's engine. A few days after cutting, the boys came to ted the hay into windrows, piling up the drying sweetness. Red River Croft was contoured by neat lines of hay, like an old map.

As tractor and tedder passed back and forth, clouds made of swallows and sand martins parted the air then stitched it back again. I had no idea so many birds would flock together after the cutting, dropping down in waterfalls, intent on feeding, hypnotised by the bounty. On every row, gangs of small birds settled to pick at the insects and seeds caught by the process of cutting and tedding, accompanied only by wing-whispers and gentle shooshing as they rose up and down and moved backwards and forwards. They were joined by clouds of dragonflies and damselflies, iridescent and spotted with colour, settling onto the drying grasses and gaps between the windrows where glistening dampness began to seep.

In the continuing warm dry spell, the sweet perfumes intensified. There is nothing quite like the aroma of freshly cut meadows – vanilla essence, overtopped by chamomile and bergamot, perhaps. Each turning of the hay produced a little more perfume until grasses and flowers had only hints of green and smelled as lovely as the head of a new-born baby.

Fragrances rose and swirled around the valley. They were almost visible. In my mind's eye they were like laundry billowing on a long line. I ambled around, prodding the neat rows with my stick until each poke released yet more scent. Several turnings and teddings meant the seeds containing the future meadow were spilled everywhere. Hundreds and hundreds of small birds picked at the ground – goldfinches, pipits, larks, song thrushes and many others. They were so intent on feeding they ignored me, the Mackenzie boys, the machinery, Dram, and the raptors who sailed over us all. It was strange to see so many birds reduced to such quiet whispers and murmurings, their feathers reflecting the honey-infused light.

After a few days the windrows were ready for baling, but a sudden change to the forecast threatened heavy rain and wind. Using the elderly baler took time; the Ducklings normally needed an afternoon off work just to get started. It would be disastrous if the windrows were soaked after so much good drying. The piles of concentrated sweetness would be ruined. The boys decided using their old baler would not be fast enough. The call went out for help. It was answered by Donald 'Tosh' Mackintosh from Red Point Farm who came with his large modern baler.

The main gate to the lower croft was taken off its hinges; curious cattle and sheep were driven away. Tosh's enormous tractor inched and scraped its way between the gate's strainer-posts, the tall baler pushed and pulled in behind. In a speedy, efficient gathering, large round bales were produced by machinery more than twice my height. As fast as the bales were extruded, they were loaded up by the Mackenzie boys with their much smaller tractor and long trailer and rushed to their big barn at Port Henderson to beat the rain. In crofting communities here and on the islands, this is the way of life – people coming together, collaborative working, mutualism at the township scale, symbiosis between crofts.

*

Each year, the sheer density and abundance of growth in the meadow has produced a large number of hay bales. I was astonished at the first harvest and proud of subsequent ones. 'A good harvest off good ground,' Duck had said. Yet, each year, plenty of ground on the croft remains uncut – the steep embankments, the peats, the margins of ditches, the riverbanks and across the river, a long sweep of ground that machinery, no matter how small and agile, cannot reach. In these places, dense swathes of scabious, knapweed, vetch, red clover, sneezewort, chamomile and meadowsweet carry on flowering throughout August and into September. They appear again and again, growing through and held up by grasses, sedges and rushes. These patches have continued to provide protective cover and food for corncrakes since their first appearance, and for other wildlife as summer wanes. And they have been a continuing source of insects for swallows and sand martins preparing for their long flights south.

After the very first harvest, I wandered slowly around the croft, savouring the evening and thinking about what had been achieved. All around the cut edges the layering of the meadows was exposed. Throughout the margins were the funnel-shaped nests of large spiders. Every metre or so, using clever design and architecture, they had built a structure made from three or four tall, sturdy stems of grass and vetch held together by fine, powerful threads. Sitting inside each nest, a round-bellied spider. There must have been hundreds and hundreds across the fields before the grass-cutting started.

The following year, two days after the big harvest and when all the machinery had gone, including Tosh's extra-large tractor and baler, I stood at the top of the bank and leaned on the gate, watching swallows diving and breathing in the still richly scented air. Even when a harvest is complete, the perfumes linger, caught here and there in the uncut patches along the river and up on the high banks. I could see the flash and glint of dragonflies even from on high. Each caught a ruby or two on their wings from the lowering sun.

I thought about the old traditions – memories of my maternal grandfather and his horses, paternal relatives in Ireland and their hayricks, the black-and-white pictures I had seen in Gairloch Museum, Cathma's photographs of her family in Erradale. But here in front of me were new memories. I had photographed the haymaking, adding to the calendar of images for my family. I half wondered whether the wild creatures below me were also storing memories – potential food supplies, safety and shelter – ready for future generations. And then I saw them, ghost-whispers of crofters in these very fields. Setting to work, raking the hay into tall piles. Another image, of the two horses Cathma's family used to pull the cart. And beyond the river, my own grandfather, laughing as he tickled his heavy horses into motion.

I am there too, following behind, with a fistful of flowers and nodding grasses.

The hay, the harvest, the corncrakes, swallows and spiders are all part of the hope I feel now for the future, hope that lies in these small meadows, in these semi-wilded margins and raggle-taggle micro-habitats. It is contained within leaf-drop and seed-spill, in fungi, bacteria and ultimately in decay and dormancy. And so, at summer's end, when the by-products of another hay harvest are shed and stored in the earth, the year ahead is already written into the soil. Here, within this small place, the sources of new life and renewal are being carefully catalogued in a library for the future.

(ii) Heather in full bloom

After the noise and bustle of haymaking, our meadows are hushed. The cut sections green again quickly but the margins along the riverbanks, springs and ditches, and around patches of scrub and trees, are tall and golden. They are busy too, quietly busy with birds and insects seeking food and shelter. All the valley shimmers in terracotta light; the air continues to hum and thrum quietly. Swallows and sand martins throng, darting high then falling, skimming over the meadows and, if I stand still, close enough for me to feel the turbulence of their passing.

South Erradale is a symphony of perfume, light and colour; every cubic metre is filled. Apart from the birds feeding frantically ahead of their imminent departure, everywhere and every living thing is somnolent, as if lethargy seeps out of the very air itself. There is a reason for the relative quiet – the heather is in bloom and it has a singular effect. The nectar-filled flowers of heathers, principally common ling, cross-leaved heath and bell heather, release a distinctive scent when they open. From a few plants the aroma would not be noticeable, but when whole hillsides bloom synchronously the cumulative effect is powerful, the fragrance at times overwhelming.

Swallows ready themselves for migration at the height of the heather bloom, when everywhere, apart from the valley floor, is drenched in purple and soaked in the dense and intoxicating perfumes. More often than not, heather in full flower coincides with a spell of warm, golden weather. They are interdependent, one leads to the other. As a result, the air feels as thick as honey, as sweet as mead. The accompanying humming and buzzing are astounding. There are bees, flies, beetles and wasps everywhere. Hillsides quiver with insects. Their droning overwrites almost every other sound. Even among the high peaks and along the steepest stretches of our windy coast, the swathes of blooming heather are accompanied by great numbers of insects, especially bees. Only at night, when the cool aromas of rock and crag creep downslope and in through windows and doors, do the sweetness and humming diminish.

As more flowers open, the air thickens still further. Pale lavender turns to bright purple, pink to fuchsia, and rose to plum. All around the croft, insects flit across the last fading summer flowers in search of every remaining drop of goodness, bouncing from stem to stem and dancing over the wetter patches, while flocks of little meadow birds chase after them or settle among the drooping grasses, picking at the last seeds. In late afternoons, warmth oozes like syrup falling from a spoon; it slurps across hills and drips down into the valley. The balmy air, filled with resinous scents of pine and myrtle mixing with heather perfumes, feels more like a warm bath sparkling with scented bubbles. We are arraigned like royalty in gold and purple.

Swallows frenzy on the wing in swooping displays of lapis lazuli, sapphire, obsidian, with flashes of pale cream and amethyst. Periodically, sun-warmed sea breezes mingle with crisp air from the mountains so that, at different times of the day, it is possible to taste salt, rock and moss, sea and high mountains, until we are overwhelmed again by the heathers in full flower.

*

Moorland filled with heathers is an ancient landscape though not a truly wild one. Heath and moor dominated by a small number of species was instigated by human activity many thousands of years ago when people began clearing trees in significant quantities. Layers of charcoal found in lake sediments alongside large amounts of heather pollen reveal stories of repeated woodland clearances associated with the use of fire. For millennia in these environmental records, the history of fire and heath occur together. Fire, used first to clear areas of trees for cultivation, was then needed to maintain open pasture, because once heathers grow beyond a certain height they become woody and unpalatable for grazing animals. This partnership between fire and heath cumulatively expanded and strengthened, leading ultimately to today's dominance of heather moor in the cultural landscapes that are the British uplands. Over time, the purpling of Scotland's hills became as iconic as its national flower, the thistle, and today tourists flock to the Highlands in late summer and early autumn to enjoy the spectacle.

There is an old saying – 'gorse for bread ovens, peat for fuel, bracken for bedding, rock for building and heather for thatch' – suggesting a long and well-established practical relationship with heather moorland. But another from Ireland – 'gold under furze, silver under rushes, famine under heather' – implies a much darker history, and one that stretched across the sea to the Highlands. In the long story of people and hill country, fire and heathland became part of the farming system of Scotland. Heathers had multiple uses, from thatching and brooms to medicine and the 'moorland tea' beloved of Robert Burns, its effects as a soporific perhaps related in some way to its heady perfume. Heather has also been used for at least three thousand years in fermented drinks. Archaeologists working on the Isle of Rum found remnants of fermented heather upon a shard of pottery.

*

Everywhere the purples, pinks and fuchsia of ling and bell heather ripple with the movement of bees. Even on small tufts and clumps clinging to the rocks and in the cracks and crevices on the highest mountains, heather grows and insects buzz. Years ago, we clambered up Stac Pollaidh in Assynt on a very warm late summer's day. The children were hot and thirsty but uncomplaining. The air was still and clear and bright. The narrow trail wound up and around the eastern flanks of the mountain through dense swathes of heather. Even as we climbed up, our laughter and chattering were almost drowned out by the sounds of bumble bees. We paused by a cluster of stones, where the path turns suddenly steeper and leads onto the knobbled summit, to have a drink and catch our breaths. All around us were thousands upon thousands of bees. The mountain seemed covered by a motile carpet of insects. We carried on, sweating in the dense, aromatic and throbbing air. As soon as we reached the top we saw the weather out to the west had changed. A large bank of near-black cloud appeared to be rushing towards us, and within minutes we were lashed by hail, shocked and cowering from a violent summer thunderstorm which seemed to have grown out of nothing. Lightning began to strike all around us. We lay down and flattened ourselves against the cliff immediately below the summit. To our left were a group of deer doing exactly the same; to our right, gouts of steam and sulphur where lightning had struck a large boulder. With the first lull we set off downhill. Rob and the boys ran ahead. My daughter and I could not match their pace. We found shelter in a howff, a small rough shelter, on the flanks of the mountain as lightning repeatedly struck the ground. Inside, uncountable numbers of gently humming bees coated every available rock surface. Their wings rippled in unison. Their humming rose and fell in sine waves, matching the emotions we felt – shock, relief, terror, concern for the boys, puzzlement, joy, wonder. When the bees began to leave, small groups soon becoming a river, we knew the storm had passed and there would be no more lightning. To this day the bee-covered, heather-clad, deeply scented slopes of Stac Pollaidh have never been forgotten. A short walk along the Seaweed Road past purpled slopes and thronging bees takes me right back to the companionship of a bee-filled cave in a lightning storm.

*

As the heathers reach their full potential, the whole valley of Erradale seems intoxicated; Red River Croft flushes with brightness and sweet scent. The colours of autumn are threaded through everything, along the shore, above and below water, in the fields and up on the hills. The green grasses of late summer are soon tipped with copper, and in between the patches of still-purple heathers across the slopes, the ground looks washed with bronze and gold. At other times the air is so full of moisture the world appears faded and worn, as if in an old sepia photograph, almost colourless, yet with hints of yellow and orange like drifting tobacco smoke. Clouds of small birds continue to roam through the humid air; they rise up here and descend there, picking at fruits, seeds and insects. Once, as I paused to watch bees dancing on a patch of scabious, a horde of goldfinches landed all around me in the long grasses of our top field. They looked like tattered flecks of Christmas wrapping paper, all shiny gold, silver and red, as they clustered noisily, chattering away, their joyful voices full of unreadable words.

Scabious flowers are purple and blue, some pink and near-white. They grow in abundance following the hay harvest and well into early autumn. I only realised how important these small buttons of mauve were after our first year cutting the meadows. Their longer flowering period offers insects sources of nectar when so many other species have finished and are setting seed. Their pretty blooms extend the purpling of our field margins and moorland for another few weeks. On the croft they finally die away in October. After just one season of hay-cutting I discovered that their tiny purple flowers scribe the Seaweed Road's old, original route, where it diagonally traverses the steep embankment in our top field and out of the gate, and line a broad track from the river crossing to meet the newer section of road between croft-gate and the cliff.

*

Just as their arrival on Red River Croft heralds summer, swallows are a signpost to autumn. They are calendrical markers and mood changers. I remember them from childhood summer holidays, though I rarely saw them living on the Lancashire coast, where swifts filled the summer skies. All summer long in South Erradale the swallows swoop and glide across the crofts.

As the meadows begin to stipple with bronze, the peat bogs are rinsed with henna, lavender cloaks of heather on the valley sides are dusted with ground ginger and the dusky purple hills are sprinkled with umber. Now the swallows line up on overhead wires, gossiping and chitter-chattering, happy, boisterous and defiant in the face of oncoming autumn. These high-wire line-ups mark the end of summer and their readiness for departure, but as the swallows fill the air and dive in and out of the old byre, the profound sadness I once felt as autumn began does not last long.

The sea calls. Just as the south calls to the swallows and sand martins, I hear the sea. After the energetic and bustling days of flower-burst, seed-setting and haymaking, the ripples of scabious point my way to the shore. Now my mind and body respond to calling waves and seashore songs. It is time to go to the leaning post at the top of the cliff, the place around which the entire year swirls.

Early one evening, when the sea was the colour of clotted cream and the sky an opaque gold, I stood at the cliff-top vantage point on the Seaweed Road, looking away from the sea and back to Red River Croft. From there the house and fields look wholly enclosed by the mountains, as if the entire croft sits in an armchair made of deep time. A small flash of white and dark brown in the air above the croft caught my eye. It was a sea eagle. His white tail was spread and had momentarily caught the sunlight. Turning his head one way and then another, he swooped low around the river and over my head before heading north towards Opinan as if he, too, followed the Seaweed Road. I wondered how the sea-log seat might look to him – just a wisp of grass on a rusty scarf of beach perhaps. Then I spotted a tractor moving along the distant road – one of the Ducklings hard at work. The eagle seemed to sail over us all, inhabiting another dimension of colour and animal scent, of fish in the sea and waving grass in the fields.

The aroma of myrtle and heather was strong under the fierce gaze of the lowering sun. Invisible molecules of honeyed perfume were vibrating to the tune of the breeze. I imagined them popping and coating everything, and wondered if the eagle was aware of the scented lake beneath him. He rose higher and higher, riding away on waves of fragrance. I turned to swim back to the house like a fish plunging through the deep and colourful waters of a scented Inner Sound, thinking of all the wild bounty in this small, crofted, semi-wilded place.

(iii) Red berries, dappled light

Without fail I hope all Septembers will be as radiant and golden as our first. Over the intervening years there have been many days of rain and wind in between the sunshine and warmth, yet always the distinctive richness of the almost-equinoctial light elicits responses from everything – mountains, sea, river, woodlands, croft, me. When a sea breeze follows the river inland, it stirs life and motion into the pale, drying and expiring meadows. Fluffy seeds float by, carried by gentle, rippling air currents; streamers of light and colour flow around and through everything. Among the blondeness and paleness of grasses, other meadow plants appear gilded and burnished. Intermittent rain magnifies these rusts, coppers and bronzes so they appear polished and fiercely glowing, but gradually the showers wash away or dampen down any remaining seeds. Skeletons appear – umbrellas, kites, footballs, and castles in splinter-thin, fabulous, almost-dying architecture. Meadow birds feed furiously wherever they can, dashing back and forth in noisy gangs. And when the rains have gone, mists rise slowly from the valley bottoms in wisps and wraith-clouds. Then the sun is reflected in every single droplet of water, countless billions of microscopic stars flaring and turning the world into a single supernova.

Occasionally there comes a particularly calm and chill morning when the fields and riverbanks, shrubs and hedges are completely covered in shawls made of the finest grey and silver silk. Every flower, leaf and stem vanishes. Created by the first cold tendrils of mist drifting around the lower valley and settling on cobwebs, the woven spider-silks twinkle as if studded with millions of sparkling rhinestones. When the sun rises and rays of light sweep across them, they flash like coloured sequins sewn by their thousands onto the tulle of a ballroom dancer's dress. Walking around the croft breaks the glistening filigree and lacework, and with each step the shimmering silver strands are released to fly about on unseen wafts of air, some catching in hair and on faces, others trailing higher and higher until they disappear in a last flash of rainbowed light. But such conditions are rare so close to the sea.

Sap-green vibrancy in the valley and rich purples and violets of heather-covered hills subside into the greys and ghostly pinks of drying, fading flowers. Leaves darken to umber or bleach into blonde. Rose-gold light spills over everything. Years ago, I drank oolong tea in a clear glass cup. It was a rich orange-ochre and dense with scents of honey and hazelnuts fresh from their shells. Oolong is traditionally prepared by allowing *Camellia sinensis* leaves to wither and curl slowly in sunlight so their distinctive aromas and colours become concentrated by the process of dry shrinkage. In September this land can seem so steeped in the perfumes of shrivelling leaves and flowers that each in-drawn breath becomes a sip of golden tea.

In the areas cut for hay, the colours of autumn soon sprinkle the last soft greens and yellows. In the remaining tall margins and uncut areas across the river and along the riverbanks, bracken slowly turns from summer green to copper, rowan leaves crimp and rust, and yellow pennies start their fall from the birches. After the headiness of recent weeks even the cheerful, bee-filled drenches of heather lose not only their colour and brightness but their perfume too.

Fast-moving pillows of grey mostly from the south and west start to arrive, carrying showers and rainbows. They herald the onset of autumn, and where latterly our days were filled with vivid, lancing light, sunrises now speak of change. Long arcs of ruby red and vermillion sweep over the summits and broaden into orange and yellow. The mountains themselves flash with autumn colour. Swirling cloud-shrouds seem to alter their moods and change our perspectives, but they remain for me a solid and reliable backcloth to life, their great age and strength still tangible and reliable. The lower hills stretch their arms out protectively on either side of our little valley; in their embrace, autumn can be seen creeping down towards the sea. And there is comfort to be had in all these grand forms and changing colours.

In one small plot close to the road leading up to our house, rowan trees grow particularly densely and vigorously. They stand tall and red-berried above the thicknesses of furze. The gorse is full of birds, and over many years they may have been responsible for the surprising density of trees, carrying fruit from other old rowans to their gorse-protected nests. The rowan trees here owe their safe-from-grazing existence to both birds and furze. Neither deer nor sheep can penetrate the gorse bank or the thick clumps of bramble surrounding it.

In small patches of woodland where grazing density has been low, the first tiny orange splashes appear, droplets of blood red in patterns a forensic scientist would recognise. On the steep slopes of nearby Loch Bad a'Chrotha and Loch Bad na h-Achlaise, the dark-green, birch-dominated woodlands are studded by mounds of scarlet in the same way as the gorse bank at home. Here, the rowan trees are spread out quite evenly. They too owe their distribution to the work of birds. When the berries mature into glowing crimson, the trees themselves stand out against the rusting greens like bright buttons.

*

Around me on the croft there are pockets of air still plump-full with the perfumes of heather, myrtle, drying grasses and the last blooms of dog-rose. But soon salt and iodine blow up from the shore, occasionally with aromas I associate with more wintry, seas. Mountains taste and smell quite differently. The crispness of rock, moss and running water feels rich, and redolent of height. As early autumn winds blow back and forth, I find those scents even at low levels. They are proxies for the high peaks whose remoteness my mind's eye can forage from remembered climbs. In that vision I look down at myself, trundling along in the lower places, just as an eagle might watch a creature too small and slow to bother with.

Like spring, this is a wonderful time of year to climb in the hills, for long, bright days provide conditions benevolent enough to allow safe summiting. In the years of ill-health, low-level walks have been my consolation – merely to walk about the mountains' feet, or simply to watch the peaks from the croft, has been both a joy and a blessing. Each time the autumn equinox drew close, I found solace and comfort in rich, deep colours around me. But again and again, I itched and yearned to be closer to the mountains.

On one beautiful September day I walked slowly with Rob and Dram through moorland vegetation and clusters of mixed pine and birch woodland. Rob had brought me away from the croft for a change of scene and, knowing how I longed for the hills, thought I should spend some time among them. Here at last I could breathe in the perfumes of peak and crag.

We had come to a quiet glen close to Beinn Eighe. From the shores of Loch Maree a newly installed 'hydro-road' reached deep into hidden, remoter valleys between high peaks. I chafed mentally at not being able to walk the familiar trail that runs almost parallel but at much higher altitude, for it is a lovely route and climbs quickly to fabulous views. But the road was well built and smooth and easier for me to negotiate using sticks and a less painful experience. The light was dappled and flickered intensely, making my eyes water. Tussock grasses were singed with orange and contrasted sharply with the lingering purples of heather and scabious. The wind was lively. Clouds ran swiftly between the great hills; gusts scooted around us. For a while we sat under a grand old Scots pine with a flask of coffee and watched as showers billowed and rippled along the loch like the flowing manes of galloping horses.

Once I would have grumbled at the sight of a hydro-road seen from the high footpath despite its green-energy credentials, but it was clear the hydro-scheme builders here had done a reasonable job. The structure housing the turbines and all the other necessary gear is partly hidden under a great artificial slope of rock, peat and moorland vegetation, cleverly carved out by diggers and bulldozers and designed to mimic the hillside. And as you move through the valley it vanishes entirely from view. Where Scots pine woodland was lost completely to the road, young native trees have been planted, but many large areas of ancient woodland are preserved. Scattered throughout the old-growth forest are enormous grandmother trees and, around them, tiny saplings seeded from the woodland's heart – nature working in tandem with engineering.

So much wonderful scientific research attests to the role played by grandparent trees, about the invisible threads binding ancient with young. The connections are real and measurable, physical and chemical, tree roots bonded to fungi in the 'Wood Wide Web', in an underland neural net. We paused again to sit among these grand old beings and watch the wind play in the leaves – flicker, flash, flicker, flash. Beyond the glen, sunlight chased shadows on Slioch and Loch Maree. In the shelter of the grand, spreading pines, heather and bilberry grew tall. Dragonflies skipped from moss-covered rock to tree trunk to boulders in the nearby burn. The air was warm and sweet, the colour of white wine. The place felt old. It reminded me of my grandmother's bedroom, of sunlight pouring in through small window panes to fall in thick beams across her polished furniture, its wood radiating heat and memories. And I thought then of my own role as grandmother, about my invisible pandemic ties to our grandchildren, of the 'Zoom' gatherings, telephone calls, photographs, messages, cards, gifts and letters. I wished in that moment for tree-like tangible, physical connections, threads with form and substance beyond the simple contacts of 2-D audiovisuals. I was overcome with longing, with the desire to be physically connected, rooted in their worlds, passing on stories and songs and hugs, so many hugs. Instead, I placed my hands on the trunk of one giantess. I leaned in further and hugged her, my cheeks against the rough bark, eyes closed and tears flowing, and willed messages into her body, messages I was certain could be translated and sent all the way to the little ones.

Further on and higher, by a small dam and fencing, were scars of the hydro-works still. Yet everywhere were signs of healing – great moss-clad boulders left untouched, presumably by design, patches of exposed peat sprouting with new life. And above the sound of waterfalls in the relaxed shade of yet more enormous ancient pines, the drone of insects and the diligent busyness of birdsong riffling through the branches sounded like the sea and whispered of recovery and healing.

★

People have been modifying this mountainous country for millennia. These are anthropogenic landscapes. Yet not all human activity is destructive. We *can* work successfully with nature as long as we understand we are as much a part of the natural world as the mosses and lichens, deer grass and dragonflies. And while those lives may seem fleeting and small, trees will outlive us by centuries and the hydro-works will eventually vanish. It is quite overwhelming, to think of how this place might look in one hundred years – one or two skeletons of grandfather and grandmother trees among a throng of younger individuals; what was once a broad 'road' covered by a deep blanket of vegetation; familiar mountains once again ushering in the autumn colours.

Many of these Highland estates, including this one with its new hydro-scheme, are 'deer forests' with a longer history than most might suppose, for only since the early eighteenth century were cattle numbers reduced in favour of deer and grouse. The Gaelic word for 'deer' – *fiadh*, or *feidh* – comes from the Old Irish *fiad*, a word that can also mean 'wild' or 'free'. It is also tied closely to an Old English word for 'forest' – *frith* – and in the past both deer and forest would have been plentiful, their mutual existence closely linked. Today a deer-hunting 'forest' refers to country that contains few trees. Yet deer forests were protected in law as far back as the seventeenth century and used specifically for hunting. As early as the mid-sixteenth century they included areas of land known as 'hained woods', where cattle, sheep and people were removed, cleared for the benefit of hunters including, even then, visitors from the Lowlands. It is highly likely some of these deer forests have been private hunting grounds for almost six hundred years.

In the spirit of rewilding, there are new forest plantations springing up in the great glens and hills of the Highlands. Provided trees are planted in the right place for the right reasons, there will ultimately be many benefits. But where old and ancient woodlands are kept preferentially and selectively, the rewards appear to be faster and greater. Grandmother Scots pines left to their own devices can, within just a few years, generate considerable new growth. They appear almost to encourage it. Science has revealed their relationships with other tree species is as powerful and mutualistic as their relationships with fellow Scots pines. This means that the 'Wood Wide Web' expands more rapidly under old forest, leading to the faster production of trees – growth that can outpace tree-planting by humans.

On a much smaller scale, this is what has been happening on Red River Croft. In the patches left completely untouched, saplings of rowan, willow, birch and cherry have sprung up. In areas grazed intermittently or managed for hay, wildflowers and grasses have flourished. Orchids, reliant on undisturbed, fungi-rich soils, have spread; the 'seed bank' in our soils has been replenished; flowers listed by Dixon almost a century and half ago have bloomed once more; and species associated with mature woodland have flowered, recalling the forests that once grew here.

The result is a place with the ability to magnify light, colour, sound and scent. In the amber light of September, all who live here, human and non-human beings, appear to be studded or rimmed with precious metals and gems. We are arrayed in gold, copper and bronze and decorated with rubies, garnets, agates, citrines and diamonds. And as the autumn equinox approaches, even though the days will now tangibly shorten, we feel both rich and truly blessed.

NATURAL CYCLES

Our living world ebbs and flows in cycles. Based on observations and images gathered across a decade, this book ties many events in nature to the annual solar cycle. On Red River Croft, calendrical markers are expressed by a singular partnership between sunsets and sunrise, landforms crafted by deep time, and local natural phenomena. As I learned more and more about our Highland home, these events were gathered up in notes, observations and photographs and bound together in small parcels of time. For me, they created a profound and personal sense of connection between earth, sea and sky. The developing bond had a spiritual dimension. It felt transcendent.

Over time, this place transformed into a radical space, where the heavenly churns in unison with the terrestrial, and where physical processes and living organisms behave as one. I became deeply embedded within it, finding solace and succour through the most difficult times, through pain and loss, heartache and anxiety. The natural world has offered outrageous beauty, extreme and powerful weather events, and close encounters with some of our most remarkable wild plants and animals. Over the last decade, I discovered more about nature and geography than in all my preceding years.

Seasonal changes in landscape and wildlife coupled with celestial movements have the potential to form a calendar anywhere on earth, and are an opportunity to find order in nature. This has been recognised and achieved by cultures around the world for thousands of years, in unique and remarkable partnerships between human and physical geographies.

Beyond the small incremental changes we may observe as the seasons pass, there are other, greater natural cycles. Science has shown how salt marshes and sand dunes often follow repetitive sequences of growth and degradation, in which sediments and biomass are removed by erosion and then rebuilt. Strangely, these patterns of change often occur in measurable human timescales, for example, multiples of eleven or twelve years, while others, like glaciation, occur at multi-millennial scales. Both are influenced by the sun's natural cycles of magnetic activity, and, if we are lucky, we may glimpse moments of cyclic phenomena in the Northern Lights.

Years before coming to live here I used to joke with friends that changes in my own life chimed with repeating patterns of sunspot activity, in the same way some natural systems follow sunspots and solar flares. I would laugh and say personal events and circumstances were guided by the eleven- or twelve-year periodicity geographers have observed in ecosystems and astronomers observe in our star – phases of childhood, young adulthood, New Guinea, motherhood, academia, life on a croft – in equally balanced phases of transformation. During 'Sunspot Cycle 22' I was a full-time stay-at-home mother with my four children, and in 'Cycle 23' a full-time physical geographer working in a university. 'Cycle 24' has been filled with northern light, a red river, otters, sea eagles, peach sands, mountains and bog myrtle. While I learned about crofting and nature here in the Highlands, eight grandchildren have been born. They are as much a part of my 'Cycle 24' as Red River Croft.

The notion of being personally tied in some way to the grand solar cycles is fanciful nonsense perhaps, yet when I stand at the old fence post on the cliff-top by the Seaweed Road, swept up by the wind, and gravity loosens its grip, a physical representation of this idea appears, scribed in the mountains, islands and sea.

Change is perhaps becoming normal. Nature is very responsive to other forces, but can be resilient in the face of enormous pressure, while at other times succumbing to great stresses. Although shifts in our solar cycle occur at immense timescales, beyond the lifespans of humans, our climate, at the planetary scale, is undergoing rapid and potentially irreversible changes, ones we *can* detect, measure and understand. We are yet to experience the more devastating types of climate impact seen elsewhere, but there are many signs of modification and adjustment all around us. On Red River Croft we have seen swallows arriving late, bees emerging in January, marsh marigolds blooming in late August instead of May. We have experienced Gobag storms arriving one after another in rapid succession, and even in summer. Surrounding peatlands are drying out more quickly and yet the river is flooding more often. For the time being, such events remain within the boundaries of lived experience and written or oral histories, for there have always been extreme events and extreme years. But their frequency is increasing; their power is growing.

Many of us feel unsettled, disturbed by alterations to the patterns we have come to know over our lifetimes, to patterns we expect to find in the natural world. Yet some refuse to see or acknowledge our collective roles in increasing the pressures on physical and natural systems and in causing additional stress to the non-human beings who live alongside us. Here in the Northwest Highlands many believe we live in highly degraded landscape. And it is true – there have been great losses in the natural world: evidence from past records of plant and animal numbers shows how overfishing, overhunting and overgrazing have dramatically reduced biodiversity. With wider agreement about such loss and change, we may be able to agree on what might be done to restore and reinvigorate this land. Crofting is uniquely placed to help habitats and ecosystems in the Highlands and Islands; crofters can and should be custodians of a fragile countryside, of traditional farming methods and thus of nature herself. Perhaps there could be a broader general acceptance of crofting as an environmental concept as well as practice.

With support, we could allow rewilding where appropriate (Red River Croft's riverbanks and field margins are an example of this), rewet and manage peatlands as carbon stores, return to traditional haymaking to help very rare and vulnerable (Red List) species such as corncrakes, protect instead of burn scrub, and grow more trees. With new partnerships between crofters and large estates, we could restore badly degraded hills and glens and instigate a return to former conditions – the complex mosaic of mixed woodland, pasture and hill grazing of the so-called *fiadh* (deer, free and wild) forests. We could chase the 'wildlife dollar' by encouraging hunting with cameras rather than guns. In the face of predicted and rapidly building pressures resulting from planetary warming, resilience is vital, such changes ever more necessary. As I typed *fiadh*, autocorrect replaced it with 'faith', and my mind filled with the notion of faith: faith in the future, a future in which we enhance nature at every opportunity, with every skill, trick and talent we possess, a future of renewal in forests and peatlands, coasts and crofts. Faith in wildness and the natural world.

*

Despite the repeating patterns, nothing is fixed; we are as malleable as the silts of a salt marsh or the sands on a beach; we respond to the winds and to sunlight, to sounds from the sea and whispering meadow grasses as they answer to the turning of the earth and track the solar year from solstice to solstice, equinox to equinox. All this tells me is that I too am elemental, as much a part of the natural world as the curlews and corncrakes singing outside my window, the dung beetles and frogspawn. We are all intertwined. All the non-human beings I have met are just as important to the world as any of us. It reminds me that my life, with all its wonders and losses, happiness, and traumas, is as closely bound to the wilds as it ever could be.

In her book *Braiding Sweetgrass* Robin Wall Kimmerer asks if it possible to become naturalised to place, to become indigenous, and I am sure the answer to her question is yes – if you love the place enough, it is reciprocated. Here at the heart of a great windswept amphitheatre made by elementals and by deep time I have learned from the croft and its river, from the coastal edgelands and grand mountain country, and from the many habitats and different organisms living within them. Nature was my teacher; the winds, my guide and solace; the calendar, confirmation I had listened.

ACKNOWLEDGEMENTS

I could never have begun without the children asking questions, encouraging me to write things down. 'No one is listening to you,' they said, 'but we would all read your diary.' I did not believe them but began to write anyway – a blog born out of notes and scribbles, tales of life here in the far northwest of Scotland, stories for my family who would be visiting but not living here. My friends asked, 'What is it about the far north that lures you there? Ah, okay. Your blog. We see it now, the love.'

Encouraged by my husband, Rob, by our children, Robert, Liz, Tom and Joe, and their partners, Sarah D, Ben, Christy and Sarah T, I wrote for our steadily growing family. Since we moved here all four children have married and now there are eight grandchildren. This is all for them. But I hope the book spreads ripples even further, out into the wider world, like a pebble thrown into a pond.

The blog was found by the lovely lass who became my agent, Jenny Hewson at Lutyens & Rubinstein. Jenny has nurtured, cajoled and encouraged, but most of all she has supported me with kindness and enthusiasm. My early words were gathered and edited by writer Melissa Harrison into her beautiful book series, *Seasons*. Other essays were published by Jay Armstrong in the journal *Elementum*, each one uniquely paired with well-known artists and photographers; a great honour. And Katharine Norbury included a short piece in her *Women on Nature*. These wonderful women offered help and guidance twinned with joy and understanding. They gave me confidence; told me I could write; helped me find my feet in this strange new world away from academic peer review and the scientific method.

Encouragement and inspiration have been gifted by other writers, especially Robert Macfarlane; I am indebted to him for his support. And it has come from others whose work I greatly admire: Nicola Chester, Caspar Henderson, Ginny Battson, Julian Hoffman, Joanna Pocock, and the *Caught by the River* team.

Support, knowledge and opportunities to learn have been generously given by experts on nature, mountains, wildlife, rivers, the sea: Nigel Hester, Ann Lingard, Liz Bradshaw, Chris Townsend, Donna Rainey, Dr Jenny Jones, Dr Vanessa Holden, Dr Ann Power, Peter Cunningham and Colin Simpson. I have learned so much from these lovely folk.

Joy in the beautiful, the wild and magnificent has been shared with artists and photographers: Mark Appleton, Sam Bannister, Lynn Bennett-Mackenzie, Rowena Dugdale, Alison Dunlop, Jill Holmes, Mark Littlejohn, Susi Petherick, Jane Rushton, David Sandum, Lyssie Stevens, Nick Wilcox-Brown and Rob Williams. Such talent.

Friendship has been gifted by the people of South Erradale: Cathma Thomson and her family – Kenny, Mali and Donny – Jan and Mark Appleton, Jamie 'the Post' Johnston and family – Kate, Carianne, Caitlin and Jody – Trudy Mackenzie and daughters Eileen and Kirsty, Steve Phillips and Lynne Wall, Lachie, Iona and Sandy MacInnes, Ian MacInnes, Sam and James Phillpotts, Brian Sutherland and May Wilcox, Lulu Stader, Lucy Cairney and family, and Birgit Joost (whose physiotherapy expertise helped me walk again). By the people of Opinan and Port Henderson: Donald 'Duck' Mackenzie and his 'Ducklings' – Neil, Kenneth and Matthew – Alison Dunlop and Ross Hood, Mark and Rachel Littlejohn, Mike and Sharon Bulmer, Drs Mike and Linda Hayes, Granny Nina (who would take Dram-the-dog to Katy's croft for afternoon tea), and Richard and Sally Cameron. By the people of Red Point: Danielle Warren, Dave Downie and Donald 'Tosh' Mackintosh. And thanks must go to Dr Tom Cripps and Debbie Dillon for their hard work ensuring the safe and continued use of the Seaweed Road from South Erradale to Opinan.

New friendships have been found and forged on social media. Thank you to all my followers for your continued support on Twitter, Instagram and Facebook, and for the blog at www.annieworsley.co.uk.

Thank you to my editors Arabella Pike and Sam Harding at HarperCollins, the project team led by Katy Archer, and copy-editor Kit Shepherd. This book has been a long time coming; they have shown great patience.

I cannot thank my mother in person, but she is responsible for so much. She taught me how to be inquisitive, ask questions, go on adventures, write stories, draw and paint. She showed me the wonders of nature, even those to be found in the polluted town of my childhood. 'There's beauty everywhere,' she said. Thanks, too, to the remote montane communities of New Guinea. They showed me how to walk lightly in the forests and how we humans are no different to, and certainly no better than, all the other living organisms upon which we depend.

Finally, thanks are offered to the wilder lives of this place, the otters and birds, insects and flowers, trees, mosses and grasses, to the soils, the Red River and high mountain summits, ever-changing sea and magical winds. Together they were my friends,

282

teachers and guides, voices in my ear when doubts crept in, bringers of joy and enablers of understanding. They made an elemental of me. They knew me, even when I was lost.

SELECT BIBLIOGRAPHY

Chester, Nicola, *Otters* (Bloomsbury Wildlife, 2014).

Dixon, John. H., *Gairloch and Guide to Loch Maree* (fifth edition, Nevisprint, 2004).

Drummond, Peter, *Scottish Hill Names: The Origin and Meaning of the Names of Scotland's Hills and Mountains* (second edition, The Scottish Mountaineering Trust, 2010).

Gange, David, *The Frayed Atlantic Edge: A Historian's Journey from Shetland to the Channel* (William Collins, 2019).

Macfarlane, Robert, *Landmarks* (Hamish Hamilton, 2015).

Mackenzie, Osgood, *A Hundred Years in the Highlands* (fifth edition, The National Trust for Scotland, 1994).

Murray, John, *Reading the Gaelic Landscape: Leughadh Aghaidh na Tire* (Whittles Publishing, 2014).

Shepherd, Nan, *The Living Mountain* (second edition, Canongate, 2011).

Schueler, Jon, *The Sound of Sleat* (Picador, USA, 1999).

Wall Kimmerer, Robin, *Braiding Sweetgrass: Indigenous Wisdom, Scientific Knowledge and the Teachings of Plants* (Penguin Random House, 2013).

★

Booklets published by Gairloch Museum (www.gairloch museum.org):

Gairloch Museum, *The Crofting Township of South Erradale* (2013).

Gairloch Museum, *Flora's Barn and Tigh Eachainn Mhor* (2013).

Gairloch Museum, *The Ruins and Features of South Erradale* (2013).

Gairloch Museum, *The Wells of South Erradale* (2013).

Malone, Dorothy, *Exploring Gairloch's South Side: From Kerry Bridge to Craig* (2014).

Thomson, Cathma, *Childhood in South Erradale and More*, transcribed by Anne MacInnes (2013).